A Conversation with God

If You Could Ask God Any Question, What Would It Be?

Alton Gansky

THOMAS NELSON
Since 1798

NASHVILLE   DALLAS   MEXICO CITY   RIO DE JANEIRO

Published in Nashville, Tennessee, by Thomas Nelson. Thomas Nelson is a registered trademark of Thomas Nelson, Inc.

Thomas Nelson, Inc. titles may be purchased in bulk for educational, business, fund-raising, or sales promotional use. For information, please e-mail SpecialMarkets@ThomasNelson.com.

Scripture quotations marked CEV are from THE *CONTEMPORARY ENGLISH VERSION*. ©1991, 1992, 1995 by American Bible Society. Used by permission.

Scripture quotations marked HCSB have been taken from the HOLMAN CHRISTIAN STANDARD BIBLE®, © 1999, 2000, 2002, 2003 by Holman Bible Publishers. Used by permission. Holman Christian Standard Bible®, Holman CSB®, and HCSB® are federally registered trademarks of Holman Bible Publishers.

Scripture quotations marked NASB are from the NEW AMERICAN STANDARD BIBLE®, © The Lockman Foundation 1960, 1962, 1963, 1968, 1971, 1972, 1973, 1975, 1977, 1995. Used by permission.

Scripture quotations marked NIV are taken from the HOLY BIBLE, NEW INTERNATIONAL VERSION.® NIV.® © 1973, 1978, 1984, by International Bible Society. Used by permission of Zondervan Publishing House. All rights reserved.

Scripture quotations noted NKJV are from THE NEW KING JAMES VERSION. © 1979, 1980, 1982 by Thomas Nelson, Inc. Used by permission. All rights reserved.

Scripture quotations marked NLT are taken from *The Holy Bible, New Living Translation*. ©1996, 2004. Used by permission of Tyndale House Publishers, Inc., Wheaton, Illinois 60189. All rights reserved.

Scripture quotations marked NRSV are taken from the NEW REVISED STANDARD VERSION of the Bible. Copyright © 1989 by the Division of Christian Education of the National Council of the Churches of Christ in the U.S.A. All rights reserved.

Library of Congress Control Number 2010940133

ISBN: 978-0-7852-3165-3

Editor: Lila Empson Wavering

Associate Editor: Jennifer McNeil

Design: Whisner Design Group

Printed in the United States of America

11 12 13 14 15 QGT 9 8 7 6 5 4 3 2 1

If the pleasures of love can attract a man to a

woman, if hunger and loneliness can make a

man travel miles in search of food and shelter,

how much more will the desire for truth

and holiness make a man seek God?

Saint Augustine of Hippo

"Come now, and let us reason together," says the Lord.

Isaiah 1:18 NKJV

CONTENTS

GOD

From the beginning, people have struggled to know God—who He is, what He does, and how they can know He really does exist.

BIBLE

The Bible is central to Christianity and is made up of histories and letters written hundreds of years apart. People want to know that the books in the Bible are the ones God intended to be there.

THE FUTURE

Much of the Bible focuses on the end of the world—the end times. What is going to happen then is the subject of much mystery and misunderstanding.

PAIN AND SUFFERING

The most difficult questions people have to deal with involve some sort of heartache. People have trouble understanding why this is so, since God is good.

JESUS

Jesus is the most important person who ever lived and is the center of Christian faith. People have many questions about Jesus' life and work.

KINGDOM OF GOD

The kingdom doesn't refer to place so much as it refers to authority. The kingdom of God is the keystone of New Testament teaching.

HEAVEN AND HELL

Eternal life, eternal punishment—both are nearly impossible for people to believe, but the Bible teaches both are real. The concept of eternal, though difficult, can be understood in this present life.

HUMANITY

The book of Genesis shows God taking a hands-on approach to creating Adam and Eve, something He didn't do with the rest of creation. God designed people to be different from the other animals.

CHRISTIAN LIVING

All people have a limited amount of time on the planet. Everyone dies. What people do before that day is their legacy—that is their mark on the world.

TODAY'S WORLD

God is all-knowing and all-seeing. His perspective on the world may be just what people expect—or it may surprise them.

Introduction

A prudent question is one half of wisdom.

Francis Bacon

In 1951, MGM released a small-budget movie titled *The Next Voice You Hear*. Starring James Whitmore and Nancy Davis (later to be Nancy Reagan), the movie shows the effects of a strange voice that comes over the radio each night at 8:30 for a week. The voice breaks into the scheduled broadcast and has a powerful impact on a man and his family. The voice, it turns out, belongs to God.

The next year saw the release of *Red Planet Mars*. It was marketed as a science-fiction movie, but it turned out to be more than that. A scientist, played by Peter Graves, believes he's contacted intelligent life on Mars only to discover that the signal is not coming from the red planet but from somewhere else, somewhere far more mysterious. The movie implies that the scientist, and the rest of the world, is really hearing a direct communication from God. To contemporary audiences, such fare might seem quaint and simplistic, but it does show our innate desire to hear a word from God.

Imagine hearing God speak. Better yet, imagine being able to ask God direct questions and then listen to His response, or to pull Jesus aside to ask for some insight on a pressing question. This book is an effort to show what that might be like. We are a curious people, and the more we think about spiritual matters, the more questions we have. It's healthy to think about such things.

What would you ask if you knew you could deliver your question to the Creator? Would it be a broad philosophical question, or would it be something close, personal, maybe born of pain and desperation? Perhaps you would question the presence of suffering and evil. Maybe you'd ask something about Jesus, say, His resurrection. Or perhaps you'd wonder whether your life has significance or not. There are hundreds of questions; each has its own unique set of complexities. This book attempts to answer fifty-five such questions and to do so in the voice of God, Jesus, and biblical characters.

Of course, no one can speak for God but God. We have used this approach as a literary device, a means of breaking away from dry philosophy and theology to give the questions new life. Together, the publisher, the book producer, the editors, and I have tried to create something that engages the mind and heart of any person—believer or not—who has questions about and for God.

Compelled by a soul-deep respect for our God and His revealed will, we've undertaken to make it possible for readers to ask the questions common to all people and enable them to "hear" what God has said about the topic. This is a high and sometimes daunting goal and one not taken lightly. Prayer and thought went into every chapter. We've avoided taking the "easy path" and the temptation to just make up answers, especially with those questions that have been debated for centuries, nor did we shy away from topics simply because they were difficult. In every case, we sought to build our answers on solid biblical interpretation and did so only after careful, prayerful consideration.

Taking what God and Jesus have already revealed, every response in this book is rooted in the Bible. Every chapter comes with biblical references situated at the back of the book so you can read the Bible verses for yourself.

The material for the fifty-five questions is set in contemporary times and is meant to speak to the lives of twenty-first-century people. Some questions require more detail than others. Some questions have easy answers, while others are not so clear. Again, in every case, we tried to remain true to what has been revealed in Scripture.

We've also made an effort to do away with what is often called *Christianese*. Engineers, architects, cooks, and mechanics all have a specialized language. The same is often true of churches. Such unique phrases can be confusing to those not familiar with the terms, and at the same time they can be overused to the point of failing to communicate in a fresh way to those who are familiar with the terms. We've tried to avoid such usage to make this work accessible to everyone.

So why do this? Why undertake this task in this way? Too often, discussions about God and Jesus are confined to books only theologians would enjoy. Most of us need and want a more direct approach. The chapters are purposely short so you can read as few or as many as you like in one sitting. You set the pace.

Let me give a few suggestions. First, take your time. These are important questions and deserve a little thought. The British politician and philosopher Edmund Burke said, "Reading without reflection is like eating without digesting."

Second, read the book in any order you wish. If one section is more interesting to you, then start there. Skip around if you want. The book has been designed for that.

Last, let the material percolate. Some of the issues covered in this book are of great importance. We suggest that you look up the referenced verses in your own Bible or that you read the references listed in the notes to see for yourself what God's Word says in context and to enhance your own connection to God and to the Scriptures. Note that the verses cited are reprinted in the back, but those quoted directly in the text are not included there.

We hope you not only enjoy this book but find it useful as you think about the who, what, and why of God, and about the people who walked with God and with Jesus in the pages of the Old and the New Testaments. Some of these people contribute their voices to the conversations:

- *Abraham*, whose name means "father of many," is the father of two nations through his sons, Ishmael and Isaac.
- *Andrew* was one of the original twelve disciples of Christ.
- *Asaph* served in King David's court as a musician and songwriter.
- *David* was a warrior, a ruler of great skill, a builder, a poet, and a musician. Most of the writings in the book of Psalms—the Bible's hymnbook—were penned by him.
- *Eve* was the first woman, the first wife, the first mother, the first grandmother, and the first mother to lose a son to violence. It was through Eve and her husband, Adam, that sin entered the world.
- *James* was the half brother of Jesus. He would later become head of the church, following Peter. (Several other people named James also appear in the pages of the New Testament.)
- *Jeremiah* is often called the "Weeping Prophet." He was a man with deep commitment and a strong personality, someone who was not afraid to speak truth to the powerful.
- *Job*, perhaps the most beleaguered man in history, went from great wealth and influence to abject poverty and back again.
- *The apostle John* was a faithful disciple of Christ and is sometimes referred to as "the disciple whom Jesus loved." He was one of the inner three, which allowed him to witness things not seen by the others.
- *John the Baptist* and Jesus were related through their mothers. His message was direct and pointed: "Repent, for the kingdom of God is at hand." Those who did repent, he baptized—by the thousands—in the Jordan.
- *Jonah* is one of the most famous and most unusual prophets of the Old

Testament. He spent three days (a foreshadowing of the three days Jesus spent in the tomb) in the belly of a large fish "appointed" by God.

- *Joseph*, Mary's husband, showed great courae and deep spiritual strength in believing Mary's miraculous conception of Jesus.
- *Joshua* succeeded Moses as the leader of the Hebrews, and he was the one who led them over the Jordan and into the promised land.
- *Judas* arranged for Roman soldiers, temple guards, and servants to take Jesus into custody. When Judas saw all that Jesus endured, he committed suicide.
- *Lazarus* of Bethany was one of a handful of people whom Jesus brought back to life.
- *Mary Magdalene* became a follower when Jesus cast seven demons from her, freeing her from years of torment.
- *Matthias* was the replacement decided on by the Twelve after Judas's suicide.
- *Micah* was one of the minor prophets. One of his prophecies named the future birthplace of Jesus—about seven hundred years before the event.
- *Moses* is remembered most for being God's choice to lead His people out of bondage in Egypt.
- *Paul* wrote about half the twenty-seven New Testament books, and he is mentioned in several others.
- *Peter*, a fisherman by trade, followed Jesus from the beginning. He was the natural leader of the disciples and became the first pastor of the first church.
- *Simeon* was a deeply spiritual man who spent much of his time at the temple in Jerusalem. His one desire was to see the Messiah before he died.
- *Solomon* followed David, his father, on the throne. God rewarded him with wisdom and riches. Most Bible historians consider him the richest man to have ever lived.
- *Stephen* was vocal about his faith and preached a long sermon about Jesus. His message was so direct that it angered the crowd to the point that they stoned him to death, a horrible and painful way to die.
- *Timothy* provided support and help to the apostle Paul.
- *Titus* was a travel companion with Paul and worked among the non-Jewish converts.
- *Urbanus* was called a "fellow worker" by Paul.

It is our hope that you enjoy a deepening of your relationship with God as you read what He says to us today through His words in the Scriptures and as you relate the experiences of biblical personalities to your own life.

Ask, and it will be given to you; seek, and you will find; knock, and it will be opened to you. For everyone who asks receives, and he who seeks finds, and to him who knocks it will be opened.

Matthew 7:7–8 NKJV

*You have looked deep into my heart, LORD,
and you know all about me. You know when
I am resting or when I am working, and from
heaven you discover my thoughts. You notice
everything I do and everywhere I go. Before I
even speak a word, you know what I will say,
and with your powerful arm you
protect me from every side.*

Psalm 139:1–5 CEV

GOD

From the beginning, people have struggled to know God—who He is, what He does, and how they can know He really does exist.

I
God, who are You? What are You?

A survey of history shows one thing: humans are a curious lot. Humans are good at many things—building tall buildings and bridges that span the widest gorge, for instance—but the thing humans seem best at is asking questions. Many questions asked are trivial in nature; others, however, reach to the deepest parts of the soul. Few are those who have gazed into the night sky and not wondered about God. While many ridicule the thought of God, far more wonder who He is and what He is like.

From the beginning, men and women have wondered about God and his nature. In his book Knowing God, *J. I. Packer wrote, "Once you become aware that the main business that you are here for is to know God, most of life's problems fall into place of their own accord."* [1]

 God, who are You? What are You? Is it possible for us to know the answers to these questions, or is it impossible for mere humans to understand You?

GOD

That's a simple question. It's also a question with a complex answer. I'm unique in all creation. Before there was history, I was. Before there was a universe, I was. Before there was anything, including time itself, I was. I am the Creator of all things. All that you see, you see because I brought it into being. There is no one like Me. There are no other gods. [2]

My uniqueness makes it difficult for humans to understand Me. Humans relate to one another because they are similar. Every human knows what it is to laugh, weep, feel joy, draw back in fear, and love. When one human looks at another, he or she sees all the similarities shared by people. I, on the other hand, have no counterpart. No one fills the universe as I do; no one has the same kind of power; no one shares all My knowledge; and I alone am unbound by time and space.

In many ways, however, I am similar to you. This is natural because when I created man and woman, I created them in My image.[3] That means we share many attributes. Does that surprise you? It shouldn't. Many of the things that make you unique in your world are attributes that make Me unique in the universe.

People who have not taken the time to learn about Me think of Me as a "thing." What you must understand is that I am not a thing, but a person. What makes a person? A person has three characteristics: intellect, emotion, and will.

I am a Being with intellect, which means I think. I'm not a distant, invisible, force. I am someone who reasons and communicates. In other words, I have thoughts. You are the direct result of those thoughts.

But more than someone who thinks, I am someone who feels. As you read the Bible, you will find that many emotions are attributed to Me: joy, anger, sadness, love, forgiveness, and even jealousy. Don't let that last one unsettle you. Jealousy is not the same as envy. *Envy* is wanting what someone else has. I don't feel envy. *Jealousy* is the fear of losing what you have. When a husband is jealous over his wife, he worries that he might be losing her. I am jealous for all My creation, and especially you. You, and every other human, matter to Me.

I also have will. Some people call it volition. *Will* means that not only can I think and feel emotions, but that I also make decisions. I have free will and the ability to make choices, as do you. I'm not a mindless force; I'm a reasoning Being. Don't think of Me as a thing, but as a person.

PAUL

As an apostle, I had two primary goals: first, to make the world aware of Jesus and His sacrifice; second, to make sure Christians everywhere understood as much as they could about God and His Son, Jesus. I have to confess, that was not always easy. To describe God is to describe the indescribable. I spent most of my adult life trying to make clear to anyone and everyone how special God is.

We Hebrews had many names for God. Each described some aspect or element of His character. For example, *El Shaddai* means "almighty God." *El Elyon* means "the God most high." The Old Testament is filled with such names, all of which attempt to help us understand who God is and what He is like. The name most commonly ascribed to God is Jehovah. The ancient Hebrews pronounced the name Yahweh. It means "I Am" and refers to God's eternal nature. That name alone appears more than seven thousand times in the Old Testament. The nature and magnitude of God are so great that it's impossible to have a single name for Him.

JESUS

Humans share many attributes with God the Father. You think, you have emotions, and you have will just as He does. But some attributes you do not share. For example, God is omnipotent. That means He is all-powerful. Nothing is beyond His strength and ability. God is omniscient. He knows all things. There is no limit to His knowledge. Not only does He know everything that is, but He knows everything that was and everything that will be. He even knows everything that "can" be.

God is eternal.[4] Don't confuse that with immortal, which means that God cannot die. True as that is, *eternal* means that He has always been. There has never been a time when God wasn't; there will never be a time when God isn't.

God is supreme and absolute. No one is greater than He is, and He is not dependent on anyone.[5] God is the only One you can call perfect. He is holy and sinless.[6]

While you share some of His attributes and some of His nature, He remains different from you. During my earthly ministry, I passed through a region called Samaria. While resting at a well, I encountered a woman, and we carried on a conversation in which I corrected her view of God and worship. I told her, "God is spirit, and those who worship Him must worship in spirit and truth."[7]

Here is where many people become confused. God has no physical form. As I told the woman at the well in Samaria, God is Spirit. To properly understand God, to properly worship Him, you must first understand that He occupies everyplace at all times. There is no place where God is not. The prophet Amos had a vision of the Lord, who said He was on both the mountaintop and the ocean bottom.[8] This means He can occupy your home and your heart.

God cannot be seen. As I told the disciples, "No one has seen the Father except the one who is from God; only he has seen the Father."[9]

GOD

Because of this, many have assumed I don't exist. Throughout the centuries, artists have attempted to portray Me in human form. Michelangelo saw Me as a large man with a white beard reaching a finger out to give Adam the spark of life. As a symbol, such artwork is fine, but it doesn't capture the reality of My existence.

I live in and beyond the realm that you see. Heaven is my home. Any attempt to picture Me will fail. As advanced and remarkable as I created your brain, it is incapable of fully understanding Me. This is not arrogance on My part; it's just a statement of fact. Your brain has a limited capacity, and I'm an unlimited Being.

Don't let this dissuade you from searching to know more about Me. A swimming pool cannot hold the whole ocean, but it can hold enough to tell you a great deal. The highest purpose a person can have is to seek Me and to know Me. I have put My yearning in you. Don't set it aside.

Remember, I am a Who and not a what. I am a person, and you share many of My qualities and abilities. You are a person because I'm a person; you have emotion because I have emotion; you have the power of choice because I have the power of choice.

I am your Creator. I am your God.

One of my prophets said, "You will seek Me and find Me when you search for Me with all your heart."[10]

I am knowable.

2
God, how can we believe that You created us?

There is perhaps no more contentious debate than that of origins. Lawsuits have been filed against schools and teachers for teaching some form of creationism in the classroom. The "Scopes monkey trial" put the topic in the newspapers of 1925, and it's been there ever since. To some it may seem a minor point of disagreement; to others it is a life-changing cause. How humans came to be is more than an exercise in academics; it is foundational to belief in God and beliefs about God. The teaching of evolution is so prevalent and its proponents so insistent that any other voice is shouted down and the speaker called a fool.

Beliefs about origins matter at every level of life.

 God, did You really create us? If so, how can we know? So many educated people teach that we are the result of chance, not direct creation. Can they be right?

GOD

Yes, you are My creation.[1] You are My design.[2] You are My art. Many people deny that; they want you to believe that accident and fortunate happenstance resulted in all you see and all you are. Does that sound right to you? Does that *feel* right to you? It doesn't. Here's why: there is an unbreakable link between you the created and Me the Creator. There is within you and within everyone the ability to recognize My handiwork. The proof of creation is all around you.

When I created the universe, I put your world in just the right spot in its galaxy. If it were much closer to the center of the Milky Way, life would be impossible. The same is true for planet Earth. Look at the other planets. Each one is beautiful in its way. There are rocky planets and moons as well as gas giants like Jupiter and Saturn. Yet your planet is the only one close enough to the sun to have heat and far enough away to maintain an atmosphere in which you can breathe. Is that an accident? The night sky testifies to creation.[3]

You are 70 percent water living on a planet that has water covering two-thirds of the surface. The oceans, the plants, and the weather make it possible for you and all living things to live and thrive. The other planets are lifeless. Only the one I made for you can support complicated life.

Some scientists have used their knowledge to declare that I don't exist, but a great many scientists know how complex and intricately designed life is. Biology is proof of My creation. Your body is an engine that converts food into energy, which in turn contributes to growth and life. That is no accident. In your blood are cells whose sole purpose is to find, recognize, capture, and dispose of contaminates. Scientists call this miracle *phagocytosis*. The process is extremely complex. I made it so.

JESUS

The key to seeing creation is the willingness to look. Evidence is everywhere: from the complexity of plants to the intricacies of your mind. There is no lack of evidence, only a lack of belief.

You might wonder why there is such a reluctance to believe in a personal creation. There is a reason. To believe that God created everything is to believe in God—and that admission demands a change in the person. Some people would rather believe that everything came to be by accident than believe there is a God to whom they are accountable.

Questions regarding creation cause the believer to think of his or her relationship with God. For that reason, many choose to believe in other things. This is not new. The apostle Paul dealt with such people in his ministry. He wrote, "They exchanged the truth of God for a lie, and worshiped and served created things rather than the Creator—who is forever praised."[4]

You can see how sad this is. To avoid obligation or admitting that there is a God, people will embrace almost any other idea and think they're making an intelligent decision, but in truth they have missed wisdom.

SOLOMON

I am often called the wisest man who ever lived. Of course, I take no credit for my wisdom. God offered me a gift, and wisdom was my choice.

The event is recorded in the Bible: "God gave Solomon wisdom and very great discernment and breadth of mind, like the sand that is on the seashore. Solomon's wisdom surpassed the wisdom of all the sons of the east and all the wisdom of Egypt. For he was wiser than all men."[5]

That supernatural wisdom gave me insight into the actions of men but also into the way the world worked. The more I learned, the clearer God's creation became. I wrote thousands of proverbs. Here's one of them: "Remember now your Creator in the days of your youth."[6] Look around you; search for the truth, and you will see God's fingerprints over the world and over you. Knowing we have a Creator makes us wise.

GOD

Think of birth—not just human birth but any birth. How is it possible that you, because of an intimate act between your parents, could come to be from microscopic cells? How can the same genetic material that makes your bones hard and solid also make the soft, clear lens of your eye? There are more cells in your body than there are galaxies in the universe. Sixty thousand miles of blood vessels run through your body. The very act of breathing—drawing oxygen from the air and using it to keep cells alive—is a miracle of design.

Some make boastful noise about creating an organic molecule or recombining strands of DNA, but, as remarkable as that is, it's a tiny accomplishment compared to creating life that thinks, functions in a social environment, reproduces, grows the food it needs, and cares for others.

The greatest proof of personal creation doesn't come from philosophical arguments or books on apologetics. The greatest proof comes from an open mind and open eyes.

Not long ago, an atheist went on a solo camping trip. He wanted time alone to think. In the mountains of California he found a beautiful area to pitch his tent. There were no other campers in sight; he was alone in My creation. On the second day of his trip, he rested in front of his tent. Next to him grew a small flower. It captured his attention. He was a well-educated man and had studied botany. He had been taught how plants draw nutrients and water from the ground and how chlorophyll converts sunlight into energy. He then thought about how plants reproduce and about the roles that insects like bees play in continuing certain plant species. The more he thought, the more he wondered about the complexity and the beauty of organic structures like plants and animals.

That night he stared at the stars and listened to the sounds of life in the forest. And he thought. The more he thought, the more convinced he became that he lived in a world of design and not accident. That night, he and I became family.

JESUS

You were created to grow and prosper. You were created to experience life. You were created to learn and explore everything around you. There is no sin in learning. Still, your race has a tendency to find substitutes for the Father. In the past, some people have created false gods to please themselves. Today, some people do not want a Creator, especially a Creator who wants a personal relationship, a Creator who can make demands.

It is easier for many to believe in random chance rather than in God, who wants nothing but the best for them. King David knew he was a created being. He said, "I praise you, for I am fearfully and wonderfully made. Wonderful are your works; that I know very well."[7]

GOD

If you will open your eyes, open your mind, and open your soul, you will find evidence of My creation of the universe and, more important, My hands-on creation of you. The more you know, the more proof you will have. I am your Creator.[8]

3
God, who are we to You?

All people want to know they matter to someone—that their lives have meaning and value. It is so easy to feel insignificant in a world with a population approaching seven billion. What is one person in a sea of billions? In view of the fact that humans live such a short time, just eighty years or so, their lives seem inconsequential. So it's not unusual to ask about ourselves and our lives from God's point of view.

If God is all-powerful, and people are weak by comparison; if God is all-knowing, and people's knowledge of life and the universe is limited; then it seems fair to wonder if people have any real value.

 God, who are we to You? Do we have any value to You? You are so great and we are so tiny that it is hard to believe that You can have any interest in us.

God

This is not a new question. Even the most faithful of My people have struggled to find a believable answer. No man was more faithful than Job, and he asked, "What is man that you make so much of him, that you give him so much attention?"[1] Centuries later, King David wrote this question: "What is man that You take thought of him, and the son of man that You care for him?"[2] The question was so important to him, he asked again: "Why do we humans mean anything to you, our LORD? Why do you care about us?"[3] The question is so universal among My followers that it was repeated a thousand years later by the writer of Hebrews: "What is man, that You remember him? Or the son of man, that You are concerned about him? You have made him for a little while lower than the angels; You have crowned him with glory and honor, and have appointed him over the works of Your hands; You have put all things in subjection under his feet."[4]

But you should know something, and you must never forget it: You are significant. You always have been and you always will be significant. There are several reasons to believe this. First, I created humans in a personal way.

We've already discussed that. Just remember that you are special because of your special creation.

Another reason, which many overlook, is revelation. *Revelation* means "to unveil, to uncover." Let Me ask a question: how much could you know about Me and My plans for you without My revealing it? You could learn many things from studying nature, but nature can teach only generalities. I have made an effort to give you a special revelation.

I value you very much, and I want you to understand as much as you can about Me and My redemptive plan. Over the centuries, I have inspired prophets and apostles to record My message that is given in the Bible. I imagine you'll have questions about that too. For now, just understand that I took the initiative to reveal Myself to you through miracles, prophets, My Son, and the Bible. If you had no value to Me, I wouldn't have bothered.

JESUS

I reminded My followers that one of My purposes was to declare the Father to them and to the world.[5] This I did because of the love We have for you. That one word is the key: *love.* You are the object of God's love. He not only gave you the world, but after sin entered the world, He made it possible for sin to be forgiven and the relationship to continue for eternity.

Love sent Me to the world; love sent Me to the cross. God didn't send Me to condemn the world but to save it—to save you.[6] You are worthy of Our sacrifice.

JEREMIAH

My entire ministry was spent trying to bring a wayward people back to their God. In the two books of the Bible I wrote under God's inspiration, I used one phrase repeatedly. I believe I may have used this phrase more than any other writer in the Bible. This phrase will help you understand what you are to God. As a prophet, God gave me a message for the people. Time and time again, I quoted God as referring to "My people." Not *the* people," but "*My people.*"

The passing centuries have not changed that. The entire history of God and humankind has been about maintaining a relationship in this life and the next. "Long ago the LORD said to Israel: 'I have loved you, my people, with an everlasting love. With unfailing love I have drawn you to myself.'"[7] There are dozens of times when God refers to you as His people.

GOD

Some have imagined that I sit in heaven and gaze down on people as if they were ants, but that is far from the truth. I see people of great value, people I love. Yes, I see the sin and it grieves Me. I see the bitterness and hear the words of those who deny My existence, but My love for humankind has not wavered. There have been times when I've had to be harsh for the good of the future, but I've never taken joy in it. I declared once that "I know the plans I have for you . . . plans to prosper you and not to harm you, plans to give you hope and a future."[8]

Abraham holds a special place in history. He was a man of great faith, and I considered him a friend.[9] Is it so difficult to believe that we could be friends? Man and God; God and man—friends.

JESUS

Toward the end of My ministry, when My betrayal, arrest, and crucifixion were close at hand, I took My disciples aside and gave one of My last sermons to them. I taught them about the importance of following My teachings, but I also wanted them to understand how much they meant to Me. I told them that the greatest love a man could exhibit was to lay down his life for his friends. That was what I was about to do. I then told them, "You are my friends if you do what I command. I no longer call you servants, because a servant does not know his master's business. Instead, I have called you friends."[10]

GOD

It is so seldom discussed, but we are partners in My work on earth. For some, this is too much to imagine. My plan for salvation was established at the beginning of the world, and it has always involved people like you. My Son sacrificed Himself for you and for the world, but before He did, He selected disciples, who became apostles and established the church to spread the message of salvation. Into your hands We placed the greatest message the world can hear. I could do this only if I loved and trusted you.

27

When I see you, I don't see a slave, someone to order around, someone to do My bidding. When I look at you, I don't see just a worshipper; I see a member of My family. Jesus taught His disciples to pray; He taught them to begin with "Our Father in heaven."[11]

Jesus

It was much more than just a passing phrase. I wanted everyone to understand that every believer is a part of the family of God. You are a child of God, and that is why He loves you so.

When you serve your Father, you are not serving some distant God; you're not doing so because you fear retribution; you're not doing so simply because you've been told to be obedient. You serve your Father because He is your Father. And He loves you because you are His child.

God

You should also know that if you've placed your faith and trust in Me through My Son, Jesus Christ, you are a Christian. That word—Christian—is used so often that few know its origin or its meaning. Two thousand years ago Jesus' followers were first called Christians.[12] The people who coined the term meant it as an insult, but it became a badge of honor. Christian means "little Christ." Being called a Christian is to be labeled as someone who reflects Jesus. When I see you, I think of My own Son.

The answer to this question could go on forever, and in many ways it will. Nonetheless, I have one more item to help you understand what you are to Me. You are a saint.[13] That doesn't mean you're perfect, and it doesn't mean that you have the power to work miracles as the apostles did, but it does mean you are special.

The word saint has a special meaning. It describes someone who has been set apart for a holy purpose. The saint is a dedicated believer, someone who's doing his best to lead a spiritual life as taught in the Bible. Saints come in all shapes and sizes, all ages, all educational backgrounds, and all races.

What are you to Me? You are the object of My love, the focus of My attention, part of My every thought. You are My child, part of a family greater than you can imagine. You are a little Christ. And you are a saint.

4
God, what does it mean that You are love?

Some people contend that love is the world's most powerful force. Most popular songs deal with love in one way or another. Love has caused men and women to sacrifice everything for the ones they love. When a family member dies, the love felt for them is seen in the grief the survivors display. Love cannot be ignored.

The ancient Greeks had several words for love (Greek is the original language of the Bible's New Testament). They used eros *to refer to erotic love;* philos *when they spoke of deep friendship; and* agape *when they spoke of God's love*

It seems that the phrase "God is love" is one of the most quoted lines ever. People have been talking about love for nearly two thousand years, so it must be important.

Q We are told that You are love, but what does that mean? How can a person be love? And of all the emotions, why love?

GOD

Love. There's a word for it in every language. Almost everyone experiences love, and everyone longs for it. Love is an integral part of being a human. It is part of My design. Ideally, parents love their children, husbands love their wives, wives love their husbands, and close friends share a kind of love. Over the years, psychologists have come to understand just how important love is. Love is a requirement for happiness. In those rare and tragic cases in which an individual receives no love, he or she struggles to make sense of life.

Love is essential to relationships. When I made Adam and Eve, I intended there to be two directions of love: vertical and horizontal. My ideal was for them to love each other with every fiber of their beings, to receive My love every moment of their lives, and to love Me in return.

Love is more than an emotion. You have a wide range of emotions that run the extremes from admiration to hate, from joy to depression, and from contentment to fear. You have more emotions than you probably know, and you experience some of them every day. Of all the emotions you have, the most powerful, most lasting, and most enabling is love.

Like you, I feel love. There are no bounds to My love. Not only do I experience love but I also must express it. Here's one thing you must understand: My love is not subject to whims or emotions. My love is grounded in reason and activated by deliberate choice. I love because I choose to love. I love you because I want to love you. Love is at the core of My Being. I created because of love; I have intervened in history because of love; and I involve Myself in the entire human race because of My love.

JOHN

Many of the apostles are remembered by the topics they emphasized in their ministries and writings. The apostle Paul is known for emphasizing grace and the inclusion of all people in the church. The apostle Peter is remembered for encouraging those under great persecution. It is my honor to be referred to as "the Apostle of Love."

I earned this title through the preaching in my writing. For me, nothing was more important than making sure the world knew of God's love for them. God's love motivated me to teach my students and followers to love one another. For example, I wrote, "Dear friends, let us continue to love one another, for love comes from God. Anyone who loves is a child of God and knows God. But anyone who does not love does not know God, for God is love."[1]

God's love is unique. There is nothing else like it in the universe. He loves in a way only He can. His very nature and essence is love. But be careful here. It is true that God is love, but that does not mean love is God. God is a person, and love describes His nature.

GOD

Love is part of My nature. I cannot *not* love. My love must be expressed, and I express it to you. You are the object of My love, the reason for My love. But My love is different. It is not subject to whims and mere emotion. My love is grounded in reason and is activated by deliberate choice. I choose to love.

For many, love is something they feel, a moving within them. Most people will describe love as an emotion felt inside a person. You know that sensation. It is like feeling something moving inside the core of your being. But love is more than that, especially for Me.

My love is more than just goodwill; it is a desire to see the very best for you. My love is not based on the attractiveness of the one I love; it is not based on how witty, humorous, or intelligent the person is. My love goes beyond that. My love is grounded in righteousness, which is another aspect of My nature. I do not violate the one to save the other.

My love is based in My perfection, not the perfection of the one being loved. I love sinners and the righteous; not because the righteous are righteous, and not because the sinners are sinners.

My love is meant to draw you to Me, to cement our relationship. I love you with an everlasting love.[2]

JESUS

On many occasions, I talk about God's love through stories and parables. I used illustrations that people in the first century could understand. One of My favorite examples was that of a shepherd. His life was hard and others often looked down on him, and yet the shepherd provided a much-needed service.

I told the people that I was the Good Shepherd, the kind of shepherd who would lay down his life for the sheep. I used the illustration so that My listeners would understand that I would not abandon them should danger come.[3]

I made it more personal than that. I taught them that like a good shepherd I know My sheep and My sheep know Me, just as the Father knows Me and I know the Father. By that I meant God was expressing love through Me to the world. To prove My love, to prove God's love, I laid down My life for you. No one stole My life from Me; I gave it freely for your salvation and the salvation of everyone who believes.[4]

JOHN

I wrote about that in my Gospel. I quoted Jesus, who said, "Greater love has no one than this, than to lay down one's life for his friends."[5]

One thing I know is that real love is not just our love for God. Real love is His love for us. God loved us so much that He sent His only Son as a means of restoring our broken relationship.[6]

God

The best testimony to My love can be found in the words of those who have received it, who have experienced it. Job, a man who lost everything, still found it within himself to love and be loved. He looked forward to the time after his death when he would see Me. He said, "I will see him for myself, and I long for that moment."[7]

The apostle Paul faced many hardships, endured many beatings and was the recipient of the worst kinds of criticism, yet he continued his work because of the love that we shared. He wrote to a group of Christians living in Rome that he was convinced nothing could separate him or other Christians from My love.[8]

I am love's author, its champion, the One who gives love, the One who receives love. My love is designed to benefit you, and My love for you brings Me great joy. Yes, I am love.

5
God, is Jesus really Your son?

"Like father, like son." No one knows how long that phrase has been around, but it's a common understanding. Simple observation proves the point. Certainly there are sons who differ from their fathers in many ways. Not every athletic father has an athletic son, for instance. Still, experience teaches us that sons have many of the qualities of their fathers. Is that also true of God the Father and Jesus the Son?

What did Jesus mean when He said that anyone who saw Him also saw the Father?[1] And why did Jesus call Himself both the Son of God and the Son of man?[2] How could that be?

 God, is Jesus really Your Son? What does that mean? How can You have a Son?

GOD

Your question is one of the most important a person can ask. It has deep theological implications. It is also a personal question. Personal for Me, and personal for you. I can answer the first portion of your question with one word: yes. But you are really asking a deeper set of questions, and that requires a closer, more thoughtful look.

To understand this, you must first understand the answer to this question: Was there ever a time when Jesus wasn't? The temptation is to think that My Son came into existence at His conception. That kind of thinking is understandable but inaccurate. Humans come into being at conception. Jesus, however, has always been. If that puzzles you, then you are not alone. Still, it's not too difficult to believe.

When I inspired the Bible writers, I led them to record this truth several times. For example, the apostle John started his gospel this way: "In the beginning was the Word, and the Word was with God, and the Word was God. He was in the beginning with God."[3] John started his gospel talking about Jesus before Jesus' birth.

Joseph

As Jesus' earthly father, I struggled to understand this. It was beyond my experience. It was beyond *everyone's* experience. When I say I was Jesus' earthly father, I mean that I was Mary's husband. From a Jewish point of view, I was Jesus' legal father. It was my privilege to care for Him during the early years of His earthly life. God, through dreams given to me and angelic visits to Mary, made it clear who Jesus' father was.[4, 5] I couldn't explain it all then, but I recognized the truth of it. Jesus existed before His birth.

Jesus

I went to John the Baptist so he could baptize Me in the Jordon. I did so to signal the start of My ministry to him and to others. When I arrived, he shouted to the huge crowd that had come out to hear him: "This was He of whom I said, 'He who comes after me is preferred before me, for He was before me.'"[6] What the crowd didn't know was this: John the Baptist was, in human terms, My cousin and was born six months before I was.

A comment I made during my earthly ministry stunned the religious leaders. It also stunned My followers. I said, "I tell you the truth . . . before Abraham was born, I am!"[7] It amazed everyone who heard it because Abraham lived and died eighteen hundred years before I uttered those words. There's a lot in that one statement, but for now, just know that I was preexistent—that is, like God the Father, I have always been.

God

Jesus took on physical form. Bible teachers call that act "the incarnation." *Incarnation* means "in the flesh." John the apostle described the act: "The Word became flesh and dwelt among us, and we beheld His glory, the glory as of the only begotten of the Father, full of grace and truth."[8] When John used the term *Word,* he was referring to Jesus before He took on physical form.

Jesus was born of Mary, a virgin. His physical conception was a miracle. There are many reasons for that, one of which was to maintain My role as Jesus' Father. He was not conceived in the usual way. What happened to Mary is unique in history and will never be repeated. That very personal miracle established Me as Jesus' true and only Father.

At His birth, angels rejoiced, shepherds visited, and wise men from a distant land came to worship Him. All of them recognized Jesus as My Son. Jesus was born at just the right time. It was all part of God's plan. But when the right time came, I sent My Son, born of a woman, subject to the law. I sent Him to buy freedom for those who were slaves to the law, so that I could adopt them as My very own children.[9] Jesus became a child so you could become My children.

JESUS

Those who have studied My teachings know that I often spoke of God as My Father. I used the phrase "My Father" many times.[10] I never hid the truth. Of course, there were many who did not believe Me. That was true then, and it's true now.

Even Satan, when he came to Me during My time in the wilderness, would begin his temptation with "If You are the son of God."[11] He knew.

Still, a great many saw the truth and were not embarrassed to acknowledge it. First, My Father acknowledged Me as His Son. As one Bible writer put it, "When he brought his firstborn Son into the world, God said, 'Let all of God's angels worship him.'"[12]

I thought that all men should honor the Son just as they honor the Father. What honors Me as the Son of God also honors God the Father.[13]

John the apostle put it this way: "God's love was revealed among us in this way: God sent his only son into the world so that we might live through him."[14]

During My ministry, I had many friends, and perhaps none were more supportive than Martha, the sister of Lazarus and Mary. At a difficult time in her life, I questioned what she believed, and she said to Me, "I have believed that You are the Christ, the Son of God, even He who comes into the world."[15]

My friend and disciple Simon Peter made a similar confession when he said to Me, "You are the Christ, the Son of the living God."[16]

GOD

One thing you must understand is that being the Son means more than having a family relationship. Jesus as My Son sets an example for all those who could be part of the family of God, My family. No one will ever replace Jesus as My Son. But anyone who can believe and act on that belief can be a son or a daughter of God.

Yes, Jesus is literally My Son. Although He existed before time began, before all creation—indeed, He was the agent in creation—His incarnation and birth created a way for people like you to relate to Me.

As My Son He did many things. He represented Me to the world; He taught My truth to anyone who would listen; He sacrificed Himself so that the price could be paid. He loves Me that much. He loves *you* that much.

One reason He was born to a virgin was to prove that Jesus is My Son. Jesus worked miracles to prove His divinity; He taught with the kind of authority and truthfulness that no other person could match. As My Son, He led a perfect life, a sinless life. He did so not to prove His superiority but so that He could be the spotless, blameless sacrifice that was needed.

Like those in the past, there are those today who try to change the world's image of Jesus. Some want to make Him a prophet, which He was. Some want Him to be nothing more than a great teacher, and He was the greatest of all teachers. Some people see Him only as a sacrifice on the cross. He was all those things but so much more.

There have been many prophets, many insightful teachers, and some irresistible leaders, but there is only one Son of God, and His name is Jesus. To make Jesus a mere man requires stripping away some of the most important elements of His being. He is a King in the line of David; He is the Christ, the Messiah, the Anointed One; He is the Savior of the world; He is your Lord and Master; and He is and forever will be My Son.

What the prophets said is true. So you should pay close attention to their message, as you would to a lamp shining in some dark place. You must keep on paying attention until day-light comes and the morning star rises in your hearts. But you need to realize that no one alone can understand any of the prophecies in the Scriptures. The prophets did not think these things up on their own, but they were guided by the Spirit of God.

2 Peter 1:19—21 CEV

BIBLE

> *The Bible is central to Christianity and is made up of histories and letters written hundreds of years apart. People want to know that the books in the Bible are the ones God intended to be there.*

6
How do we know the Bible is accurate?

The Bible is the most successful book in all history. No other writing can match it in the number of copies printed, the number of copies in a typical home, or the number of translations available to the consumer. The sixty-six books in the Bible make it more of a library than a single volume. But the Bible was penned by forty different authors on three continents in three languages and spanning a fifteen-hundred-year period. Logic would seem to say that it couldn't possibly be error-free under those conditions.

Christians recognize it as the source of moral authority and biblical history. It is at the heart of most churches, quoted countless times every Sunday, studied by children and adults alike, and continues to move and challenge minds today. Every day people turn to it to look for comfort, wisdom, guidance, and teaching about how God has worked in human history. It is hard to believe, though, that the Bible is trustworthy given its multiple writers and languages. It seems more likely that the truth would become distorted over that many years.

God, how do we know the Bible is accurate and truly Your word? What makes it different from other books? Can I trust the Bible?

GOD

So many people think of Me as an immaterial, impersonal force. They don't think of Me as a person but rather as a "Great Something" out there. But as we've already talked about, I'm a person with intellect, emotion, and will: I think, I feel, and I choose My actions.

I am a Being who communicates. Sharing My thinking, My plans, My desires, is important to Me. I want you to know many things that are needed to live a godly and worthwhile life. How can I make you aware of these things if I don't first take the initiative to communicate? The Bible is a collection of books that reveal interactions over the ages between My creation and Me. It is an honest and accurate book.

You should know what the Bible is. It is a compilation of books inspired by Me and recorded by men of God and received by the people of My church, and it is the sole written authority for spiritual living.

From the very beginning, I intended the Bible to be your way of understanding My thoughts. When you read the Bible, you are reading material that has guided the lives of men and women for centuries.

To understand the Bible, you must first know a few terms. When the word *Scripture* was used in Jesus' day, it referred to what you now call the Old Testament. The word *Bible* simply means "book." The word came from a town named Byblos, a city famous for papyrus. Over time, *Byblos* became *Bible*.

Scripture had a different meaning. It referred not to the Book itself but to the contents of the Book. You can say that the Bible holds the Scripture. When a Christian today speaks of the Bible, he or she means both the Old Testament and the New Testament. *Testament* is a word that means "contract," so you have the "old contract" and the "new contract." The way I dealt with My people prior to Jesus is recorded in the Old Testament; the way I related to people after that time is called the New Testament. Jesus became the new contract.[1]

Paul loved Scripture so much that when he was a prisoner for Christ in Rome he sent a letter to Timothy asking him to bring the parchments and scrolls and a cloak to ward off the cold. He wanted a cloak to keep his body warm, and he wanted the Scriptures to keep his soul warm.[2] In that same letter Paul said, "All Scripture is God-breathed and is useful for teaching, rebuking, correcting and training in righteousness, so that the man of God may be thoroughly equipped for every good work."[3]

JESUS

Your questions ask about the trustworthiness of the Bible. Part of the answer lies in the term *God-breathed*. That term is often translated as "inspired." The original writings of the Bible were done in three languages: Hebrew, Aramaic, and Greek. The New Testament was written exclusively in Greek. Greek is a detailed language, while Hebrew is a poetic language. Greek is the language of lawyers, philosophers, and engineers; Hebrew is the language of artists.

It is not an accident that the term *God-breathed* is used. We wanted you to understand that the teachings in the Scripture come from God, and they were written by men moved by the Spirit of God. The Bible says exactly what God wants it to say.

The Bible is unique because its content comes from God. It includes history, poetry, prophecy, and much more. Each book in the Bible reveals a little about the writer of the book but even more about the nature of God.

God the Father, working through the Holy Spirit, carried the writers along so that what God wanted written was written.[4] In a way, you could say God's fingerprints are all over the Bible.

God

In the centuries before Jesus entered the world, I spoke to prophets—many prophets. I would get My message to the prophet, who would speak to the people, saying, "Thus says the LORD."[5] That phrase appears more than four hundred times in the Old Testament. Those statements, that teaching, those admonitions were written down for the benefit of future followers.

Many of the great men of the Bible were not ashamed to say that I had spoken through them. Moses recorded My words when I said, "Go, and I will be with your mouth and teach you what you shall say."[6]

King David said, "The Spirit of the LORD speaks through me; his words are upon my tongue."[7]

The prophet Jeremiah recorded what I did for him: "The LORD reached out his hand and touched my mouth and said to me, 'Now, I have put my words in your mouth.'"[8]

Over the centuries, the Bible has been found to be historically accurate and correct in every issue it speaks to. Although the Bible is not a scientific book, it mentions several scientific principles, including the water cycle.[9] Rain makes its way to lakes, then into oceans, and then back into the atmosphere through evaporation. Every schoolchild knows this now, but King Solomon was talking about it three thousand years ago.

The Bible makes many statements about nature that would not be proven for thousands of years. You might be surprised to learn that the Bible speaks of the earth as a sphere, not flat as it is depicted in other ancient books. Approximately twenty-seven hundred years ago, the prophet Isaiah described Me as "He who sits above the circle of the earth . . . who stretches out the heavens like a curtain and spreads them out like a tent to dwell in."[10] While many ancient books describe the earth as riding on the back of a turtle or some equally strange object, the Bible describes the earth as suspended in space, saying, "God stretches the northern sky over empty space and hangs the earth on nothing."[11] How could Job, who lived nearly four millennia ago, know the earth hung in space?

If you go out on a clear night and gaze skyward, you can see approximately a thousand stars. The human eye can do no better, and yet the ancient prophet Jeremiah spoke of uncountable stars in the sky.[12] This kind of evidence shows My inspiration of the Bible.

Prophecy is another proof you should consider. Prophesying is the act of foretelling the future. There are hundreds of prophecies in the Bible, many of which have been fulfilled with great accuracy. Many of these had to do with Jesus. In the small book of Micah, the birthplace of Jesus is predicted: "You, O Bethlehem Ephrathah, are only a small village among all the people of Judah. Yet a ruler of Israel will come from you, one whose origins are from the distant past."[13] The prophet Isaiah foretold that Jesus would be born of a virgin.[14] Both of those prophecies were stated many centuries before Jesus' birth.

The prophets under My inspiration spoke not only of Jesus' birth but also of His death. A thousand years before it happened, King David described the crucifixion.[15] The detail will amaze you. Isaiah did the same thing.[16] Those men spoke about a form of execution that wouldn't be used for centuries.

The Bible is accurate in everything it speaks about. It is trustworthy because I have been involved with its creation and protection through the years. Those who study the Bible find more and more proof of its divine composition even though human writers were involved.

But the Bible is more than a curiosity, it is My Word—the Word of God. It is the basis of Christian behavior. In its pages, you will read of My involvement with humankind from the beginning to the creation and spread of the church.

JESUS

One Bible writer put it this way: "The word of God is living and active and sharper than any two-edged sword, and piercing as far as the division of soul and spirit, of both joints and marrow, and able to judge the thoughts and intentions of the heart."[17]

Some people rebel against the Bible because it contains teaching that requires commitment and a change in the way they live. Of course, that's the point.

God

For centuries, the Bible has been examined from every angle. It has been tested and found true. Those who read it are blessed. You will be blessed when you open its pages.

7
How do we know if we understand the Bible correctly?

> *The Bible is a unique book, unlike any other. Perhaps that is why there are so many interpretations. Pastors teach that God was active in the Bible's creation, revelation, inspiration, and compilation. They say it's a holy book because holy means "set apart for a purpose." It's not clear, however, just what makes the thirty-nine books of the Old Testament and the twenty-seven books of the New Testament holy. Even so, millions of people look to the Bible to guide their lives.*
>
> *The Bible has been quoted in defense of everything from UFOs to racial superiority. Some people seem to have gone to great lengths to twist its teachings to their own purposes. But other people say that the content of the Bible doesn't say anything of the kind. They say it isn't difficult to interpret. They say it is straightforward revelation. It's quite confusing.*

 How do I know if I'm understanding the Bible correctly? Aren't there many equally valid interpretations? How can I keep from reading the Bible incorrectly?

GOD

From the beginning, I intended the Bible to be a record of My work and love for humanity in general and for you specifically. Can you think of another book that is simultaneously intended to be read by everyone and still so personal as to change one life at a time? There is no other such book.

I am a communicator. Follow My work through history, and you'll see countless times when I've made Myself known to humankind. When you hold My Bible, you hold a condensed account of My work. Through the ages, I've spoken to people in many ways.[1] Because I am a communicator, I made you a creature of communication. Think of the many ways you convey ideas to those around you: it's all done with words. Words allow you to form thoughts and share those thoughts with others. You speak to Me in prayer with words. I can communicate in other ways, but My words remain the most powerful.

The Bible is a compilation of spoken words and works. But language spoken or written is not always correctly understood. Consider just one language: there are probably two hundred thousand words—more if you count obsolete terms and compound words.[2] When I inspired the human authors, I guided them to just the right words. Of course, those words were in different languages than the one you speak.

Nonetheless, the Bible is still accessible and easy to understand if you are willing to take things a step at a time. Here's the good news I want you to understand: believers have help.

HOLY SPIRIT

This is one of My roles. God the Father has pulled back the veil to reveal Himself and make His message known. I enabled writers like Moses, Isaiah, David, Matthew, Luke, Paul, and all forty men to record everything accurately and correctly. No prophecy or account in Scripture was thought up by the prophet himself. I was in these godly men so they gave the true messages from God.[3]

I have another job. When someone like you comes to the Bible genuinely wanting to understand its message, I'm there with you, helping you draw the truth from the printed page. You do not read alone. By being open to My leading and with faithful study, you can learn more than you imagine about God and His work.

The apostle Paul understood this. He mentioned it in his letter to the church in Ephesus. Listen to what he wrote: "The Spirit will make you wise and let you understand what it means to know God. My prayer is that light will flood your hearts and that you will understand the hope that was given to you when God chose you."[4]

See the phrase "light will flood your hearts"? Bible students call this illumination. When you come to the Bible with faith and intellectual honesty, I turn on the light of understanding. I was involved in the creation of the Bible, and I'm here to help you understand it.

Jesus

From the beginning, people have been misinterpreting the Scriptures, sometimes on purpose to suit their goals. I faced opposition during My earthly ministry. Several groups caused the most trouble. Here's the irony: all of them were deeply religious, but not deeply spiritual. Consequently, they twisted Scripture or just ignored the parts they didn't like. That is the wrong way to go about things. Although these groups—Pharisees, Sadducees, experts in the laws of Moses, and other religious leaders—appeared to be knowledgeable, they weren't. I told them, "You search the Scriptures, for in them you think you have eternal life; and these are they which testify of Me."[5]

That was a message I had to deliver more than once.[6] Had they been true students of the Old Testament, they would have seen that My coming, My ministry, My death, and My resurrection were all foretold. Interpreting Scripture properly is important. When I taught in the synagogues and other places, I would interpret Scripture for them, starting with the books of Moses and working through the other writings.[7]

God

You should know several things to read and study the Bible properly.

Belief is not a requirement for any other book, but it is essential for anyone who wants to see the wisdom and truth in the pages of the Bible. Anyone can open a copy of the Bible and read it. Many do and find comfort, wisdom for daily living, or simply interesting history. But the Bible has more in it. When you read with the eyes of faith, you can see the deeper layers of meaning. Countless Christians have noted that they see something new every time they come to a familiar passage. You see, an unbelieving heart rebels against what it reads. Academics who don't believe have tried to dismiss the Bible as the product of superstitious, ancient, unsophisticated people. Academics who believe see the opposite. The Bible has proven repeatedly that it is worthy of your belief.

You must be willing to think. Modern people are taught to read quickly. Most books today can be read that way, but not the Bible. Reading the Bible is more like enjoying a fine meal; linger over it. Read a passage, and think about it. Ask questions. Read it in different translations. Let it take root in your mind. You will find that the more you think about it, the more answers will come to you.

Do you have a willingness to be taught? The Bible is a teacher, a mentor, but only to those who are willing to learn. If you start with your conclusions frozen in place, then you will draw nothing new or beneficial from the words of the Bible. Don't set your intellect aside. The Bible challenges the mind and the heart. Be willing to wonder; be willing to think on what you read.

The nature of the Bible is progressive. The Bible covers a large segment of history, from creation to the end of the first century. I revealed Myself and My plan over time. Abraham knew a great deal, but I revealed even more to Moses. By the time I sent My Son into humanity, the amount of revelation was greater still. After the church was formed and functioning, there was even more information. The great men and women of God in the Old Testament longed to know what one could know from reading the New Testament. The New Testament has priority.

JESUS

Don't misunderstand. The Old Testament books are important. I gave them credence by teaching and quoting them. The New Testament takes priority because it is the most complete revelation.

GOD

There is a human tendency to read meanings into the Bible that were never intended, to read between the lines without first understanding the lines themselves. When you read the Bible, apply a simple, normal, plain interpretation. I did not include tricky phrases or hidden codes. It is a book for everyone. There is plenty of symbolic language, but it is easy to recognize.

The Bible is designed to be read *from* not read *into*. Always remember to receive information from the Bible, and don't try to insert your own meaning into it. There are many figures of speech. Plain, normal interpretation takes these for the poetic expressions they are. For example, when it says in the book of Psalms, "How priceless is your unfailing love! Both high and low among men find refuge in the shadow of your wings,"[8] it doesn't mean I have feathers.

When the prophet Jeremiah called Me his strength and fortress,[9] he didn't mean to imply that I am a stone building. Poetic speech is part of the Bible. Just use common sense, and you won't be misled.

For some reason, people tend to neglect this next point. One of the best ways to learn and understand the Bible is to be part of a good, Bible-based church. Most pastors have gone to seminary where they learn the best techniques of interpretation. They are trained in biblical languages like Greek and Hebrew. They have access to many fine commentaries and reference books. They also have years of experience that they are willing to share with you. Church is a resource that shouldn't be overlooked.

Take everything in context. That means you should not pull verses out of context and twist them to some other purpose. What does the passage preceding it say? What about the one that comes after? Any person would be offended if their comments were repeated out of context. I feel the same.

When it comes to interpreting the Bible, take your time, read deeply, ask questions, and most of all, pray for guidance.

8
God, why were You different in the Old Testament?

It's been said a dozen different ways and repeated by many people: "The God of the Old Testament resembles the devil of the New Testament." The statement might be clever, but is it accurate? Did God have one character before Jesus was born and a different one afterward? It is often argued that God was cruel in the Old Testament while He was loving in the New Testament.

Some would have us believe in a bipolar God, one who vacillates between sweet forgiveness and bitter retribution. If this is true, then it is difficult to know which God to follow. It is important, perhaps even imperative, that we know if God's nature has changed over time.

 People tell me You were different in the Old Testament than You are in the New Testament. Why is that, God?

GOD

Your question is a good one, but it is not new. It has been asked many times. The words used may differ, but the unspoken meaning always comes through clear. Those who use the comment to show a disparity in My behavior show they don't understand what the Bible reveals about Me.

The allegation goes like this: My work in Old Testament times paints Me as a wrathful, vengeful, ready-to-strike-down-everyone God. In the New Testament, I'm a soft and cuddly God. From that assumption rises the idea that the Bible is inconsistent and therefore not to be trusted. After all, how can the "two" Gods be reconciled?

Let me put this to rest. The two Testaments show the same Me. The assumption that the Old Testament shows Me as perpetually angry is simply not true.

At times, the first thirty-nine books of the Bible do record severe judgments that originated with Me. I take no pleasure in passing judgment. I am Love, but I am also Justice. Justice and love go together.

From the beginning of time, I have expressed My love for you and all humans. The Old Testament is filled with expressions of My love. In fact, because the Old Testament makes up close to 70 percent of the Bible, it contains more expressions of My concern and hope for My people than the New Testament does!

For example, the psalmist wrote, "Just as parents are kind to their children, the LORD is kind to all who worship him."[1] Jeremiah reminded the people of his day that My love endures forever.[2]

The reverse is true. The New Testament shows My love but, like the Old Testament, makes no secret that I am a just God. On many occasions, the New Testament makes clear that sin will be judged.[3] My character is the same throughout the Bible.

JONAH

I can speak to the extent of God's love. My story is well known.[4] I was a prophet of God, but not a very obedient one. He sent me to a city of Nineveh. My message was to be one of judgment. Instead of doing as God directed, I ran the other way. You probably know the story of the great storm that battered the ship and crew until I was tossed overboard. God had selected a great fish to swallow me. It really happened. Three days later, and after much repenting, I was released. I traveled to Nineveh, and for several days I proclaimed the message God had given me: "Forty days more, and Nineveh shall be overthrown!"[5]

Why did I run? The two biggest reasons are these: first, the people of Nineveh were not God's chosen people; second, they were known everywhere as a vicious, terrifying people. They used to hang the bodies of their enemies over the wall that surrounded their central city. As far as I was concerned, going to that city was a death sentence.

Still, I went and proclaimed God's judgment. They had exactly forty days to repent. One thing that kept me going was the knowledge that the city and its horrible inhabitants would be destroyed and that I could watch it all happen. Accounts like this cause some people to think that God as revealed in the Old Testament is evil, but those who read the whole story know the difference.

You see, the people—pagan, warlike, cruel—listened to God's warning and repented. They repented publicly, and God poured out forgiveness. That upset me. I know it was unkind of me, but I wanted God to judge them, to wipe them from the face of the earth.

I was angry. God told me in clear terms that I had no right to be angry. He spared a city that had more than 120,000 children so young they couldn't tell their right from their left.[6]

I'm sure you see the point. In the book that bears my name, we see God as desiring to forgive, not just judge, and mine is an Old Testament book.

JESUS

Moses told his people that God is not a man that He should lie or change His mind.[7] God told the prophet Malachi, "I, the LORD, do not change." The same, by the way, can be said of Me. I am the same yesterday, and today, and forever.[8]

Humans can change over time. Good men can grow bitter, and bitter men can grow joyful. A woman filled with hate can learn to love. A trusting man can become cynical. God does not change like that. He is as He was and was as He is.

One thing that does change, however, is your understanding of Him. In any relationship, people get to know one another better, and their perceptions of one another change. The more you know God, the more your perception of Him changes. The Bible should be taken as a whole. Augustine of Hippo, who lived a few centuries after My ministry, said, "The New Testament is hidden in the Old; the Old is clarified by the New." It's an accurate assessment.

GOD

I can know every detail about you and your life, even your future, but no human can know all there is to know about Me. The immensity of My person and nature is beyond full understanding. That is why David wrote that such knowledge was beyond his capabilities.[9]

Over the centuries, I have revealed more and more of Myself as human-kind has been able to comprehend. There is much more to learn once on My side of eternity.

Jesus

Much of the Old Testament is a record of the Father's drawing rebellious people back into His arms. The laws and decrees served to show the world their need for a Savior. The apostle Paul wrote a great deal about this. He said, "The law was our tutor to bring us to Christ, that we might be justified by faith."[10] What some consider harshness in God's attitude was meant to show that no one could earn salvation. No amount of obedience to laws can make you good enough.

God

The entire sacrificial system shown in the Old Testament foreshadowed the sacrifice made by My Son, Jesus. Permanent forgiveness came through His willing sacrifice, something no animal sacrifice can do. Some have said that Christianity is a bloody religion. They're right. However, the animal sac-rifices of the past were replaced by the once-and-for-all sacrifice of Jesus.

Jesus

It would be a mistake for you to assume the Old Testament is no longer needed. While it is true that the law was given through Moses and that grace and truth came through Me,[11] the Old Testament is still as important as it ever was. It reveals aspects of God's nature not seen in the New Testament. The reverse is also true.

On several occasions I said that I hadn't come to get rid of the Law or to replace the Prophets.[12] To fully understand God and His plan, you need to see how He is revealed in the Old and the New Testaments. They are complementary, not contradictory.

God

The entire New Testament book of Hebrews was written to show that the Old Testament revelation was preparation for the New Testament. Search the Scriptures, and you will see that I am the same in both Testaments.

9
Why weren't all early writings included in the Bible?

"Banned from the Bible," has been a popular theme for television shows and books. Many of these documentaries portray the compilation of Bible books coming about as a conspiracy of church officials who accepted some books as authentic while dismissing others because they didn't like them. There's no question that if it's true, it would be an odd and dishonest way of deciding which books belonged and which didn't. And, if it's true, it would throw shadows of doubt on the trustworthiness of the Bible.

Theologian J. I. Packer said, "The Church no more gave us the New Testament canon than Sir Isaac Newton gave us the force of gravity. God gave us gravity, by His work of creation, and similarly He gave us the New Testament canon, by inspiring the individual books that make it up."[1] It's difficult to know what to believe.

There are many ancient books not included in the Bible. Many of them seem Christian in nature. Why were some of them excluded from the Bible?

GOD

The assumption is that I inspired all early writing. I didn't. Remember what inspiration means—"God-breathed." Inspiration comes from Me and guides the human authors. Just because a book was written near the time of the New Testament doesn't mean that it belongs in the Bible. A theologian said, "Through God alone can God be known."[2] The books in the Bible were inspired by Me and recognized by religious leaders as having the mark of inspiration.

Those who study the Bible use a word you should know: *canon*. It comes from a Greek word that refers to a measuring rod, like a yardstick. Sometimes you hear the phrase "canon of Scripture." That refers to the books that have been examined and that measure up to the tests of inspiration and genuineness. The early church followers—the leaders who came immediately after the apostles—spoke of the canon of the church, or the canon of truth. The reason some ancient books weren't included in the Bible is that they simply didn't measure up.

MOSES

The books you now call the Old Testament were in place long before New Testament times, in fact, centuries before. I wrote the first five books of the Old Testament. People refer to them by different names: the Law, the Pentateuch, the Torah. That information came directly from God and was so important that He ordered the five books kept with the ark of the covenant.[3] We carried that writing as we traveled in the wilderness.

Those books were so important to us that God gave this instruction to the people about choosing a king: "It shall come about when he sits on the throne of his kingdom, he shall write for himself a copy of this law on a scroll in the presence of the Levitical priests. It shall be with him and he shall read it all the days of his life, that he may learn to fear the LORD his God, by carefully observing all the words of this law and these statutes."[4]

The king was to copy the words in his own hand and read them over and over again throughout his life. We knew those words were from God, and we treated them as such.

I was not allowed to cross over into the promised land. My successor, Joshua, led the people over the Jordan and into the land God had given them. Before he did, God gave him some final instructions, which included this: "This book of the law shall not depart out of your mouth; you shall meditate on it day and night, so that you may be careful to act in accordance with all that is written in it. For then you shall make your way prosperous, and then you shall be successful."[5]

We value those books not just because they help us, but because God values them.

JESUS

It is a myth that men and men alone determined the books that would become the Bible. Men didn't determine which books were inspired; rather, they recognized inspiration. Many books were left out—and understand that many of those books came about well after the first century and were written under the names of people long dead—because they lacked in key areas.

Every book in the Bible is associated with a recognized man of God. As Moses said, the first five books of the Old Testament are associated with him. Many of the other books are associated with prophets like Jeremiah, Isaiah, and Daniel. In the New Testament, books are associated with apostles. Some are obvious. Matthew, also known as Levi, wrote the Gospel of Matthew. John wrote the Gospel of John, the three letters (often called epistles) of John, and the book of Revelation.

Mark, although not one of the inner circle of disciples, wrote the Gospel of Mark under Peter's guidance. Students of the Bible have known from the beginning that Mark's gospel is really Peter's gospel. Peter also wrote two letters that are part of the New Testament.

Luke is associated with the apostle Paul. His gospel comes from research and interviews. He also accompanied Paul on his travels, and much of the book of Acts comes from Luke's personal experience and observation.

MOSES

Books of the Bible contain prophetic elements. Prophecy isn't always intended to predict the future. It is true, of course, that many prophets announced what God was going to do, but the prophets' main concern was proclaiming God's message to the people of their day. As God told me so many centuries ago, "I will raise up for them a prophet like you from among their own people; I will put my words in the mouth of the prophet, who shall speak to them everything that I command."[6]

He also instructed us in how to recognize a true prophet: "You may wonder, 'How will we know whether or not a prophecy is from the LORD?' If the prophet speaks in the LORD's name but his prediction does not happen or come true, you will know that the LORD did not give that message. That prophet has spoken without my authority and need not be feared."[7]

Many of the Bible writers were workers of miracles. This gives them godly creditability.

57

JESUS

My inner circle of disciples, the Twelve, worked miracles. Yes, even Judas before he betrayed Me.[8] I did this to multiply My ministry, train the future leaders of the church, and to give them credibility for their future writings. Later, those disciples would become apostles. An apostle is very much like an ambassador—someone who represented Me to the world. To be an apostle, they had to have been trained by Me and to have worked signs, wonders, and miracles.[9]

There is also a recognizable power in the authentic books of the Bible. Unlike other books, the authentic books touch the heart and the mind in ways you may have trouble explaining. The writer of Hebrews expressed it this way: "The word of God is alive and powerful. It is sharper than the sharpest two-edged sword, cutting between soul and spirit, between joint and marrow. It exposes our innermost thoughts and desires."[10]

The authentic books affect readers in a way that only something from God can do. They have the power to change lives, which has been shown to be true repeatedly. In fact, that knowledge gave Paul a great sense of joy. He wrote a letter to a church in Thessalonica, and that letter became one of the books of the New Testament—1 Thessalonians. In it he said, "When you received the word of God which you heard from us, you welcomed it not as the word of men, but as it is in truth, the word of God, which also effectively works in you who believe."[11]

GOD

There are many practical reasons why early books supposedly written by church leaders or others have been rejected as inauthentic. Many were written too late to have been penned under an apostle's authority. Many lack the genuineness present in other books of the Bible. Even a casual reading shows they do not measure up. The church fathers rarely quoted from those books or used them in sermons.

The Bible is as it should be. You can trust it for information, guidance, direction, wisdom, knowledge, comfort, strength, and many more things. Every book in it has been proven genuine many times over.

Is nature the sixty-seventh book of the Bible?

> *Sunsets move us. Although cold and distant, outer space demands interest. The terror of a storm is captivating. Everywhere there is complexity beyond what chance can create. The diversity of the animal kingdom boggles the mind. Every year tens of thousands of new species are added to the list of known animals. Some people estimate that there are ten million species of animals. These include a sea horse the size of a pea and an adult snake so small it can curl up on a quarter.*

> *The great distances between galaxies are amazing. So vast are the distances that they are measured in light-years. The distance light travels in one year is nearly six trillion miles. But isn't creation more than something to look at? In some ways, nature seems like a book to be read, a book that tells a great deal about life and, possibly, how it originated.*

Q Someone called nature and the universe the "sixty-seventh book of the Bible." Is that accurate? What can I learn about You from nature?

GOD

I have revealed Myself in two primary ways. First is general revelation. Remember that *revelation* means "to unveil," so when I use the word I am talking about My making Myself known to you. General revelation is also called *natural* revelation. That seems to be what you're asking about. The second way I've revealed Myself is called *special* revelation, and that involves making Myself known through direct conversation as I did with Adam and Eve, Moses, Elijah, and others. Those accounts and many others are recorded in the Bible. That makes the Bible one aspect of special revelation. The greatest expression of special revelation is My Son, Jesus.

You are most familiar with the revelations given in the Bible, but still you are right to wonder about nature and about what nature has to say about Me. It says a great deal, more than most people realize. Nature cannot give the specifics you need to respond to love and work, but just as a painting reveals something about the artist, so the natural world reveals something about Me.

The Bible is a library of sixty-six books that vary in size. Some books, like Genesis and Isaiah, are relatively long; others are short. Based on word count, 3 John is the shortest book in the Bible. Fewest words, however, doesn't mean least important.

Nature is a book of sorts, one written without words. You, as a reader, absorb information through words; you, as an observer, receive information through thoughtful inspection.

Earlier, when we were discussing creation, I told you of an atheist who went camping and came to believe in Me because of the intricacies he found in a plant. Many people would not have bothered to look or to take the time to wonder. That experience changed the man's life. From there, he went on to study the Bible, where he found the details he needed to have a deep understanding of Me and My kingdom.

PAUL

The knowledge gained through the study of nature works both ways. My ministry as an apostle was with Gentiles, non-Jews. As a Jew, I always made certain that my missionary efforts first included them. However, I was almost always rejected. I then turned to the Gentiles, whom God intended for salvation too.

Dealing with Gentiles of that day was very different from dealing with my own people. The Jews had the Tanach, the books of the Old Testament. Often I encountered those who said, "Since we don't have the revelation of God as the Jews do, we are not accountable." They were wrong. Here's what I wrote to those people in Rome: "What may be known of God is manifest in them, for God has shown it to them. For since the creation of the world His invisible attributes are clearly seen, being understood by the things that are made, even His eternal power and Godhead, so that they are without excuse."[1]

Do you see the point? Anyone can see the reality of God just by looking around. God has manifested Himself in countless ways. By *manifest*, I mean "to show something clearly." His power, intelligence, and work are easy to see—at least for those willing to look. Since that information is available to anyone, no one can make the excuse that God has not made Himself known.

God

To see, you must look. Look upward. The existence of stars and planets, the protective atmosphere that shields you from harm, the sun itself, which is just far enough away to provide light and energy to every living thing but not so close as to harm those I created to benefit from its glow.

Look inward and take time to see how intricate your parts are. Think of what each organ does. The heart is complex and tough; the liver and kidneys purify your body; the eyes allow you to see, and all this happens without conscious thought from you.

Think about where your creativity comes from. Does an appreciation for art and music come from evolution, or do you see a purpose behind it all?

C. S. Lewis came to faith later in life. By his testimony, it was the idea of joy that made him realize a Creator must be involved.[2] He defended My existence by showing that an argument over a parking place comes from a sense of right and wrong—something he couldn't imagine arising from chance.[3] He took the time to think on these things. Those arguments didn't come from the Bible, but from observation of things around him. You have the same ability.

Think of the complexity of human emotion. Ponder all the complicated steps in the development of a baby from the joining of two microscopic, single-cell organisms. The nature of the human body—any animal body for that matter—speaks of Me as Creator and Designer.

Jesus

Don't shy away from the truth of a designer for the universe simply because seemingly bright people mock the idea. Every good and holy thing is mocked. I was mocked through My entire ministry. People even mocked Me while I hung on the cross. Denial of truth doesn't make it false. You know that instinctively.

William Paley said that life arising on earth by accident was like finding a watch in the forest and declaring, "Look what fell together from the surrounding material."[4] Paley did not go far enough. To get closer to the truth, someone would have to find not only the world's most intricate watch; a watch that was also intelligent, self-determined, self-aware, able to communicate, able to create, formed relationships with other watches, and could reproduce.

Whether you look at the cosmos or the micro-cosmos, you will see order, thoughtful design, and unending creativity. This teaches that God is orderly, thoughtful, and creative. It also teaches that God is powerful. To create all that can be seen requires great power, ultimate power. Creation reminds you that God is omnipotent—all-powerful. But don't think God is an impersonal force. God has a person. He has personality. He has emotions and intellect.

God

In the book of Psalms is this verse: "Great are the works of the LORD; they are pondered by all who delight in them."[5] No one is more blind than the person who chooses not to see. The man who wrote that verse said those who delight in My works ponder them. The person who convinces himself or who allows others to convince him that the life he lives has come about by billions of happy coincidences will not study nature and see Me.

Your mind and heart must be open to the possibility of My existence.[6] Those who choose to disbelieve before they've taken time to look will miss the evidence around them.

Nature speaks of Me. My fingerprints are everywhere. There is enough revelation in creation to convince anyone with a receptive mind.

But natural revelation was never meant to be the only evidence. While it demonstrates My existence, My power, and My intelligence, it does not give the necessary teaching for you to understand what matters to Me, what brings us close. Nature, then, could be viewed as the sixty-seventh book of the Bible, or, if you prefer, the first book, since it was in those pages that it was first revealed. But I have left nothing to chance or personal interpretation. Making you aware of creation was just the first step in revelation. Prophets and teachers came speaking the words I gave them. Those words became the Bible. Over time, more and more revelation was given.

You do not know everything yet—there is so much more to know. The Bible does not hold a record of everything My Son, Jesus, or I did. The apostle John wrote, "Jesus did many other things as well. If every one of them were written down, I suppose that even the whole world would not have room for the books that would be written."[7] Someday, however, you will see everything clearly.[8]

It is sad that an atheist, when moved by a gorgeous sunset, doesn't know to thank Me.

Nature makes known My power and glory. It moved King David to write these lyrics: "The heavens keep telling the wonders of God, and the skies declare what he has done. Each day informs the following day; each night announces to the next. They don't speak a word, and there is never the sound of a voice. Yet their message reaches all the earth, and it travels around the world. In the heavens a tent is set up for the sun."[9]

Christ is the only foundation. Whatever we build on that foundation will be tested by fire on the day of judgment. Then everyone will find out if we have used gold, silver, and precious stones, or wood, hay, and straw. We will be rewarded if our building is left standing. But if it is destroyed by the fire, we will lose everything. Yet we ourselves will be saved, like someone escaping from flames.

1 Corinthians 3:11–15 CEV

THE FUTURE

> *Much of the Bible focuses on the end of the world—the end times. What is going to happen then is the subject of much mystery and misunderstanding.*

Are we living in the end times now?

It is fascinating to contemplate the future. Maybe it's because humans are naturally curious, or perhaps it's because the future is going to arrive whether it's wanted or not. The Christian study of the future is called eschatology, *which means "study of last things." The Bible is filled with information about events yet to happen.*

Through the years, some people have tried to pinpoint the date when Jesus is supposed to return to earth. All of them have been wrong. Still, that doesn't keep people from wondering. Is this the beginning of the end? The New Testament writers taught that the church of their day was living in the end times, and that was two thousand years ago! Surely, they had to be wrong.

 God, it seems everywhere I turn someone is speaking about the end of the world or the second coming of Christ. Are we living in the end times?

GOD

Your question is an important one, and I am not making light of it when I say you're closer than ever before. You should know some things before we go much further.

First, you are a time-bound creature. Everything you see is in the same time lock. Time and your sense of it has long been a subject of philosophers and scientists. Some interesting theories have been suggested, and some have gone so far as to suggest that time is an illusion. No matter what you think of time, or how you define it, it moves on. People who suggest that time doesn't exist still grow older.

Second, I am not bound by time. I am timeless and eternal. I have always been and always will be. Time has no effect on Me, even though time is part of My creation. With Me a thousand years is as a day.[1] What seems like a long time for you is a brief span for Me.

Some have argued that because the promised returned of Jesus hasn't happened in the last two thousand years it will never happen. Such thinking is shortsighted. I deal with eternity. And you may not realize it yet, but so do you. You have an eternal soul. Time will change for you in the future. Two thousand years will seem short to you then.

I want you to understand a simple but profound truth: My calendar is not the same as yours, nor have I revealed everything to you. My timing has always been on a need-to-know basis. That includes the time of the last days.

JESUS

No one except the Father knows when the last days will be—no one, not the angels, and not even Me.[2] During My earthly ministry, I taught My disciples that neither I nor anyone else knows the time of My second coming. That was by plan. God hasn't revealed everything yet.

My coming is certain but unexpected. It is no accident that the date and time have not been revealed. I will come unexpectedly, without prior notice.[3]

I gave specific instructions to My disciples to expect My return but not to be preoccupied with trying to figure out when the end will come. Shortly before My ascension into heaven, I was asked about the future. I answered that "it is not for you to know the times or periods that the Father has set by his own authority."[4]

They were not wrong in asking, but it was important for them to understand that the Father has a right to keep His own counsel. The disciples needed to focus on continuing the ministry I started. Hazardous days awaited them. Their focus needed to be on the present even while their hearts longed for the future. I have the same requirement of you.

Your curiosity is good and commendable. To wonder is not a sin; to be consumed by end-time guessing is counterproductive. Worse, it can lead to deception. History is filled with those who convinced their followers that the end was near. Some sold all they had and fled to the hills; others turned over their belongings to the so-called prophet; some could no longer bring themselves to believe. The news has carried reports of groups storing weapons and food. None of them—not one—have been right. You must be on your guard not to be misled. I warned My disciples that many false prophets would appear and lead many astray.[5] Paul told the church not to be upset or troubled or deceived by anyone saying that the day had come.[6]

SIMEON

I was a prophet of God, led by the Holy Spirit. One desire filled my days and nights. I wanted to see the Messiah. The Holy Spirit revealed to me that I would not die before the first coming of Jesus.[7] I waited, and I went to the temple hoping each day that it would be the day.

Then it happened. Joseph and Mary brought an infant to the temple. The Holy Spirit let me know that baby was the One whom other people and I had been waiting for.

Mary allowed me to take the child into my arms. I said, "Lord, now let your servant die in peace, as you have promised. I have seen your salvation, which you have prepared for all people. He is a light to reveal God to the nations, and he is the glory of your people Israel!"[8]

If anyone can understand the longing to see the end times, I can. Like you, I wonder when that will be, but I learned patience when I first waited on the coming of the Savior. Patience is the key.

GOD

You have heard the scoffers. In his New Testament book, Peter said, "Know this first of all, that in the last days mockers will come with their mocking, following after their own lusts, and saying, 'Where is the promise of His coming? For ever since the fathers fell asleep, all continues just as it was from the beginning of creation.'"[9] There will be more and more scoffers as time draws near.

Yes, you are living in the last days, but understand there are more days than you imagine.

The early Christians used to say good-bye with a single word: *Maranatha*. It's Aramaic for "Lord, come quickly!"[10] They were eager for the Second Coming. All Christians are. Still, they had to learn to be patient with My patience.

Simeon is a fine example of a godly person waiting instead of worrying about the coming of Christ.

12

Why and when is the earth going to end?

The Bible deals not only with the past but with the future. Although no one knows when some of the events it describes will come to pass, few Christians doubt that they will come to pass. One of the most graphic statements about the future deals with the end of the earth.

Can it be possible that the earth will cease to be? Many cultures have wondered about the end. Their wonderings have become part of their ancient traditions. Science-fiction movies have portrayed the end of the world—or at least all life on earth—a dozen different ways: asteroids, runaway earthquakes, alien invasions, unstoppable diseases, and more. The end of the word may simply be that, a story, or it may be an eventuality. If so, it's hard to understand why.

Q **Is the end of the world really going to happen? If so, how and when and why?**

GOD

Yes, it's really going to happen, but many things will come to pass first, things we'll discuss later. For now, let Me say that a day is coming when the earth and everything else will pass away. That may sound like bad news, but it isn't. This shouldn't be news to any student of the Bible.

Peter wrote about it in his second letter: "The day of the Lord will come as unexpectedly as a thief. Then the heavens will pass away with a terrible noise, and the very elements themselves will disappear in fire, and the earth and everything on it will be found to deserve judgment."[1]

Before going any further, you need to understand why I would inspire such a verse. I know it sounds terrifying. First, understand this: That is not the end. It is not the last line of the story by any means. There will be a new heaven and a new earth.

In this case, "day of the Lord" refers to the final consummation of all that is and the beginning of what is to come. It indicates a time of My direct involvement in the present to change the future. It is associated with judgment. Peter was writing about the final part of the day of the Lord: the Last Day of the last days.

On that day, all you see will cease to be in one cataclysmic, thunderous event. The stars and the galaxies will disappear, and the earth will dissolve.

JESUS

You wonder how this can happen. I hold all things together by My power and will. I was before all things, and in Me all things hold together.[2] I uphold all things by the power of His word.[3]

I hold the universe together at the atomic level. When that day arrives, I will let go and all atoms will release their bonds. The word Peter used is often translated as "burn up," but it also carries another meaning: "to dissolve."

This creation will pass in a moment; everything in creation will be gone. But as mentioned, there will be a new heaven and a new earth. Peter, just two verses later, reminded his readers that a new heaven and a new earth—a place where righteousness dwells—await them.[4]

The phrases dealing with the end of heaven and earth can be puzzling, and they are impossible to ignore. Christians are motivated by the knowledge that new things are on the way, a better world and a better life for believers. The replacing of this tired and stained world with a new creation from God is exciting. It motivates believers to holy thoughts and behavior.

Isaiah wrote, "All the stars of the heavens will be dissolved and the sky rolled up like a scroll; all the starry host will fall like withered leaves from the vine, like shriveled figs from the fig tree."[5]

The old will make way for the new—and that's a good thing.

GOD

Did you know that sin affects more than just humans? Sin has had a negative impact on every living thing and the universe as a whole. Paul wrote, "The creation itself also will be delivered from the bondage of corruption into the glorious liberty of the children of God. For we know that the whole creation groans and labors with birth pangs together until now."[6]

Do you see the joy of a new creation? The world and everyone on it has been made less than they can be. When the time comes, I will return creation to its original state by making it new again.

As I said in Isaiah, "I will create new heavens and a new earth. The former things will not be remembered, nor will they come to mind. But be glad and rejoice forever in what I will create."[7]

JESUS

Although the new heaven and the new earth are still in your future, one man has seen what it will be like. The apostle John was unique among all men. While many prophets received visions that revealed the Father's nature and desires, only John received a detailed look at the new heaven and the new earth to come. He was an eyewitness to something that has yet to happen. He recorded what he saw:

"I saw a new heaven and a new earth, for the first heaven and the first earth had passed away. Also there was no more sea. Then I, John, saw the holy city, New Jerusalem, coming down out of heaven from God, prepared as a bride adorned for her husband. And I heard a loud voice from heaven saying, 'Behold, the tabernacle of God is with men, and He will dwell with them, and they shall be His people. God Himself will be with them and be their God. And God will wipe away every tear from their eyes; there shall be no more death, nor sorrow, nor crying. There shall be no more pain, for the former things have passed away.' Then He who sat on the throne said, 'Behold, I make all things new.' And He said to me, 'Write, for these words are true and faithful.'"[8]

Keep in mind that the end of the physical world is not the end of you. Believers live on through eternity. Christians live on in resurrected bodies and will live in the new heaven and the new earth. The old, sin-fractured creation will be done away with, and it will be replaced with a new creation.

GOD

You have lived in a difficult world filled with sorrow, death, trials, troubles, and uncertainty. It is My desire to build for you a place where such things no longer exist; a place filled with joy, happiness, and undiluted fellowship with Me. It is hard to think of leaving the familiar for the new, but a person who is moved from a shanty to a mansion seldom complains.

There is much to admire in this creation, but there will be more to come. No human can understand what it is like to live in a universe without sin. No illness. No sadness. No death. You will have the opportunity to live in such a place!

JESUS

What I taught My disciples remains true today: "Don't let your hearts be troubled. Trust in God, and trust also in me. There is more than enough room in my Father's home. If this were not so, would I have told you that I am going to prepare a place for you? When everything is ready, I will come and get you, so that you will always be with me where I am."[9]

Eternal togetherness has always been the goal. All that We do, We do with you in mind.

13
What's ahead for us in the future?

Henry Ward Beecher, a nineteenth-century minister, said, "Every tomorrow has two handles. We can take hold of it with the handle of anxiety or the handle of faith." Most people wonder about the future. Some worry about it, and others long for it. Apart from death and taxes, to paraphrase Benjamin Franklin, no one knows what the future holds. Perhaps that's why so many have turned to psychics and fortune-tellers. Some believe that people like Edgar Cayce and sixteenth-century prognosticator Nostradamus had the necessary skills to look forward in time. But it seems doubtful that any human can look beyond the present.

Since God is God, He knows and creates the future. It seems doubtful that any human can look beyond the present. But what information has God revealed?

Q **You said there were other events that would happen before the new heaven and new earth. What's ahead for us in the future?**

GOD

The future is My domain. I see all possibilities and outcomes, but I am not merely a passive viewer. I have plans—plans that go back to the beginning of time and extend into the eternal future. You are part of those plans. All major events are already realities to Me, but they need to be worked out in your time.

Eschatology is the study of the last things. That is possible only because I revealed to the prophets and the apostles some of what is ahead. Not every detail has been recorded in the Bible, but enough has been recorded to give you an idea of what to expect.

My greatest desire is to restore our fellowship. I am your God, and you are one of My people. You are incomplete without a vital, vibrant, personal relationship with Me through Jesus Christ. Redemption has always been the goal. Your eternal life and happiness remain My greatest concern.

The world is an unholy place. As God, I am by nature loving but also just. The future holds great promise for My followers; it also holds a time of judgment.

JESUS

You are in good company when you ask about the future. The disciples asked many similar questions. They wanted signs about when My second coming was near; they wanted to know about future events.

Science-fiction writers have focused on the extreme possibilities. Either the future is filled with happiness and peace, or it is a dark, evil place. H. G. Wells showed a bleak future in his novel *The Time Machine*. Those writers have sensed the difficulties to come and some of the joys. The Bible is the only book to outline what is to come. It is from the Bible that you get the only picture of what truly lies ahead.

The future hinges on My second coming. While My coming will be sudden, the events leading up to it will happen over time. Many of those events are tragic. I told My disciples, "You will hear of wars and rumors of wars; see that you are not alarmed; for this must take place, but the end is not yet. For nation will rise against nation, and kingdom against kingdom, and there will be famines and earthquakes in various places: all this is but the beginning of the birth pangs."[1]

"Wars and rumors of wars" wasn't what My friends wanted to hear, but it was what they needed to hear—same as you. There have always been wars, the result of a world contaminated by sin. Pick any time in history, and you will discover scores of wars going on. The closer the time draws to My second coming, however, the more wars will increase. One of the natural outcomes of sin is governmental instability.

Where there are wars, there will be famines. Darfur, Ethiopia, Somalia, and many other countries provide contemporary proof of that.

Earthquakes will increase. Earthquakes are a natural function of the earth. The earth is dynamic, and geological plates shift. Earthquakes around the globe will increase as the end times draw closer.

I also told the disciples that the future held difficult, painful times for them: "Then they will deliver you up to tribulation and kill you, and you will be hated by all nations for My name's sake. And then many will be offended, will betray one another, and will hate one another. Then many false prophets will rise up and deceive many. And because lawlessness will abound, the love of many will grow cold. But he who endures to the end shall be saved. And this gospel of the kingdom will be preached in all the world as a witness to all the nations, and then the end will come."[2]

Does this describe things you've seen? Persecution began with My crucifixion. It escalated shortly after My ascension into heaven. The first wave of persecution came from the religious leaders who hounded and arrested some of the disciples. A deacon named Stephen became the first Christian martyr when those same religious leaders stoned him to death. Soon Christians were forced to flee their homes.

Rome began its own brand of persecution because Christians refused to utter the words "Caesar is Lord." The number of martyrs grew. The word *martyr* comes from the Greek word for *witness*. Those early martyrs died because they spoke of Me. As bad as it was, it would grow worse over time. Today, thousands of Christians continue to suffer at the hands of persecutors, and many of them are killed. Hard as it is to hear, the future holds more of that.

STEPHEN

As Jesus mentioned, I was the first to die for the faith.[3] I had no desire to be a martyr, but I have no shame about it. My death came by stoning. I was tossed into a pit, and my attackers threw stones at me until I died of my wounds. At that time, the great apostle Paul—then called Saul—sided with my killers. He later came to faith and changed the world with his preaching, teaching, and writing.

I bring that up so you will understand that out of the worst situations, God can bring good. Paul went from persecutor to proclaimer. It's a fair issue to wonder why God allows persecution. Christians have never been promised a trouble-free life. Every apostle but one died as a martyr, and he endured hardships and torture. Wherever there has been persecution, the church has thrived. It's a hard truth but true nonetheless. In the persecutions to come, many will come to Christ.

On a personal note, my death was painful, horrible, and ugly, but I've experienced the greatest joy after my passing. For believers, the future always holds the glory of heaven.[4]

GOD

The fact that eternal good comes from persecution does not mean I will tolerate such behavior forever. There comes a time when I must judge the world. That will happen on a global scale during the Great Tribulation. The coming tribulation is My judgment against sin, not against My children. I will take them from the earth before I pour out My wrath. All Christians look forward to that day.

STEPHEN

The details boggle the mind. Paul wrote about it: "The Lord himself will come down from heaven, with a loud command, with the voice of the archangel and with the trumpet call of God, and the dead in Christ will rise first. After that, we who are still alive and are left will be caught up together with them in the clouds to meet the Lord in the air. And so we will be with the Lord forever. Therefore encourage each other with these words."[5]

Did you notice that the dead in Christ will rise first? I will be in that group. Followers of Christ receive a bodily resurrection. We were made to live in a body. This old body will be changed into something new and imperishable. Again, I have to quote Paul: "Listen, I tell you a mystery: We will not all sleep, but we will all be changed—in a flash, in the twinkling of an eye, at the last trumpet. For the trumpet will sound, the dead will be raised imperishable, and we will be changed. For the perishable must clothe itself with the imperishable, and the mortal with immortality."[6]

JESUS

That, however, is not My second coming. What Paul refers to is often called the Rapture. The word *rapture* does not appear in the Bible, but it is a convenient term to reference the event. You may have noticed that the believers are "caught up" in the air to join Me. The Second Coming always refers to My physical return to earth.

After the believers are removed from the world to be with Us in heaven, My Father will bring tribulation to the world. During that time a man will arise called the Antichrist. There have been many such men, but this person will lead the world even further from faith: "This lawlessness is already at work secretly, and it will remain secret until the one who is holding it back steps out of the way. Then the man of lawlessness will be revealed, but the Lord Jesus will kill him with the breath of his mouth and destroy him by the splendor of his coming. This evil man will come to do the work of Satan with counterfeit power and signs and miracles."[7] He will claim to be the Christ.

I taught, "If anyone says to you, 'Behold, here is the Christ,' or 'There He is,' do not believe him. For false Christs and false prophets will arise and will show great signs and wonders, so as to mislead, if possible, even the elect. Behold, I have told you in advance. So if they say to you, 'Behold, He is in the wilderness,' do not go out, or, 'Behold, He is in the inner rooms,' do not believe them. For just as the lightning comes from the east and flashes even to the west, so will the coming of the Son of Man be."[8]

GOD

The Tribulation will last for seven years, and then Jesus will return to earth and put an end to the Antichrist and the trouble he has caused. Every believer will return with Jesus. This will usher in a new millennium, a thousand-year reign of Christ—a thousand years of peace for the world.[9]

Then come the judgments. The best known of these is the Great White Throne judgment. John saw it in the revelation I gave him: "I saw a great white throne and Him who sat upon it, from whose presence earth and heaven fled away, and no place was found for them. And I saw the dead, the great and the small, standing before the throne, and books were opened; and another book was opened, which is the book of life; and the dead were judged from the things which were written in the books, according to their deeds."[10]

For the believer, there is no future judgment for salvation. Jesus took care of that on the cross. Their works will be judged, but only for the purpose of rewards.[11]

What else does the future hold for you? Your inheritance. You should know that those who serve the Lord receive an inheritance, an eternal reward.[12]

This is just an outline of things to come. The future is in My hands.

14
Why should we work if the world is going to end?

She was a faithful Christian, one of those people who preferred to talk about faith, God's love, and Christ's sacrifice over any other subject. She was young, a senior in high school—an important time in her education. She spent a great deal of time discussing Jesus' return and became convinced that the Second Coming was close at hand: so close that it made no sense to continue studying or taking final exams. That was four decades ago.

It seems wrong for her to think Jesus' return was imminent. After all, He didn't come in all those forty years. It seems more likely that she exchanged the hope of all Christians for an excuse to avoid work.

 If Jesus is coming soon, and if the world is ultimately going to come to an end, why should I work or try to achieve anything worthwhile?

GOD

Millions have asked this question and they've done so from the beginning. How many of them were right? The question springs from the misconception that we work because we have to. When I created Adam, I had work in mind for him and for you. From the beginning, Adam was to tend to the garden. It was as much for Adam's benefit as the garden's. Work is part of the human experience.

Let's begin with the obvious answer. As we've noted, no one other than Me knows the date of Jesus' return. It could be three hours from now; it could be three centuries from now.

The early church was taught to live with expectancy. It wasn't their job, or yours, to pick the date. They were to be faithful in their Christian lives and in worship, hoping Jesus would come that day but knowing it could be a long way off.

The future events we've discussed are meant to motivate you to a godly life, not cause you to avoid your responsibilities. There is a time for everything. Solomon wrote about that in the Old Testament book of Ecclesiastes: "There is a time for everything, and a season for every activity under heaven."[1] Since you do not know when the end will come, you should find the work you love and do it. I did not create you to be idle.

Jesus

The knowledge of My second coming should motivate you to work, not cause you to reject it.[2] Christians have work to do. The work you do and the way you do it set an example to others. Paul, as great a man as he was, refused to be a burden to anyone. He worked for his bread and advised the church to separate from those who refused to carry their own load.

He put it this way: "We command you, brethren, in the name of our Lord Jesus Christ, that you withdraw from every brother who walks disorderly and not according to the tradition which he received from us. For you yourselves know how you ought to follow us, for we were not disorderly among you; nor did we eat anyone's bread free of charge, but worked with labor and toil night and day, that we might not be a burden to any of you, not because we do not have authority, but to make ourselves an example of how you should follow us."[3]

Paul never forgot to praise those who worked with him.[4]

Titus

I traveled with Paul and others on missionary journeys. I saw for myself that Paul worked so as not to be a burden on the churches. It was customary among Jews of that day for a father to teach a craft to his son. It was expected. Even Jesus worked as a carpenter before beginning His public ministry. Paul was a tentmaker. Tentmaking was a noble profession then. Paul often donned his leather apron and performed the demanding work of stitching heavy material into tents.

All who traveled with Paul saw his hard work and willingness to support himself. His work was more than just following a tradition; it spoke of his faith and dedication. His work was a testimony to others.

I can assure you that Paul believed in Jesus' imminent return. He encouraged Timothy to keep at the work he was called to: "In the presence of God, who gives life to all things, and of Christ Jesus, who in his testimony before Pontius Pilate made the good confession, I charge you to keep the commandment without spot or blame until the manifestation of our Lord Jesus Christ, which he will bring about at the right time."[5]

Paul's motto was, "Keep working until Jesus comes again."

GOD

Work is a testimony to others and to Me of your faithfulness. There is much to be done, and that work has been passed to the church. Remember, church is not a building; church is a group of believers. The people who make up the church have a great deal of work to do.

JESUS

Almost every disciple I called, I called from a place of work. As I walked beside the Sea of Galilee, I saw two brothers, Simon called Peter and his brother Andrew. They were fishermen and were casting a net into the lake. "Come, follow Me," I said, "and I will make you fishers of men." They left their nets and followed Me.[6]

In another case, I pointed out how much work remained to be done. I had been traveling through the cities and villages, teaching in the synagogues, proclaiming the gospel of the kingdom, and healing diseases. There were so many people without a leader. They were distressed and dispirited, like sheep without a shepherd. I said to My disciples, "The harvest is plentiful, but the workers are few. Therefore beseech the Lord of the harvest to send out workers into His harvest."[7]

GOD

The knowledge that Jesus can return at any moment should motivate you to good and faithful work. Don't become confused here. When I speak of work, I don't mean just church work. The work you do for a living is important—it has value. But of greater value is the way you do the work. Whatever you do, do it with all your might as if working for Me and not just your employer.[8]

Work that is done well reflects not only on you, but on Me. Do your work well, and do it in a way that brings glory and honor to your Savior.

Yes, the day is coming when normal work will cease. Look forward to that day. Pray for that day, but continue to work.

Work not only helps others, but it helps you. Work keeps your mind sharp and gives you a sense of value and purpose. Your ultimate fulfillment comes from a relationship with Me, but work makes you a contributing member of society.

There was a time in your history when the monastic movement was at its zenith. Many educated men went to monasteries to pray and withdraw from society. Their dedication is admirable, but the unexpected result was that the best and most educated men left their communities, communities that could have benefited from their skills and knowledge. I don't ask that you withdraw from the world around you. Your world needs to see what a Christian is and how a Christian behaves.

Every life makes a difference. Whether you're a mechanic, an architect, a doctor, a minister, a bricklayer, or some other occupation, your attitude and words will have an impact on your fellow employees and employer.

What you do makes a difference.

15

How should we prepare for the end of the world?

Christian author Dorothy Sayers wrote, "The only Christian work is good work done well."[1] Simple wisdom says, "God did not create us with two hands so we could sit on them." But what kind of works should people be doing between now and the coming of Christ? Some, fearful of the event, have gone to extremes storing food and weapons.

Is this what Jesus meant for people to be doing? If Christian teaching is correct, shouldn't the Second Coming be a glorious thing, something to be longed for, hoped for?

 Since the second coming of Jesus may be close or far away, what should Christians be doing to prepare for the end of the world?

GOD

Let's be clear. There is nothing you can do to push up or delay the events of the end times, but there are things you should be doing.

One thing we haven't discussed is the need for you to be vigilant. As Jesus taught, "Be on guard! Be alert! You do not know when that time will come."[2] In his own way, Paul repeated the instruction: "Let us not sleep, as others do, but let us watch and be sober."[3]

JESUS

Paul went into detail when he wrote to the church in Rome: "Do this, knowing the time, that it is already the hour for you to awaken from sleep; for now salvation is nearer to us than when we believed. The night is almost gone, and the day is near. Therefore let us lay aside the deeds of darkness and put on the armor of light. Let us behave properly as in the day, not in carousing and drunkenness, not in sexual promiscuity and sensuality, not in strife and jealousy. But put on the Lord Jesus Christ, and make no provision for the flesh in regard to its lusts."[4]

Live as if I'm returning tomorrow; plan and work as if you have a lifetime. Remember that the timing is not your business; faithful, worshipful, meaningful work is. Set aside what Paul called the "deeds of darkness" and live and work in the light.

I gave instruction to the disciples about what they should do in the time remaining to them. By extension, that instruction applies to you. There is work you should be carrying out until My return. Here's what I said then: "All authority in heaven and on earth has been given to me. Go therefore and make disciples of all nations, baptizing them in the name of the Father and of the Son and of the Holy Spirit, and teaching them to obey everything that I have commanded you. And remember, I am with you always, to the end of the age."[5]

It was to be their work and that of the church to make disciples. As you know, a disciple is a learner—someone who sits at the feet of a teacher. My disciples became apostles. The word *apostle* means "sent-out one." *Apostle* was the term that would be used for an ambassador. An ambassador represents one country to another. That's what My followers became: people who represented the kingdom of God to the rest of the world. Christians do the same kind of work today.

I sent the first disciples into the world—not just to Jerusalem or the Holy Land, but to the world. Their work was to teach others what I had taught them and to make them part of the church. This they did, and they took the work seriously.

MATTHIAS

I may have the least recognizable name in the New Testament. That's all right with me. I didn't become a follower of Jesus because I wanted to be well known. I wanted to be His disciple and help further the kingdom of God He taught about.

One of the first things the disciples did after Jesus ascended into heaven was select a replacement for Judas the traitor. Jesus had called twelve disciples to be part of His inner circle. After Judas killed himself for betraying Jesus, the disciples decided to cast lots to bring the number of close disciples back to twelve. They prayed and then cast lots. I was selected and added to the eleven.[6]

Why is this important? Here's an interesting fact. Apart from that single mention of my name, I never appeared in the New Testament again. Does that mean the disciples were wrong to do this? No, although sometime later Saul would meet Jesus while on the road to Damascus and be changed from a religious zealot who persecuted the church to Paul the apostle. He was the lasting replacement for Judas, not me. But even though I am not famous, I still had a role to play, and that's why I'm sharing this story with you.

I worked for my Savior until my death. There was work to do then, and there's work for you to do today. We knew then what you must know now: Christians do what they can, where they are, with the skills they've been given to spread the news about Jesus. That is what we do until the end of the age. I wanted Jesus to find me working when He returned. That's something every Christian should want.

God

What specifically should you be doing until Christ comes again? What is the best way to prepare for that day? Be a person of faith, because that is the only preparation you can make. Be personally ready for Jesus' return. Other events will take care of themselves. The real question is this: what should you be doing to help humanity prepare for the end of the age?

Do the work of Christ. Jesus was clear about the work I sent Him to do: "The Son of Man has come to seek and to save that which was lost."[7] Seeking and saving. You can't do the saving part; that's Our work. However, you can spread the news about Jesus by word and by deed. Let others see Jesus in you. Do not hesitate to share what you know about Jesus, what you learn from the Bible.

Living a Christlike life brings other responsibilities. Followers of Christ do works of benevolence and humanitarianism. "Pure and genuine religion in the sight of God the Father means caring for orphans and widows in their distress and refusing to let the world corrupt you."[8]

Unfortunately, many of My churches have shied away from this, calling it a social gospel, but it is so much more than that. Your actions speak louder than any sermon.

Jesus

You may be familiar with the parable of the good Samaritan. The story is so famous that nonprofit organizations use the title, and there are even laws called good Samaritan laws. A religious leader asked Me, "Who is my neighbor?"[9] To illustrate the point that faith changes the way we see others, I told the tale of man who, while on a journey, was attacked by bandits, robbed, beaten, and left for dead. Religious people passed him, stepping over him as if he weren't unconscious in the road. Along came a Samaritan who administered first aid, took him to an inn, paid for a room, and gave the innkeeper money to take care of the man. For this to make sense, you need to know that Jews of the day hated Samaritans and would often travel out of their way to avoid stepping foot on Samaritan soil. Yet this hated outcast was the one who did the work of God.

After I told that parable, I told the people to "go and do likewise."[10]

GOD

There always has been and always will be a need to teach new Christians how to grow to maturity so they, too, can contribute to the Christian work leading to the end of the age.

One of the central goals of My plan is to have My people "reach unity in the faith and in the knowledge of the Son of God and become mature, attaining to the whole measure of the fullness of Christ."[11] New believers are like infants needing to be fed milk first then, as they grow, solid food.[12]

It is the obligation of each Christian to grow in the faith, and there is always room to grow. Growth is part of the life lived in faith. No human knows it all. Learn, live what you learn, then teach what you've learned. You may have heard preachers say this, but the church is always one generation away from extinction. What is known needs to be passed on to new believers.

Every Christian should be involved with worship, praise, and prayer. To My disappointment, I have heard many say, "I don't need to go to church. I can worship right where I am." That is only half true. Any believer can worship anywhere, but believers should always be involved in church, the only institution that Jesus founded.

Worship should be thought of as a privilege more than work, but you should be involved in the effort. Jesus set the example: "He came to Nazareth, where He had been brought up. And as His custom was, He went into the synagogue on the Sabbath day, and stood up to read."[13] Worship, prayer, and praise were part of His ministry, and they should be part of your life.

This need has changed since the first century, although people occasionally need a reminder not to neglect their meeting together for encourage-ment.[14]

There is work to be done between now and the time Jesus returns. Your best preparation is to be busy going about My work and the work of the church, remembering that by doing so you are preparing for the coming of Jesus.

The Lord said to the man, "You listened to your wife and ate fruit from that tree. And so, the ground will be under a curse because of what you did. As long as you live, you will have to struggle to grow enough food. Your food will be plants, but the ground will produce thorns and thistles. You will have to sweat to earn a living; you were made out of soil, and you will once again turn into soil."

Genesis 3:17–19 CEV

Pain and Suffering

The most difficult questions people have to deal with involve some sort of heartache. People have trouble understanding why this is so, since God is good.

16
God, why do You allow natural calamities to kill so many people?

We've all seen the headlines, watched the unsettling videos on our televisions, heard firsthand reports over the radio. Natural disasters. They come as no surprise, but no matter how many there are, news of massive destruction and death shakes everyone to the core as heartbreaking images stream into our living rooms.

Such events cause people to question the existence of God, or, at the very least, His power to do anything about such cataclysms. When the dust settles, many ask, "Where was God?" The question doesn't come from just mean-spirited people; it also comes from people of faith. How does one reconcile a loving God in the aftermath of disaster?

 God, why do You allow earthquakes, tsunamis, floods, and other natural calamities to kill hundreds of thousands of people?

GOD

An earthquake in Haiti took 300,000 lives in 2010. In 2004, a tsunami killed more than 250,000 people in lands around the Bay of Bengal. A 1931 flood destroyed four million lives. We can go further back. In May of 526, an earthquake wiped out a quarter-million lives. Spanish flu took the lives of 100 million people worldwide. Do the numbers surprise you? There have been far worse. The death toll of the Great Chinese Famine, which spanned the years 1958 to 1961, approached 43 million.

I know those numbers and hundreds more like them. I know more than that. I know the name of every person who drowned in a tsunami, perished in an earthquake, was cut down by an epidemic, or succumbed to hunger. To many people these numbers are statistics, but to Me they are much more. Rich or poor, good or evil, young or old, I know them all. I know every hair on their heads,[1] every dream they had, every hope they harbored, and every loved one they left behind.

The question is fair and understandable. Many ask the question in anger, and I understand the emotion. But are you ready for My answer? Generally, when someone challenges My knowledge or ability, they are not seeking understanding. They're lashing out. Some have a right to be hurt and troubled. Death is common, but it is not natural for humans. I did not design Adam and Eve to die. Death came to humanity through sin, not through intention.

One of the oldest books in the Bible is the book of Job, and it tells the story of a man who lost everything: family, wealth, position, and his health—and I allowed it. It may sound cruel to you, but I do nothing out of cruelty. Job had reason to complain, but I made it clear to him that he did not and could not understand all that I do or, for that matter, what I don't do. In the end, he said, "Surely I spoke of things I did not understand, things too wonderful for me to know."[2]

Are you wrong to grieve over such massive loss of life that occurs in a natural disaster? Of course not, but remember that your point of view is limited by space and time. You do not see all history and the future as I do. You do not see what happens to those souls. I deal with eternity, and My perspective is unlimited.

JOB

I experienced great loss. My pain is beyond what most people experience. Even so, the death of my loved ones was a tiny number compared to what the world has seen from natural disaster. I did my best to remain faithful, but my mind raced to make sense of my sudden loss. In my day, family was everything to a man. Children were his future. Their sudden deaths robbed me of the will to live. I was one of the richest men of my day, and then I lost it all. I never lost my sense that God was in control, however. I did lose my ability to understand God's sometimes-inscrutable ways, but I never lost His reality and involvement in my life.

Like you, I had an expectation about fairness. I felt God should bend to my ideals instead of the other way around. When you see massive loss of life from natural desire, you feel it is unfair. Perhaps it is. But fairness has nothing to do with it.

JESUS

A group of My Jewish brethren came to Me one day to complain about Pontius Pilate. Pilate held no love for Jews. In fact, he hated us all. On several occasions, he caused the death of those he was supposed to govern. He would play an important role in My own death. In one case, he caused a group of Galileans to be killed while they were offering sacrifices. To My brethren, his behavior was as unfair as the death of good men. I said, "Do you suppose that those eighteen on whom the tower in Siloam fell and killed them were worse culprits than all the men who live in Jerusalem?"[3] The answer was no. All men die. Only two men have never died: Enoch[4] and Elijah.[5]

Every human is destined to die.[6] Sometimes death comes unexpectedly, as with those eighteen men who died in the tower collapse. Those men were no more sinful than the men nearby who weren't killed. When someone dies in an accident, it is not God's judgment against them. Some people die because of the foolishness of others, as in auto accidents. Some die because of natural disasters.

GOD

You live on a dynamic planet. Earthquakes, hurricanes, tornadoes, and other natural disasters are part of how the earth functions. I am not the cause of every drop of rain, or every tremor in the ground.

That is not to say I cannot influence the weather. I can and have. Moses warned My people about idol worship. He said, "If you do, the Lord's anger will burn against you. He will shut up the sky and hold back the rain, and the ground will fail to produce its harvests. Then you will quickly die in that good land the Lord is giving you."[7] Sound harsh? The idol worshippers of that day sacrificed their children to gods who didn't exist. The warning sounds harsh, but worse are the acts that idol worshippers committed.

JOB

I lived under the assumption that trouble and pain came only to the wicked. But fairness has nothing to do with death and disaster.

I learned that I had to do some things to understand my sudden change in fortune. First, I don't know enough to question God. There are those who think they do, but I can assure you, no person does. Second, I came to understand that good and bad things happen to everyone. I might live a life of privilege and security, but I can't say I deserve it more than others do.

I came to understand that God is with us in the storm. We are not promised an easy life, but we are promised light in darkness, hope in a hopeless situation. All through Scripture, you find faithful people of God who suffer in life but continue to believe, driven by their love for God.

Through my trials, I came to understand that there is more beyond this life. I told my friends, "I know that my Redeemer lives, and He shall stand at last on the earth; and after my skin is destroyed, this I know, that in my flesh I shall see God, whom I shall see for myself, and my eyes shall behold, and not another. How my heart yearns within me!"[8]

GOD

The world you live in is not your final destination. There is more beyond. Many people of faith have suffered. "These men of faith died without ever receiving all that I had promised them; but they saw it all awaiting them on ahead and were glad, for they agreed that this earth was not their real home but that they were just strangers visiting down here. When they talked like that, they were looking forward to their real home in heaven."[9]

JESUS

Tsunamis will occur again. So will earthquakes and hurricanes. These should be taken seriously. Wisdom needs to be exercised about pending disasters. You and others should be ready to help in times of crisis. God will take care of things on this side of eternity; you and others can work on earth to ease pain and restore the stricken.

Many centuries ago, a prophet named Habakkuk faced difficult times. It had been revealed to him that his people would be taken captive by an invading army. He could do nothing to prevent it, but he could decide how he would face the coming difficulties. He learned to trust God when he could fully understand why things happen as they do. He wrote: "Though the fig tree does not bud and there are no grapes on the vines, though the olive crop fails and the fields produce no food, though there are no sheep in the pen and no cattle in the stalls, yet I will rejoice in the LORD, I will be joyful in God my Savior."[10]

GOD

There is no satisfying answer when people ask why. People want a perfect world, one without storms and earthquakes, but the physical world does not work that way. Physical forces are part of a physical world. The new heaven and the new earth will be different, but for now, you must be wise, prepared, and trusting that I know what I'm doing. I cause all things to work together for good even if you can't see it now.[11]

17
Why is there so much suffering?

> *Suffering has been a topic of conversation since the beginning of man. Some speak eloquently of it; others speak disparagingly. No matter what one thinks of suffering, no one denies its existence. Suffering comes in many variations. Approximately thirty thousand people die each day from hunger. Most of them are children. Some disasters are caused by humans.*
>
> *The hungry suffer one way; the oppressed another. There is mental, emotional, physical, and economic suffering. Some suffer as individuals; others in groups. No one likes suffering, and many prefer to look the other way. Still, evidence of suffering is everywhere: jails, hospitals, convalescent homes, mansions, shanties. History is a record of human suffering. Is that fair?*

 God, everywhere I look I see suffering—hunger, pain, oppression. Why is there so much suffering in the world?

GOD

Suffering is part of the human condition. It can't be avoided. You see it everywhere you look. I see every bit of it. I see it at the individual level. I count every tear. Suffering was never My intention. You will notice the Bible opens in a garden paradise and closes in a garden paradise after I have redeemed the world from sin. I caused this to be recorded in the first book of the Bible: "The LORD God had planted a garden in the east, in Eden; and there he put the man he had formed. And the LORD God made all kinds of trees grow out of the ground—trees that were pleasing to the eye and good for food. In the middle of the garden were the tree of life and the tree of the knowledge of good and evil."[1]

Sounds idyllic, doesn't it? It was. The first man and woman lived in comfort and in a world where suffering didn't exist. As you saw in our discussion of the end times, I will return things to the way they were intended to be. The book of Revelation is the written record of a vision I gave to the apostle John.

He saw much of what the future would hold, the good and the bad. He saw great suffering, but he also wrote in the last chapter: "The angel showed me the river of the water of life, as clear as crystal, flowing from the throne of God and of the Lamb down the middle of the great street of the city. On each side of the river stood the tree of life, bearing twelve crops of fruit, yielding its fruit every month. And the leaves of the tree are for the healing of the nations. No longer will there be any curse."[2]

Suffering is temporary, but the bliss of heaven is forever.

JESUS

A great deal of suffering comes from man's inhumanity to man. It has been that way for millennia. The dictators of history are easy to recognize, but ordinary people treat others poorly—at times cruelly. This includes some governments and corporations.

I am well acquainted with suffering, and I mean beyond what I experienced after My arrest and the event leading to the crucifixion. I was born into suffering. Mary gave birth to Me far from her home. Rather than giving birth on her own bed, she and Joseph had to settle for an animal pen. My first bed was a stone feeding trough, and My first ceiling was the night sky.

For Mary and Joseph, it was a time of great anguish and fear. Then things grew worse. Sometime after My birth, wise men from the east came looking for Me. They had seen and followed a star to Jerusalem. While in the city, and being the men of influence they were, they spoke to King Herod. Herod was an evil man who, in his great paranoia, killed members of his own family who he thought were after his throne.

The wise men asked where the king of the Jews was. Herod considered himself the king of the Jews. Experts in Bible prophecy quoted Micah 5:2 to him: "You, Bethlehem, in the land of Judah, are not the least among the rulers of Judah; for out of you shall come a Ruler who will shepherd My people Israel."[3] He then asked when the wise men had seen the stars. After the men left, feeling threatened, Herod ordered every child two years old or younger to be killed. Imagine the cries of anguish as Herod's men snatched infants and toddlers away from their parents and killed them in full view of the family. Can you imagine greater suffering?

My family escaped to Egypt and stayed there until Herod died. My first years of human life were spent as a refugee. One man caused that suffering.

MARY MAGDALENE

Much of my life was spent in suffering. Until Jesus healed me, I was plagued with illness and worse.[4] Jesus freed me from all that. His miracle made me a new person. I became His follower. He had a great many female followers. I was to them what Peter was to the male disciples. Our roles were different, but we were all followers.

I saw Jesus at many stages of His ministry. I listened as He taught, watched Him thwart the religious leaders as they tried to entrap Him, and I saw Him work countless miracles. The New Testament recorded thirty-five of Jesus' miracles. He did many more. Of those thirty-five miracles, seventeen of them were physical healings. If you add exorcisms, the number is twenty-three.

Jesus healed leprosy, blindness, paralysis, crippled limbs, fevers, and much more. Throughout Jesus' ministry, He faced and alleviated suffering. He released me from the afflictions that had plagued me for years, but greater suffering was coming my way. I was one of the people who stood at the foot of the cross. I saw what the Romans had done to Him. The blood, the swelling, the disfigurement made Him almost unrecognizable. His mother, Mary, stood beside me. As bad as it was for me—and it was too horrible for words—it was worse for her.

I saw His death, and I saw the persecution of the church as it began in Jerusalem and spread throughout the world. Christians are not exempt from suffering. In fact, in some places it's expected.

GOD

There is a widespread misconception that when a person turns to Christ he will be protected from all future suffering. That idea has not come from Me, nor is it taught in the Bible. In truth, the Bible teaches otherwise.

Peter wrote: "Dear friends, do not be surprised at the painful trial you are suffering, as though something strange were happening to you. But rejoice that you participate in the sufferings of Christ, so that you may be overjoyed when his glory is revealed. If you are insulted because of the name of Christ, you are blessed, for the Spirit of glory and of God rests on you. If you suffer, it should not be as a murderer or thief or any other kind of criminal, or even as a meddler. However, if you suffer as a Christian, do not be ashamed, but praise God that you bear that name."[5]

At times, those who are righteous suffer because of their righteousness; some suffer because they are disciples of the One who suffered. In a sense, you share in His suffering.

James, who led the church after Peter left Jerusalem to minister in Rome, saw the church through the early persecutions. He witnessed hundreds of his congregation suffer at the hands of hateful men, and he encouraged them: "Follow the example of the prophets who spoke for the Lord. They were patient, even when they had to suffer. In fact, we praise the ones who endured the most. You remember how patient Job was and how the Lord finally helped him. The Lord did this because he is so merciful and kind."[6]

As you've noticed, Paul was a blunt man. In a letter to the young pastor Timothy, he said: "Everyone who wants to live a godly life in Christ Jesus will suffer persecution."[7]

Suffering is part of the human condition, and it will continue until the end of the age. From the beginning, for instance, I have encouraged those who can help to do so. I demanded that farmers not harvest the corners of their fields so they could leave food for the poor to harvest.[8] Suffering began because of sin; love and action can alleviate much of it.[9]

JESUS

No matter how bad the suffering, what lies ahead for believers will more than compensate for it. "I consider that the sufferings of this present time are not worthy to be compared with the glory that is to be revealed to us."[10] I know the pain you feel; I also know the glory that awaits you.

18
Why are some people rich and others poor?

Ask one hundred people on the street if they would like to be wealthy, and there's a good chance every one of them will say yes and say it with enthusiasm. To most people, wealth equals acceptance, security, and freedom.

And it seems that some extremely rich men aren't happy. W. H. Vanderbilt said, "The care of $200 million is enough to kill anyone. There is no pleasure in it." And multimillionaire John Jacob Astor commented, "I am the most miserable man on earth." John D. Rockefeller said, "I have made many millions, but they have brought me no happiness. I would barter them all for the days I sat on an office stool in Cleveland and counted myself rich on three dollars a week." Andrew Carnegie noted, "Millionaires seldom smile." Henry Ford complained, "I was happier when doing a mechanic's job."

Life often seems unfair, God. Why do some people who don't care about You become rich and famous, while other people who love You become targets of persecution? There are those who are good and kind yet struggle to get by, while selfish people seem to be rewarded. Why is that?

God

Wealth is a misunderstood concept. Would it surprise you if I said I have no problem with wealth or wealthy people? I don't. Job was wealthy, as was Abraham, and, of course, King Solomon was the richest man ever to live.

While I have no problem with wealthy people, wealthy people often have problems with riches. There are happy billionaires, but there are also many miserable ones. And you're right when you mention that many godless and selfish people seem to have an advantage over the godly. Sometimes it seems the unrighteous receive favorable treatment, but some of that is an illusion. They live in this fallen world just as you do.

Jesus taught this about Me: "He makes the sun rise on both good and bad people. And he sends rain for the ones who do right and for the ones who do wrong."[1] I don't play favorites.

ASAPH

Near the middle of the Bible is a long book called Psalms. It is less a book than a collection of songs. Most of the entries were written by King David, but as one of his leading musicians I also composed several psalms. Almost three thousand years ago I wrote, "I envied the arrogant when I saw the prosperity of the wicked. They have no struggles; their bodies are healthy and strong. They are free from the burdens common to man; they are not plagued by human ills."[2]

I resented the wealthy. Everything about them made me feel like a failure. I let this bitterness fester until I began to lose my spiritual footing. My resentment grew from my envy. This may be what you're experiencing.

Over time, I learned that things were not as they seemed. In some ways, the wealthy have unique temptations that are not common to others. Riches can be a snare that keeps them from finding peace with God.

JESUS

Solomon served as king after his father, David, died. He is known for many things, but his two best-known qualities are his supernatural wisdom and his wealth. He said, "He who loves money will not be satisfied with money, nor he who loves abundance with its income. This too is vanity."[3]

Despite his great wisdom and power, Solomon turned away from his faith, allowing his many wives to worship idols. Over time, he lost perspective and made decisions that harmed him and his country.

The problem with riches is that if you're not careful, they can fog your spiritual vision. I told a parable about a sower who sows seed in different kinds of soil. In the first century, and in many third-world countries, seeds were spread by broadcasting—by taking a handful of seeds and tossing them on the ground. In the parable, the seeds grow but are soon choked out by weeds. I said, "He who received seed among the thorns is he who hears the word, and the cares of this world and the deceitfulness of riches choke the word, and he becomes unfruitful."[4]

Consider this account: A wealthy young man came to Me and asked how to gain eternal life. I told him to keep the Ten Commandments. He said, "I have kept all these; what do I still lack?"

I answered, "If you wish to be perfect, go, sell your possessions, and give the money to the poor, and you will have treasure in heaven; then come, follow me." When he heard this he went away grieving, for he had many possessions.[5]

He had an opportunity to follow Me, but I knew he loved his wealth more.

God

Many who followed Jesus left behind businesses. Peter and his partners left a fishing business. This is not a requirement for salvation, but there are guidelines for how Christians handle wealth.

Paul expressed the guidelines like this: "Teach those who are rich in this world not to be proud and not to trust in their money, which is so unreliable. Their trust should be in God, who richly gives us all we need for our enjoyment. Tell them to use their money to do good. They should be rich in good works and generous to those in need, always being ready to share with others. By doing this they will be storing up their treasure as a good foundation for the future so that they may experience true life."[6]

Riches are meant to be shared. I allow and enable some people to become rich so they can use their money to achieve things for My kingdom. Many Christians tithe their income, meaning they donate 10 percent to the churches where they worship. I have followers who give away 90 percent of their income and still live well.

The problem has never been money, but the love of it. The most misquoted verse in the Bible is "Money is the root of all evil." But the verse actually says, "The love of money is a root of all sorts of evil, and some by longing for it have wandered away from the faith and pierced themselves with many griefs."[7]

Did you notice it isn't money that is the root of all evil, but rather the *love* of money? Godliness and contentment make great companions.

JESUS

This topic was part of My teaching: "Do not store up for yourselves treasures on earth, where moth and rust destroy, and where thieves break in and steal. But store up for yourselves treasures in heaven, where moth and rust do not destroy, and where thieves do not break in and steal. For where your treasure is, there your heart will be also."[8]

There is the key. What matters is not wealth but the placement of your heart. What others achieve financially is not your responsibility. You are to be a good steward of what you have. Whether you are poor or rich, your heart should be set on heaven.

Don't let this be a stumbling block for you. Pray, and I will help you understand the prosperity of the wicked and the way of the righteous.

ASAPH

I told you of the psalm I wrote expressing my frustration over the very issue you raise. I found my answer by seeking the wisdom of God. That is where you will find your answer.

GOD

Yes, sometimes the selfish, the evil, gain wealth and power. That is temporary. Others gain wealth and use it for great things. Most learn to be content with the basics of life. In each case, a choice is made. You can choose bitterness, or you can choose contentment.

19
God, do You truly care for everyone?

The Bible contains terms that can be confusing: the chosen people, the elect, those predestined. *It would seem that God is interested in only some people while ignoring all the rest. Is God that selective? Are there groups or individuals who have no hope of grace, faith, or salvation because they somehow don't fit in?*

It's a horrible scenario. The idea that God's love is selective is chilling. It doesn't seem fair that God is interested only in the people He chose. What about the rest?

 God, do You care for everyone, or is Your focus on just a few select people?

GOD

I care for everyone. My desire is that everyone experience My love and receives My gift of eternal life. It is true that I focused on the Jews. The Old Testament is the account of My dealings with the descendants of Abraham. I called them My chosen people. I selected Abraham to be the father of a nation with millions of people who call him father. I said to him: "Look up at the heavens and count the stars—if indeed you can count them . . . So shall your offspring be."[1]

My people are meant to be an example to the nations. They're faithfulness would show what a relationship with Me could be like. Out of the nation of Israel My Son would be born, the Messiah. I was stricter with them than with others. They had a great role to play in history, and as examples of My kingdom, I demanded more. Everything I demanded, however, was for their benefit as well.

Do I play favorites? In a sense, but when I do so, it is to bring about a great good. I do not, however, play favorites with individuals.

JESUS

When you read the New Testament notice two words that will help you understand Our universal love: *world* and *whoever*. Let's sample a few verses containing the word *world*:

"This gospel of the kingdom will be preached in all the world as a witness to all the nations, and then the end will come."[2] I was speaking of the end times with the disciples when I uttered those words, but you can see that the gospel has always had a worldview. The gospel is meant to be heard by every nation in the world. The target audience is everyone. Did you notice the word *nations*? In the original language of New Testament Greek, it's the same word often translated as *Gentile*. Salvation was first preached to the Jews, but it is also meant for non-Jews.

SAMARITAN WOMAN

Sometimes the world is right next door. My name is not recorded in the New Testament. I did not live the most noble of lives. My claim to fame is that Jesus talked with me and brought my sin to the forefront. I'm a Samaritan. Samaritans and Jews were not friends. To be frank, we hated the Jews, and they hated us. Jesus did what most Jews avoided; He traveled through our land. Then He did something else: He sat at a well, and when I came to draw water in the middle of the day, He asked for a drink.

Doesn't sound like much, does it? But Jesus did what no other Jewish man would do. He spoke to not just a woman, but a Samaritan woman drawing water in the heat of the afternoon. You see, I always drew water when the other women weren't around. They loathed me because I was immoral. Yet Jesus broke all the social taboos to deliver the gospel to me. When I told the other people in the village about Jesus, they wanted to hear His message too. They said to me, "Now we know that he is indeed the Savior of the world."[3]

World doesn't refer just to distant lands. Sometimes it refers specifically to people who are outcasts. Jesus brought the salvation message to someone hated by His people and her own.

JESUS

The goal of the gospel has always been to heal the broken and repair a person's relationship with God. John said of Me, "There was the true Light which, coming into the world, enlightens every man."[4] My light came to everyone in everyplace.

We can add this verse to the list: "The bread of God is he who comes down from heaven and gives life to the world."[5] I give life to those who believe, regardless of their history, ethnic group, gender, or location on the planet. I exclude no one who chooses to believe.

The other word I mentioned—*whoever*—appears many times in the New Testament and carries great meaning. Salvation is never forced on anyone. It must be accepted by choice. I said, "Whoever hears my word and believes him who sent me has eternal life and will not be condemned; he has crossed over from death to life."[6]

In the Old Testament book of Joel is a verse that is used three times in the Bible: "It shall come to pass that whoever calls on the name of the LORD shall be saved."[7] Peter used that verse as the text in his first sermon, the one that saw the conversion of more than three thousand people.[8] Paul quoted it in his book to the Romans.[9] And one of the central words in the verse is *whoever*. The gospel is a "whoever" message, and I intended it for everyone.

GOD

Jesus told a series of parables that show the love We have for the individual. Those parables are stories drawn from life, stories every listener can comprehend. Here's His first parable: "If a man has a hundred sheep and one of them gets lost, what will he do? Won't he leave the ninety-nine others in the wilderness and go to search for the one that is lost until he finds it? And when he has found it, he will joyfully carry it home on his shoulders. When he arrives, he will call together his friends and neighbors, saying, 'Rejoice with me because I have found my lost sheep.' In the same way, there is more joy in heaven over one lost sinner who repents and returns to God than over ninety-nine others who are righteous and haven't strayed away!"[10]

The beauty of the parable is its simplicity. We love and will go searching for every lost sheep. You are far more valuable and important to Us than a sheep. All heaven rejoices for everyone who comes to or returns to faith.

My Son told another, similar parable: "Suppose a woman has ten silver coins and loses one. Won't she light a lamp and sweep the entire house and search carefully until she finds it? And when she finds it, she will call in her friends and neighbors and say, 'Rejoice with me because I have found my lost coin.' In the same way, there is joy in the presence of God's angels when even one sinner repents."[11]

JESUS

The purpose of those parables and others like them is to show you how valuable you are. We care for everyone. Salvation and forgiveness are offered to everyone.

GOD

Some of the apostles had to learn that My love was meant for everyone. Even Peter had to learn that the gospel was open to Gentiles. After seeing that My power worked in non-Jewish groups, he made this confession: "I now realize how true it is that God does not show favoritism but accepts men from every nation who fear him and do what is right."[12]

Like a parent, We love all equally. As Paul said, "In this new life, it doesn't matter if you are a Jew or a Gentile, circumcised or uncircumcised, barbaric, uncivilized, slave, or free. Christ is all that matters, and he lives in all of us."[13]

20
Why is there disease?

The number of diseases is not known. That is partly because many virus-caused diseases change over time. The flu is a common example. Every few years, a new strain of flu appears. The reason there is no cure for the common cold is that it is not so common. Multiple viruses give us cold-like symptoms. The leading cause of death is heart disease, followed by cancer and stroke.[1]

There are infectious diseases, too, some of which have taken millions of lives. Smallpox, typhus, bubonic plague, and influenza have at times devastated large areas. In a perfect world there would be no disease, but the world is far from perfect.

 God, why are we affected by uncountable diseases that sicken and kill?

GOD

There is more to My creation than you can see—angelic realms and distant galaxies that hold mysteries yet to be discovered. There is a whole level of creation at the microscopic level. Scientists have identified thousands of microbes, viruses, and bacteria, some of which are harmful to people.

Such things are not new, of course. The Bible mentions or shows many diseases: fevers, abscesses, atrophy, blindness, paralysis, hemorrhaging, leprosy, and more. Diseases in the past were as horrible as those of today.

I designed Adam and Eve to live in a protected environment. I also made them disease resistant. Look at the life spans of the earliest humans. Adam lived 930 years.[2] His son Seth died when he was 912 years old.[3] The man who lived the longest was Methuselah, who died when he was 969 years old[4] By today's standards, those ages seem impossible, and in today's world they are.

Study the Genesis genealogies, and you will discover something interesting: the life expectancy of each successive generation after Adam and Eve decreased until reaching a normal life span of about seventy or eighty years.[5]

In some countries, forty is considered elderly; in others, it is not uncommon to see people live well into their nineties or later. But no matter how healthy a lifestyle one lives, or how much access to modern medicine one has, humans will succumb to some form of disease. It might be aging, or it might be a virus. A time will come when there will be no diseases. Death will be done away with. Death will be the last enemy to be destroyed.[6]

That day is in the future, and for now you live in a world that has challenges on all sides. Disease is one of them. No one is exempt from disease. Paul, as great and as faithful a man as he was, prayed to have a physical affliction removed. Here is his account: "Because of the surpassing greatness of the revelations, for this reason, to keep me from exalting myself, there was given me a thorn in the flesh, a messenger of Satan to torment me—to keep me from exalting myself! Concerning this I implored the Lord three times that it might leave me. And He has said to me, 'My grace is sufficient for you, for power is perfected in weakness.' Most gladly, therefore, I will rather boast about my weaknesses, so that the power of Christ may dwell in me."[7]

Paul suffered from many diseases, including one that affected his eyes. This was in a day when there was little medical treatment, at least what people today would call treatment. His solution was to rely on My grace and continue on.

JESUS

I went about confronting illness, often healing those with diseases.[8] I touched lepers, made the lame to walk and the blind to see, but I didn't heal everyone. Dealing with difficulties makes you strong and more dependent upon God. Don't be confused. Not every disease is from God and meant to punish. God has used diseases as judgments, but those were extreme cases. Most illness comes not from sin or judgment, but simply from living in this world.

GOD

The world has more diseases that affect humans than ever before. Many of them come from changes occurring in your environment. Human encroachment into wildlife habitats forces animals to live in denser population where disease spreads and mutates. Some of those mutated diseases jump to human hosts.

Many things, from the destruction of the rain forests to urbanization, pollution, and medications, can enhance disease. Disease is part of a changing world. Even good intentions of curing illness can lead to disease problems. Antibiotics are wonderful things, but their overuse has led to stronger strains of disease.

LUKE

I am the only physician mentioned by name in the Bible. Medical science is far more advanced than it was in my day, but the needs are the same. I saw people who cursed God for their diseases, and I saw those who sought His help in their pain.

The first thing a doctor learns in any age is that attitude makes a big difference during illness. Prayer and trust in God during difficult medical times help more than most people realize, but they don't always lead to a cure. Part of being human is fighting disease.

Our defenses are not what they were in Adam and Eve's day, but they are still remarkable, and medical science has saved untold lives and eased pain all across the globe.

No one likes disease. It doesn't seem fair. Perhaps it's not. But it is common to the human condition. Disease comes upon the innocent as well as the guilty. Some diseases, however, are spread by preventable human conduct. Most venereal diseases would pass from existence in a generation or two if there were no such thing as fornication and adultery. Other diseases, however, have nothing at all to do with sin. Innocent children contract mild and even life-threatening diseases.

GOD

Your question, like the ones before, shows a desire to live in a perfect world, but the world was perfect for only a short time. I know that a world without disease seems idyllic. It was. It will be again, but there is much that needs to happen between now and then.

I have great concern over those in the world who are ill. That is why Jesus did so much healing, but His ministry wasn't to eradicate disease of the flesh. His ministry was to eradicate disease of the heart.

Illness, unpleasant as it is, can draw you closer to Me and closer to the ones you love. The anxiety you experience indicates your love for ill family members or friends. It also forces you to think about how you can help. It has caused many to seek Me in prayer.

I do not make light of illness. Some of the laws I handed down to Moses were meant to lessen My people's exposure to disease, laws such as the prohibition against eating pork, which carries the worm that causes trichinosis. I also gave instruction on how to deal with people who might be infectious. These people were brought to the priests, who were trained to recognize certain spreadable diseases. My book of Leviticus goes into great detail.[9]

Disease has been around for a long time. Isn't it interesting that people like Paul and others never saw the presence of disease as a theological problem or a hindrance to faith? They depended upon Me for strength and endurance, and they kept their eyes fixed on the day when such things would be only a memory.

Some have made the mistake of thinking that because I allow something, I approve of it. Some have gone so far as to suggest that since I allow disease, they should do nothing to fight it. That isn't so. Part of humankind's task is to improve the lives of others. The world is blessed by doctors and medical researchers who enable you to live longer and healthier.

When stricken with a disease, whether minor or significant, My will for you is to rest, pray, and see a doctor. Consulting a physician is not a sign of thin faith; it is a sign that you're using the wisdom I've given you.

Jesus came from Galilee to John at the Jordan to be baptized by him. And John tried to prevent Him, saying, "I need to be baptized by You, and are You coming to me?" But Jesus answered and said to him, "Permit it to be so now, for thus it is fitting for us to fulfill all righteousness." Then he allowed Him. When He had been baptized, Jesus came up immediately from the water; and behold, the heavens were opened to Him, and He saw the Spirit of God descending like a dove and alighting upon Him. And suddenly a voice came from heaven, saying, "This is My beloved Son, in whom I am well pleased."

Matthew 3:13–17 NKJV

Jesus

Jesus is the most important person who ever lived and is the center of Christian faith. People have many questions about Jesus' life and work.

21
Jesus, how did You live knowing how You would die?

There are no words sufficient to describe how horrible Christ's crucifixion must have been, yet plenty of people attempt to do so. No other event in history has received more attention than what happened to Jesus just outside Jerusalem two thousand years ago. Crucifixion was, by design of evil men, the worst form of execution used. Dr. Joseph Guillotine invented the machine bearing his name to keep prisoners from suffering a lingering execution. Crucifixion had the opposite goal, and some crucifixions lasted days.

Despite its ugliness, crucifixion still captures the attention of those brave enough to face it. The word excruciating *comes from the same root word as* crucifixion. *Jesus' life can be viewed as a step-by-step march to the cross. A coin has two sides, one inseparable from the other. So it must have been with Jesus' death and resurrection.*

 Jesus, the Bible indicates that You knew the cross was waiting for You. How could You carry on with all You did knowing what lay ahead for You?

JESUS

Your question is easier to ask than it is to answer, and it gives Me an opportunity to clear up some misconceptions. My death was described in the Old Testament centuries before it occurred.[1] The New Testament is filled with reminders of the importance of My death on the cross.

My arrest, trial, torture, and crucifixion did not come as a surprise. I knew what would happen to Me. It was part of the plan from the beginning. I was not surprised. In fact, I taught from the start that My execution would come.

On My way to Jerusalem, I took My twelve disciples with Me. I wanted them to know what was about to happen, so I said, "We are going up to

Jerusalem, and the Son of Man will be betrayed to the chief priests and the teachers of the law. They will condemn him to death and will turn him over to the Gentiles to be mocked and flogged and crucified. On the third day he will be raised to life!"[2] Shortly after that, I reminded them again; this time I put a time stamp on it. "You know that after two days is the Passover, and the Son of Man will be delivered up to be crucified."[3]

Many people think that I arrived in Jerusalem during the third year of My ministry and was taken by surprise. Those who arrested Me certainly thought they had caught Me off guard, but I was waiting for them. The religious leaders were so concerned that they brought a mob of servants, the temple guard, and even a Roman cohort[4] (a cohort was six hundred Roman soldiers). Large crowds followed Me wherever I went. They were expecting stiff resistance. Instead, they found Me and three disciples and nothing more.

I wasn't caught off guard, but that didn't make it any easier. Crucifixion was horrible, but My suffering began before the cross. The religious leaders orchestrated the arrest and the trials, but the Romans tortured Me.

They tied Me to a post with my arms over My head and whipped Me with a multistrand whip. The leather strips of the whip held small weights that tore at My flesh.[5] Many people died who were subjected to this form of punishment. I knew beforehand that I would be whipped in this way as part of God's plan for Me.

Another misconception is that because of who I am, My death was different, less painful. Such was not the case. The word most often associated with My crucifixion and the torture that preceded it is *suffering*. My body was like any other man's, and I felt physical pain just as you would.

But there was much more than just physical pain. Peter wrote, "He himself bore our sins in his body on the cross, so that, free from sins, we might live for righteousness; by his wounds you have been healed. For you were going astray like sheep, but now you have returned to the shepherd and guardian of your souls."[6]

He wrote those words a long time ago, but they are as true now as then. I suffered unimaginable pain, but not just from the nails in My hands, the crown of thorns, the spike in My feet, or the shredded skin on My back. The beating I took contributed to the shock and injury, but the real pain came from taking on humanity's sins.

PETER

This began before His arrest. The Lord led us from Jerusalem, through one of the gates in the walls, and across the Kidron Valley to a garden on the Mount of Olives, a place called Gethsemane. Once there, He left eight of the disciples at the low stone wall that surrounded the Garden and took three of us into a grove of olive trees. I was there, along with James and John. The day had been busy. It was Passover, and just walking through the streets was taxing, and so we were sleepy.

Jesus asked us to watch over Him as He prayed, which is something He did several times. He moved a short distance away and began to pray. I had heard Him praying many times, but this was different. I watched Him walk away. His steps were unsteady. He fell, and then He prayed, "Abba, Father . . . everything is possible for you. Take this cup from me. Yet not what I will, but what you will."[7]

I can still hear His words in my ears. His agony was great; His sorrow was so deep that His sweat turned bloody. You know what He did after that, because the whole world knows the story. After repeating the prayer three times, He stood and waited for the mob of angry men led by Judas to arrest Him.[8]

GOD

That suffering was for a reason, one that goes beyond human understanding. Jesus, My Son, was a sacrifice for the world. He gave Himself for you, and it was not easy for Him to do.

He did this because His love for you is that great. As He said, "the greatest way to show love for friends is to die for them."[9] Read the Gospels, and you'll see that Jesus is full of emotion. Matthew recorded one of several times that the plight of people moved Jesus emotionally: "When he saw the crowds, he felt sorry for them. They were confused and helpless, like sheep without a shepherd."[10]

Jesus kept going every day, knowing the emotional, spiritual, and physical pain that waited for Him because of His compassion and love for you and the world. His love for you is the same as My love for you.[11] I showed My love in sending My perfect Son to die for imperfect people so that our relationship could be restored.

117

At just the right time, when you were still powerless, Christ died for the ungodly. Very rarely will anyone die for a righteous man, though for a good man someone might possibly dare to die. But He demonstrated His own love for you in this: While you were still a sinner, Christ died for you.[12]

Jesus

I was driven by the fact that My sacrifice would bring a new relationship between you and God. I was willing to die to open the door to eternity for you and all who believe. Under the Old Testament laws, animal sacrifices were used to atone for sin, but no animal sacrifice could do the job. That was the point of the sacrificial system: to prove that nothing you did could earn your salvation, but that My sacrifice made it possible.[13]

Peter

I taught that truth throughout my ministry. I wrote, "Christ suffered for our sins once for all time. He never sinned, but he died for sinners to bring you safely home to God. He suffered physical death, but he was raised to life in the Spirit."[14]

I did many things wrong in my life. I denied Jesus publicy. When things got tough, I ran. I often spoke without thinking or without knowing what I was speaking about. Yet I always knew that Jesus loved me. Every day, I thought about the cross. Every day.

Jesus pressed on to the cross for me. That understanding changed me forever. Like the other disciples, my life was hard. I, too, was crucified, but at my request, I asked to be crucified upside down. I never felt I was worth dying the way my Savior did. As bad as crucifixion was, it wasn't close to the burden of our sin Jesus carried to His cross.

Jesus

Peter was worth it. So are you.

22

Jesus, where did Your soul go after You died?

The Bible speaks of worlds beyond our own, places like heaven and hell, places humans cannot see. It has been said that death is not the end of existence, that the spirit lives on even though the body lies buried in the ground. But information about these mysterious places is scarce, and what there is sometimes seems contradictory.

Jesus died a physical death. There was nothing metaphorical about it. He shed real blood, felt excruciating pain, announced, "It is finished!" and then died a real death. But what happened during those days His lifeless body was entombed?

Q **Jesus, we're told that after we die, our souls go somewhere. After You died on the cross, where did Your soul go?**

JESUS

Your question has elements that theologians have debated for centuries, but the Bible contains the information you need to understand the answer. The best way to deal with your question is to look at a few specific passages.

Let Me set the groundwork. We will discuss the soul later, so for now just know that every human has an immaterial part called the soul. To be more accurate, every human *is* a soul. At death, the soul and the body are separated. It's an unnatural separation, and it's the reason most people fear death. The soul was never meant to be parted from the body, but sin brought death,[1] and now this separation is the norm for all humans.

LAZARUS OF BETHANY

I died twice. I was an avid supporter of the Savior during my earthly life, as were my sisters, Mary and Martha. Jesus often stayed with us in our house in Bethany. Bethany was near Jerusalem, so Jesus stayed with us whenever He visited the great city.

One day while He was in another part of the country, I fell ill and died. He arrived in Bethany four days after my death. I was already buried in the family tomb. Jesus brought me back to life.[2] I am one of the few who died and lived to tell about it.

When I died, my soul went to sheol, the place of the dead.

GOD

Sheol is a Hebrew word. It can refer to the grave or the place of departed souls. Prior to My Son's resurrection, all souls went to sheol. In the New Testament, the equivalent Greek term is *hades*. Hades and hell are not the same place. Hell is the place of future punishment, and the Bible always speaks of it in the future tense. That is not an accident. Sheol/hades is a present-tense place, as is heaven.

JESUS

To help My followers understand this, I told them about another man, whose name was also Lazarus.[3] The Lazarus I raised from the dead shares the same name, but his earthly circumstances were different. For example, Lazarus of Bethany was rich; the Lazarus of My account was poor and sickly.

Some call this account a parable, but that isn't quite right. I used parables as a teaching tool to help people understand complicated concepts. They were short stories about earthly events that revealed heavenly truth. In none of My parables did I use a proper name like Lazarus. What I shared that day was an account of a real event.

In summary, a man named Lazarus had suffered his entire life, and his body was covered in sores. Lazarus supported himself by begging. He often asked for help from a rich man, who denied him every time. The rich man had everything a person of that time could desire, but he was unwilling to share with anyone, especially Lazarus. Both men died and both went to sheol.

I called sheol "Abraham's bosom" in the account. It was a common euphemism of the day. You can think of sheol as having two countries, one for the good and one for the unrepentant. Lazarus found himself free of disease and in great comfort, something he never knew in life; the rich man, however, was in agony.

The rich man begged for relief, and he went so far as to beg that Lazarus be sent to him with water. Even in death, the man saw Lazarus as someone beneath him. Abraham told him no, that a great chasm separated the two places.

Lazarus of Bethany

When I died, my soul went to the glorious part of sheol. It was quite a shock to be brought back to life. It changed my view of death, and I never feared it again.

Jesus

When I died on the cross, I went to sheol, to hades. Here's how Peter put it: "They will have to give account to him who is ready to judge the living and the dead. For this is the reason the gospel was preached even to those who are now dead, so that they might be judged according to men in regard to the body, but live according to God in regard to the spirit."[4]

Paul said it this way: "When it says, 'he went up,' it means that Christ had been deep in the earth. This also means that the one who went deep into the earth is the same one who went into the highest heaven, so that he would fill the whole universe."[5]

By "deep in the earth," Paul meant the grave and sheol. If you study the New Testament, you will notice that no detail is given about this, just the fact that it occurred. The reason is that it doesn't pertain to you or anyone else who died or will die after My resurrection.

God

Jesus' death and resurrection changed everything, including what happens to you after death. Before, both the righteous and the unrighteous went to sheol: the faithful went to the pleasant, comforting side; the unfaithful went to the side experienced by the rich man. After the resurrection, Jesus led the righteous people in sheol to heaven. That side is now empty. Those on the "rich man" side await a future judgment.

Today, when a believer dies, his or her soul is immediately with Me in heaven. To be absent in the body is to be present with Me.[6]

Jesus

For believers, sheol is closed. My death made it possible for all the faithful to experience eternal life from the moment of salvation on. Not even death can stop that. I descended to sheol to preach to the faithful there what God had done and what My sacrifice achieved, and also to take them from a great place to a better place. In the group were the saints of old.

The faithful of the Old Testament days looked forward to My coming; today's believers look back upon My work. My sacrificial work was for believers of all ages. I did not come just for those lucky enough to be born after Me or for those yet to come. I died for all people of all eras, including those who died centuries before I began my ministry.

God

Salvation is timeless because I am timeless. From the very beginning, My desire has been to see all people come to salvation, to have eternal life. I want all men to be saved and to come to a knowledge of the truth.[7]

My reward is for believers of all ages.

23
Just what is salvation?

> *Words are powerful things, but only if you know what they mean. A man sat in a coffee shop listening to a group of men speak. He recognized the language as German, but, not knowing German, he had no idea what they were saying. Even in languages we do know, common words can take on a new meaning. An aerospace engineer using the word* lift *means something entirely different from what an English man means when talking about an elevator.*
>
> *This is also true for other idiom-specific terms. Some terms in the Bible and in the church are confusing to those not familiar with them.* Saved *and* salvation *are two such terms. Sometimes it seems that different people mean different things when using those terms.*

 Jesus, I hear the words *salvation* **and** *saved* **used a lot. Exactly what do those words mean?**

JESUS

Salvation and *saved* are words everyone should know. Combined, the terms appear nearly one hundred times in the New Testament. Theologians and experts in the Bible have written countless pages examining every nuance of the words. There is nothing wrong with that, but the concept is so simple that children understand it.

Both words mean "to rescue," which creates the image of someone in great danger, say, from drowning, and someone coming along and snatching him from the danger.

I appropriated that word and gave it a broader meaning. Still, the original image remains. People are in spiritual danger, drowning in their own imperfection and sin. They need rescuing, and My work and death on the cross is what rescues them.

GOD

The first thing you need to understand is that you are a sinner. The word *sin*, like *saved* and *salvation*, is used so often that it has lost some of its meaning and impact. The word means "to miss the mark." Just as an archer with poor aim misses his target, so every human misses the mark of righteousness. Those who are honest with themselves and especially with Me are never surprised by the accusation of sin.

PAUL

I suffered for the faith. Five times I received from the Jews the forty lashes minus one. Three times I was beaten with rods, once I was stoned, three times I was shipwrecked, once I spent a night and a day in the open sea. I was constantly on the move. I was in danger from rivers, bandits, my own countrymen, and Gentiles; I was in danger in the city, in the country, and at sea, as well as from false brothers. I labored and toiled and often went without sleep; I knew hunger and thirst and often went without food; I was cold and naked. Besides everything else, I faced daily the pressure of my concern for all the churches.[1]

But those sacrifices did not absolve me of my sin. Many look up to me based on my work, but I was no different from anyone else. I gave my life, my wealth, and my health to help others know the truth about themselves and about Jesus. None of that removed my sin.

I know a great deal about sin. Although I preached thousands of messages, established scores of churches around the known world, and suffered persecution, beatings, prison, and other hardships that left me a scarred man, I was still one of the worst sinners to walk the planet. I wrote this to Timothy: "This is a faithful saying and worthy of all acceptance, that Christ Jesus came into the world to save sinners, of whom I am chief."[2]

Many people think only thieves, liars, and criminals should be called sinners. But all people are sinners, and I made sure everyone knew that I numbered myself among them. King Solomon made it clear: "Indeed, there is not a righteous man on earth who continually does and who never sins."[3] No one other than Jesus can claim to be sinless. I told the Galatians, "The Scriptures declare that we are all prisoners of sin, so we receive God's promise of freedom only by believing in Jesus Christ."[4] John said, "If we say that we have not sinned, we are fooling ourselves, and the truth isn't in our hearts."[5]

But your question is about salvation. In the next verse, John wrote, "If we confess our sins, he who is faithful and just will forgive us our sins and cleanse us from all unrighteousness."[6] That is salvation.

GOD

To understand salvation, you must first understand your need for it. Sin, no matter how small or seemingly insignificant, has driven a wedge between us. I am a just God. Justice is as much a part of My makeup as love is. Sin has created a problem. You cannot rid yourself of sin; it has to be done for you. If sin isn't dealt with, then all is eternally lost. Jesus' work and sacrifice make it possible for that sin to be removed.

The word *justified* is the term used to describe the removal of sin and, therefore, the removal of the barricade between us. Some choose to remember the meaning of the word by pronouncing it *"just-as-if-I'd-never-sinned."* Listen carefully to this: When you confess your sins, when you choose Jesus as your Savior, your sins are forgiven and forgotten. You appear to Me as sinless as Jesus. Don't misunderstand. I didn't say you *are* as sinless as My Son, but His sacrifice makes it as if you are.

I can also forget your sins. Not only do I blot out your transgressions, but I also choose never to bring them to mind again.[7]

JESUS

To be saved means you were drowning in your own sin but that your sin has been forgiven and will not be brought up again. Salvation brings freedom from sin. You will not be perfect in this life, but you will be forgiven and empowered to resist temptation and to avoid sin.

Salvation brings you into a good and proper relationship with God the Father. While the original word that is translated *saved* and *salvation* means to be rescued *from* danger, it also means to be saved *to* something—to eternal life. I taught that I came to earth so people could have abundant lives.[8]

When someone is saved, his or her sins are forgiven, but much more than that happens. From the moment of salvation on, the person is changed. Of course there are still struggles and difficulties, but the process continues.

Salvation continues through a person's life. It has a past, a present, and a future aspect. You can say, "I have been saved." As Paul told the Ephesians,

"It is by grace you have been saved."[9] Believers might have been children or adults when they made their decisions. The Father honors those decisions, sins are forgiven, and new believers are granted eternal life. That's salvation in the past tense.

You can also say you are being saved—present tense. Paul used the present tense when he wrote, "The message of the cross is foolishness to those who are perishing, but to us who are being saved it is the power of God."[10] Your salvation begins at a moment in time, and it continues throughout your life.

It is also proper to speak about being saved in the future. This is the culmination of salvation. Unless you are alive at My second coming, you enter heaven through death. There, you experience the full measure of salvation.

God

You can't earn salvation. No amount of good works you do can earn salvation. Remember, *to save* means to rescue someone in deadly peril. If people could solve their problems on their own, they wouldn't need rescuing. The salvation I offer comes by grace. Grace is receiving a benefit you couldn't earn. It is a gift.

Paul said it to the Ephesians this way: "By grace you have been saved through faith, and that not of yourselves; it is the gift of God, not of works, lest anyone should boast. For we are His workmanship, created in Christ Jesus for good works, which God prepared beforehand that we should walk in them."[11]

24
How do we know if we are saved?

> Hope *is an interesting word. In English, the word most often means a wish or a desire, something longed for. A sports fan hopes the local team goes to the play-offs, but there may be reasons to doubt they will. In the Bible, though, the word* hope *seems to have a different meaning —more expectant than wishful. It's more like hope without doubt.*
>
> *Doubt, however, is a human emotion, especially when it applies to things not yet experienced. Lots of people talk about heaven, but no one has seen it. How can anyone be confident about salvation if there's no objective certainty of it?*

 How do I know if I'm going to heaven, born again, saved, whatever you call it?

Jesus

It isn't uncommon to harbor doubts occasionally. Even preachers have moments of uncertainty. This is where faith is important. Faith isn't wishful thinking. It isn't a leap in the dark. It isn't belief without facts. Faith is based on what has been revealed to you and what you have experienced.

Consider what Peter wrote about faith: "Though you have not seen him, you love him; and even though you do not see him now, you believe in him and are filled with an inexpressible and glorious joy, for you are receiving the goal of your faith, the salvation of your souls."[1]

Many people believe in Me, trust in Me, and love Me even though they've never seen Me in the flesh. They are aware of Me in a way physical senses cannot match. They have felt the joy and the assurance of their salvation. Millions follow Me even though two thousand years have passed since My time on earth. The same can be said about the assurance of your salvation and the promise of heaven.

God

Some people long for a vital spiritual relationship but fear that they've missed something. They worry that maybe they've done something wrong and will somehow miss the life to come. In their minds, they picture Me saying, "Sorry, but you just don't measure up."

Actually, no one measures up, because salvation can't be earned. Salvation exists because I love you. Heaven exists because I long to spend eternity with you. It is My desire for you to be part of My family.

Moments of doubt are common, but you can be assured of your salvation. Paul suffered for his faith, and you might expect that there would be times when he wondered if he was being punished, if he had somehow fallen out of fellowship with Me. He told his protégé Timothy, "I know whom I have believed and am persuaded that He is able to keep what I have committed to Him until that Day."[2]

Paul knew he had placed his faith in Me, and he knew that I'd be with him through every day and on through eternity. Paul had his moments, but he always came back to the belief that I would keep My promises about his salvation.

JESUS

If your salvation were tied to your goodness, your ability to avoid sin, or your good works, then you would have every reason to be concerned. However, your salvation does not rest in what you do, but in what I've done. The gift of God is eternal life in Me.[3]

PAUL

Still, it's not uncommon to want proof. Let me ask a few questions that will help you understand your standing in faith.

Do you recall asking Christ to be your Lord and Savior? My salvation experience came on the road to Damascus. I was going there to persecute the church. The Savior stopped me in my tracks. I ended up on the ground hearing Him ask why I was persecuting Him.[4] The story of your conversion experience may be far more subtle but it will still be something you remember. If you called upon the Lord, you were heard.

I wrote this assurance to the church at Rome: "If you confess with your mouth that Jesus is Lord and believe in your heart that God raised him from the dead, you will be saved. For it is by believing in your heart that you are made right with God, and it is by confessing with your mouth that you are saved. As the Scriptures tell us, 'Anyone who trusts in him will never be disgraced.'"[5]

Confess means "to agree." When you confess that Jesus is Lord, you are saying that you agree with God that He is the rightful Lord of your life. If you place your belief and trust in God through Jesus Christ, you will not be turned away.

Are you any different since that decision? Here's why I ask. When you became a follower of Jesus, the Holy Spirit began to work in your life, changing you from the way you were to someone new. You are a new creature; the old things passed away, and you became a new person.[6]

Christians are not perfect. Only Jesus can claim to have lived a perfect life.[7] People still have to battle sinful natures. Believers, however, have the help of the Holy Spirit, who guides us. Becoming a believer makes you want to live the best you can for Jesus.

The Holy Spirit works in all believers, alerting them to sins they might be tempted to commit, or convicting them of sins already committed.[8] He does this so the matter can be dealt with. Conviction is evidence of your salvation.

The Holy Spirit does something else for those who have been saved: He gives them spiritual understanding and a desire to know more about spiritual matters. In a letter to the Corinthians, I wrote, "Only someone who has God's Spirit can understand spiritual blessings. Anyone who doesn't have God's Spirit thinks these blessings are foolish. People who are guided by the Spirit can make all kinds of judgments, but they cannot be judged by others."[9]

God

How do you know if you've been saved and will go to heaven? You've made a decision to believe, to trust, and to accept Christ. You don't know everything, and you won't in your current life, but you know enough. Your salvation has changed you. It hasn't made you perfect, but the fact that you're worried about this is evidence of your salvation.

You've placed your trust in Me through Jesus. Continue trusting Us.

25
Jesus, what is Your role in salvation?

> *By definition, a paradox is a statement or proposition that is self-contradictory. In some ways, salvation would seem to be a paradox. It is simple: humans needed a Savior, so Jesus came and then died. But as simple as that is, it raises a complicated question: What did Jesus do on the cross that made the difference? Was it His willingness to die? Was it His actual death?*
>
> *An anonymous writer said, "Salvation is so simple we can overlook it, so profound we can never comprehend it." But that doesn't make anything clear.*

Q
Now that I know what salvation is, Jesus, what is Your role in my salvation? What is my role?

JESUS

Salvation is what you need; salvation is what I have provided. In that sense it is as simple a concept as you can imagine, but your question shows that you suspect there is more to it than that. And you're right. Everything that seems simple at first glance has layers of complexity beneath the surface. But just because you may not understand how atoms and subatomic particles work in salt doesn't prevent you from putting some on your food.

My role in salvation was to bridge the gap between you and My Father. This I did by living a perfect life, teaching people what they needed to know about God and their relationship to Him, and becoming a sacrifice for sin.

Jews used to practice animal sacrifice. They did so because My Father told them to. Those animal sacrifices pointed out the need for a onetime, once-and-for-all sacrifice.

GOD

Those sacrifices were meant to be acts of faith by the people and to foreshadow the sacrifice Jesus would make. They were symbolic. On several occasions I spoke through the prophets, saying, "The multitude of your sacrifices—what are they to me? . . . I have more than enough of burnt offerings, of rams and the fat of fattened animals; I have no pleasure in the blood of bulls and lambs and goats."[1]

Those sacrifices were annual reminders of sin and nothing more. It isn't possible for the blood of bulls and goats to take away sins.[2] Under the old sacrificial system, priests would make animal sacrifices—blood sacrifices—for their sins and the sins of the people. This they did every year on the Day of Atonement. An animal sacrifice reminded the people that a better sacrifice was needed to wash away sin.

JESUS

I have many titles, including King, Prophet, Messiah, and High Priest. The high priest used to enter a special room in the temple to make a sin sacrifice for the people. I am the High Priest who made the ultimate and eternal sacrifice for the sins of the world. When I arrived on the shores of the Jordan River to be baptized by John the Baptist, he saw Me and announced to the people, "Behold, the Lamb of God who takes away the sin of the world!"[3] He knew before anyone else that I was to be the sacrificial Lamb.

The best way to answer your question is to talk first about a few terms. More important than the terms are the meanings behind them. Knowing these terms will help you understand My role in salvation.

Atonement is one of those words that can be changed to provide a memory clue to its meaning. *Atonement* means "at-one-ment." Prior to My sacrifice, there existed a hostility between humans and My Father. Paul said it this way: "Christ has made peace between Jews and Gentiles, and he has united us by breaking down the wall of hatred that separated us. Christ gave his own body to destroy the Law of Moses with all its rules and commands. He even brought Jews and Gentiles together as though we were only one person, when he united us in peace."[4]

Atonement means I took your sin upon Myself and paid the price for it on the cross. That removed the barrier between you and God, freed My people from all the rules and regulations they couldn't possibly keep, and reconciled you to God.

Reconcile is another word that helps explain all that happened through My death and resurrection. It means "to settle or resolve." *Reconciliation* is a term often used in a legal sense to describe the reuniting of a husband and a wife after a divorce. It means to heal the rift between antagonistic partners. One of My roles in salvation was to heal the rift caused by sin.[5]

Sanctification is another important term. Back in the days of the temple, certain items were set apart for worship and could be used only in the temple. Those items, which could not be loaned to others to be used for common practices, were sanctified—set apart for God's use and God's use only. The word also applies to people. In the context of salvation, sanctification is the act in which you are set apart for God. The word *holy* means the same thing.

My role in salvation has made you a chosen people.[6] Salvation is more than just having your sins forgiven. It is the restoration of a relationship with God that makes you more than you have ever been.

Redemption is a familiar term. It comes from the verb *to redeem*. Today people redeem everything from bottles to bonds, but in the biblical context of salvation, redemption has a more significant meaning. It means "to buy back." It paints the picture of someone freeing a slave by paying the price on his head. Peter taught the concept with these words: "You were rescued from the useless way of life that you learned from your ancestors. But you know that you were not rescued by such things as silver or gold that don't last forever. You were rescued by the precious blood of Christ, that spotless and innocent lamb."[7]

A man could be bought from the slave market with money and then set free. Your spiritual freedom came at the expense of My life so you could be free forever. This is why one of My titles is Redeemer.

ABRAHAM

These terms and many others describe what Jesus achieved on the cross. He is all those things and so much more. In my day, I looked forward to the One who would be the sacrifice for all of us. Jesus would do His work eighteen hundred years later, but I lived through an event that made His sacrifice clear. God ordered me to sacrifice my only son.[8]

It was horrible. My son Isaac was a young man at the time. He never questioned me, not even when we traveled to Mount Moriah, not even when he carried the wood that was to be used for the fire to burn his body, not even when I made him lay himself on the altar, not even when I put a knife to his neck. I believed that God would raise him from the dead.[9]

I did not have to complete the task because, thankfully, God stopped my hand before I could harm my son. But He did not stop Himself when His own Son went to His death. When you ask what role Jesus played in salvation, you must also ask what role God the Father played. They sacrificed everything for me and everything for you.

Salvation came at the highest price.

GOD

Your role in salvation is only to believe. The word *believe* carries more than the idea of agreeing that something is true. It also means to act on what you know to be true.

In the earliest days of the church, just as the persecutions were beginning, Peter and Silas were arrested and thrown into jail. An earthquake sprang the prison doors, and all the prisoners escaped—all, that is, except Paul and Silas, who chose to stay behind. Knowing that the guards faced death if the prisoners under their watch escaped, they shouted, "Don't harm yourself!" The guard went to them and asked, "Sirs, what must I do to be saved?"

Their reply makes your role in salvation clear: "Believe in the Lord Jesus, and you will be saved."[10] Your part is belief—knowing the truth, accepting the truth, and committing to the truth. That truth will change you forever. There is nothing more you need to add; nothing more you can add.

26
Can we go to heaven without forgiveness?

Although it is unlikely you'll encounter someone who says, "I have never sinned," it is common to meet those who dismiss the whole idea of sin out of hand. It's a human trait to turn attention away from the things that are uncomfortable. People avoid thinking about death, aging, or illnesses. The old myth that an ostrich hides it head in the sand has long been disproved when it comes to ostriches, but it is still, at least mentally, practiced by humans. Like children who hide under the covers at hearing a strange sound in the night, many people would prefer to pull a blanket over the mind to avoid facing this uncomfortable topic.

If there were no solution to the problem, then pretending it doesn't exist might make sense. But there must be a solution. Could it be true that death is the only solution?[1]

Q **Jesus, everyone I know has done things they're ashamed of. All of us have done some pretty ugly things in life, but why is it important for You to forgive our sins in order for us to get into heaven? Why is forgiveness so important?**

JESUS

Sin is real, and like it or not, it affects everyone, every class, every economic status. Isaiah said, "All we like sheep have gone astray; we have turned, every one, to his own way."[2] That means everyone.

Some people dismiss sin so readily because acknowledging its existence would be acknowledging personal guilt, and no one likes to do that. This denial has gone on so long that the concept is foreign to many twenty-first-century people. Yet it is there. We see the effects everywhere.

Earlier we said sin could be described as missing the mark, like an archer missing a target. That's a good illustration, but there's more to it than that.

Sin, at its most basic, is rebellion. It is doing what you know to be wrong.

It is violating the commands of God. That was the first sin. God told Adam and Eve not to eat of the Tree of Knowledge of Good and Evil. They did it anyway. They rationalized away the command so they could do what they knew was wrong.[3]

GOD

My approach has always been mercy before judgment. Adam and Eve made a decision that had an impact on everyone, including you.

My moral code exists for a reason. It isn't there for My benefit but for yours. Good parents warn their children about the dangers in life. They would be poor parents if they didn't attempt to guide the child away from the things that would harm and toward the things that would benefit him or her.

Almost every parent knows, however, that as a child grows he or she will rebel. That's what humanity has been doing from the beginning. Like a child who wants to pull free of a mother's hand and rush into a busy street, people sometimes fail to see the outcome of sinful decisions. I see every outcome.

I made you with free will. There was a danger in that, but a people who could not make decisions of their own would be lesser beings. I love you because I chose to love you. I want to be loved the same way—by choice. By giving you choice, I empowered you to great things and made you far more intelligent than any other creature. The downside was that some would choose to love themselves more than they love Me.

Righteousness was part of your original makeup. You know what is right and what is wrong. No one has to teach you that killing your children is wrong, and yet some cultures in history became so calloused, they made human sacrifices of their children. The Nazca, the Maya, the Aztec, and the followers of Moloch and Baal were guilty of this horrible sin. Sin, left unchecked, can lead an entire people group astray.

JESUS

Sin is putting yourself above God. That is the essence of sin. There are sins of omission as well as sins of commission. A sin of commission is choosing to do what you know is wrong. A sin of omission is failure to do what you know is right. Sin, which covers a multitude of behaviors, has changed history and continues to change the future.

Moses

On Mount Sinai, God gave me the Ten Commandments to govern the behavior of the people He had just released from captivity. They had been in Egypt for three centuries, and He wanted them to know that He expected a higher level of behavior from them. Those commandments comprise God's moral law. Let me summarize them:[4]

1. "I am the Lord your God, who brought you out of the land of Egypt, out of the house of bondage. You shall have no other gods before Me." There is one and only one God. The Egyptians worshipped many gods and idols. God wanted His people to remain loyal.

2. "You shall not make for yourself a carved image." This goes along with the first commandment. The people I led out of Egypt had seen many handmade idols. They were not to follow that example. God alone was to be worshipped. Anything else was sin.

3. "You shall not take the name of the Lord your God in vain." God has many names in the Old Testament, including Elohim and Jehovah. Each name describes one of His unique attributes. His name was and is to be kept holy.

4. "Remember the Sabbath day, to keep it holy." As slaves, the Exodus people worked seven days a week. Now they were to set aside one day for rest and worship, just as God rested on the seventh day of creation.

The first four commandments taught us to value, love, and worship God. The next set shows God's rules for how we deal with those around us:

5. "Honor your father and your mother." The family relationship reflects our relationship to God. Children are to honor their parents, just as we all are to honor God.

6. "You shall not murder." Life is precious, and it is not to be taken in the heat of anger or out of revenge. This one struck me hard. Many years before, I killed an Egyptian, forcing me to flee my home in the pharaoh's palace.[5] God brought good out of it, but it is still something for which I've had to give an account.

7. "You shall not commit adultery." Sexual sin has always been

prevalent, and it always brings trouble. Sex is a powerful human drive and one that is meant to bring pleasure as well as reproduction, but human nature can and has corrupted it. This has been and is true in every generation and every people group.

8. "You shall not steal." Theft has always been a crime and a sin. When one steals, he deprives someone else of his rightful property. When neighbor steals from neighbor, problems arise.

9. "You shall not bear false witness against your neighbor." This covers the sins against honesty. God wants us to be honest in all our dealings. It was not uncommon in my day—and every generation since—to gain an advantage over a neighbor by lying or gossiping about them. God demands honesty at all times.

10. "You shall not covet your neighbor's house; you shall not covet your neighbor's wife, nor his male servant, nor his female servant, nor his ox, nor his donkey, nor anything that is your neighbor's." Coveting is more than envy, it's a consuming desire to have what your neighbor has—not just to have something similar to what your neighbor has, but overwhelming desire to take from them and give to yourself. It isn't just wanting more for yourself; it's also wanting less for your neighbor.

The Ten Commandments are a summary of God's moral law, and that has not changed. These commandments aren't just for Jews; they are for everyone.

JESUS

I added an eleventh commandment: "I give you a new commandment, that you love one another. Just as I have loved you, you also should love one another."[6] The greatest antidote to sin is love. There are those who avoid sin because they fear a lightning bolt will streak out of heaven and strike them dead. But those who love God and others avoid sin because to do so pleases God and makes the world a better place.

GOD

There are two foremost reasons why sin matters. First, sin hurts you. My overriding concern is your spiritual life and eternity, but I'm also concerned about how sin will damage you. Adulterers may start seeking sexual adventure, but they end up by hurting their spouses, their children, other people's families, and their own souls. The sin of anger—that is, cultivated anger—burns a hole inside a person. Failure to forgive leads to being deprived of forgiveness. In fact, I require that people forgive one another. My Son was clear about this: "If you forgive those who sin against you, your heavenly Father will forgive you."[7]

As a just God, I will judge sin; as a loving God, I have made provisions for forgiveness. I led Paul to say it this way: "This righteousness from God comes through faith in Jesus Christ to all who believe. There is no difference, for all have sinned and fall short of the glory of God, and are justified freely by his grace through the redemption that came by Christ Jesus. God presented him as a sacrifice of atonement, through faith in his blood. He did this to demonstrate his justice, because in his forbearance he had left the sins committed beforehand unpunished—he did it to demonstrate his justice at the present time, so as to be just and the one who justifies those who have faith in Jesus."[8]

You see above some of the terms we used in our last few conversations: *justified, faith, grace, redemption*, and *atonement*. Everything is tied up in Jesus' sacrifice. He is the reason why your sins can be forgiven; He is the reason why you have hope for the future.

Every human sins. Even great biblical heroes went astray. I was there to forgive them. I am here to forgive you.

27
Jesus, were You really raised from the dead?

> *If there is no resurrection, then there is no Christianity. There might be a shadow of the church, but faith as it is known would cease to exist. Jesus hung His credibility on the fact that He would be arrested, tortured, killed, and buried. Then, on the third day, He would rise from the grave. It is a ridiculous claim, but nonetheless, millions of people say it is true. If Jesus did not rise from the grave, then He would be little more than a good teacher—a self-deluded but good teacher.*
>
> *If Jesus didn't rise from the dead, there would be little left for Christians to believe, and the many martyrs who gave their lives would have given them for nothing. It's important to know the truth, whether Jesus really did emerge live from His tomb.*

 Jesus, the resurrection seems too much to believe. Were You really dead? Were You really brought back to life?

JESUS

Yes and yes. Your faith depends on that truth. A seminary professor stood before a class of soon-to-be ministers and challenged them about the resurrection, saying, "You don't believe in a resuscitated corpse, do you?" Not one student had the courage to say yes. Yet all Christianity rests on the fact that I rose from the dead—as promised.

GOD

The resurrection was part of My plan from the beginning. No one should ever diminish the sacrifice My Son made by going to the cross and bearing the sin of the world, but that act would have been incomplete without the resurrection. The cross and the resurrection are two sides of the same coin. Each finds its eternal meaning in the other.

Jesus' resurrection is the first of many resurrections to come. Believers will also be resurrected. Paul wrote, "We must each wait our turn. Christ was the first to be raised to life, and his people will be raised to life when he returns."[1]

Jesus is the firstfruit of future resurrections. Do you question that? Do you wonder about other people who have been brought back from the dead? People like the widow's son whom Elijah prayed over and brought back to life,[2] or Lazarus of Bethany,[3] or Eutychus, whom Paul raised?[4] In all those cases, the one raised died again. It is best to think of those as resuscitations rather than resurrections. Those men were dead in the most literal sense, and, although brought back to life, they didn't experience what Jesus did, or what believers will experience in the future.

Jesus is the first to rise from the grave who will never die again. His resurrection is, in many ways, a promise to all believers that wait for the day of His return.

JESUS

It has been popular over the years to explain away My resurrection. Some say I never died; some say I just passed out on the cross and was later revived by the coolness of the tomb.

CENTURION[5]

I was in charge of the crucifixion. I can tell you that Jesus of Nazareth was dead. As a Roman soldier and the leader of one hundred men, it was my responsibility to help carry out the orders of Pontius Pilate, the Roman procurator over the country that many today call the Holy Land. Pain and death were my specialty. I oversaw the crucifixion of many men.

Jesus wasn't the only man ever crucified. We nailed hundreds of men to crosses. If you've read the biblical account, you know Jesus was crucified between two thieves. Jesus, however, was different. I could sense it.

I watched as He was whipped and as He was forced to carry the crossbeam of His own cross. I gave the orders to impale Him with nails and tie His wrists to the crossbeam. I know what death looks like. It was my business, and I tell you Jesus was dead when we took Him down from the cross and released His body to Joseph of Arimathea and Nicodemus.[6]

I put a living man on the cross and took down a corpse. It was my job to make sure the criminals being crucified were truly dead. If I failed, it was my career on the line—it was my life on the line. Trust me, it was not something I would or could make a mistake about.

Jesus

Joseph of Arimathea and Nicodemus prepared My body for burial. That meant washing it and wrapping strips of linen from My feet to under my arms like a mummy. They used seventy-five pounds of spices and other materials to prepare My body for the tomb.[7] If I had been alive, they would have noticed. I did not pass out on the cross. I died, and everyone who saw Me that day knows it. Even if I had just swooned and everyone who saw Me was wrong, My hands and feet were tied, and I was wrapped in the linen strips. Weakened from the Roman beating, crucifixion, dehydration, the spear shoved into My side,[8] and nearly three days in a tomb without food or water, I would have been far too weak to move the large stone that closed the mouth of the tomb.[9]

Centurion

Pilate had a seal placed over the stone in front of the tomb. A cord was stretched across the large stone and its ends secured to the sides of the tomb by a wax seal that bore Pilate's personal insignia. To break that seal was to invite execution. Knowing that Jesus had said He would rise from the dead, Pilate posted guards.[10] My men would have stopped anyone from touching the tomb.

Jesus

The other theories offered to explain away My resurrection are equally ridiculous. I don't have a twin, and if I did, he could not have replaced Me. Sillier still is the suggestion that My disciples stole My body so people would think I had risen from the dead. To what end? They fled after My arrest, and only one was near the cross.[11] They hid because they feared for their lives. It was natural to assume that if the authorities crucified Me, they'd also crucify My disciples.

My disciples would later give their lives for Me, My teaching, and the church. Would such men suffer so much for a corpse in a tomb in Jerusalem?

My resurrection changed them then and has been changing lives ever since.

The resurrection was central to My disciples' preaching. In the first sermon preached after My death and resurrection, Peter said: "Listen to what I have to say about Jesus from Nazareth. God proved that he sent Jesus to you by having him work miracles, wonders, and signs. All of you know this. God had already planned and decided that Jesus would be handed over to you. So you took him and had evil men put him to death on a cross. But God set him free from death and raised him to life. Death could not hold him in its power."[12]

Peter delivered that sermon in Jerusalem to a large crowd. And in that crowd were the same people who orchestrated My illegal trials and death. He and the other disciples could not have been more exposed. He wouldn't have made such an accusatory statement to men who might take his life if he hadn't first believed what he was saying.

GOD

My Son made twelve appearances to witnesses over a six-week period. In some cases He appeared to just one person at a time; in other cases He appeared to as many as five hundred.

Paul wrote a summary: "I passed on to you what was most important and what had also been passed on to me. Christ died for our sins, just as the Scriptures said. He was buried, and he was raised from the dead on the third day, as the Scriptures said. He was seen by Peter and then by the Twelve. After that, he was seen by more than 500 of his followers at one time, most of whom are still alive, though some have died. Then he was seen by James and later by all the apostles. Last of all as though I had been born at the wrong time, I also saw him. For I am the least of all the apostles. In fact, I'm not even worthy to be called an apostle after the way I persecuted the God's church."[13]

Doubting the resurrection is not new. It began immediately after it became known.

JESUS

Even Thomas, one of my bravest disciples,[14] had trouble believing. He was not with the group when I first appeared to them. They told him what had happened, but his response showed his skepticism: "First, I must see the nail scars in his hands and touch them with my finger. I must put my hand where the spear went into his side. I won't believe unless I do this!"[15]

A week later, I appeared to them again. This time Thomas was there. I offered My hands and side for his inspection. Instead of touching Me, he fell to his knees and said, "You are my Lord and my God!"[16] He never doubted again.

GOD

Everything about the Christian faith hinges on the resurrection. Paul got to the point when he wrote: "Tell me this—since we preach that Christ rose from the dead, why are some of you saying there will be no resurrection of the dead? For if there is no resurrection of the dead, then Christ has not been raised either. And if Christ was not raised, then all our preaching is useless, and your faith is useless. And we apostles would all be lying about God—for we have said that God raised Christ from the grave, but that can't be true if there is no resurrection of the dead. If there is no resurrection of the dead, then Christ has not been raised. And if Christ has not been raised, then your faith is useless, and you are still guilty of your sins. In that case, all who have died believing in Christ have perished! And if our hope in Christ is only for this life, we are more to be pitied than anyone in the world."[17]

It is all true. Jesus rose from the dead and lives forever. Christians have a Savior who has overcome death.

28
Can I lose my salvation?

Security. Everyone appreciates a sense of security. Children often have security blankets. Adults long for that kind of security. Adults want their money, homes, families, cars, and businesses to be secure. Few things are as unsettling as insecurity. One of the government's biggest programs is Social Security. Behind it is the idea that men and women who have worked all their lives can feel financially secure after retirement.

When it comes to spiritual matters, men and women also want assurance that they haven't fallen through the cracks.

 Jesus, is there any way I can lose out on spending eternity with You? Can I lose my salvation?

JESUS

The purpose of My whole ministry and sacrifice was to draw people into a new, eternal relationship with God. That is My heart's desire. But each person must choose Me as I have chosen him or her. Early in My ministry I said, "Whoever believes in the Son has eternal life, but whoever rejects the Son will not see life, for God's wrath remains on him."[1] Every choice has a price or benefit in life, and that's especially true in the spiritual life.

Delivering eternal life is at the heart of everything I do. Anyone who hears Me and believes in the Father will have life forever and won't come into judgment.[2] The only way to lose out on spending eternity with Me is to walk away from the salvation I offer. I feel great pain over every person who does.

JUDAS

My name is one of the best known in all history, but for all the wrong reasons. Benedict Arnold's name is synonymous with *traitor* in the United States. My name is synonymous with *traitor* in almost every language in the world.

I walked away from my chance. I followed Jesus for three years. I was one of His disciples, and I even went out on missions with the others where we worked miracles.[3] I spent hundreds of days with Jesus and saw Him in every kind of context—visiting in the homes of friends, being confronted by His enemies, teaching massive crowds about the kingdom of God, taking time to talk to the individual—I saw it all. And yet I made the worst decision a man could make. I refused to listen and preferred that Jesus conform to my image of the way things should be. In hindsight, I should have conformed to His image.

I wanted a different kind of Messiah. I, like all Jews in my day, waited for the Anointed One of God. We all had high expectations. The Messiah, at least in my mind, was to come and release us from our bondage to Rome. My country was an occupied one. A hostile force had taken over, and many of our leaders rolled over for them. No matter where I went, I saw Roman soldiers, Roman businessmen, wealthy Roman ladies—Romans everywhere. Gentiles wielded the power of God's people. It ate at me, plagued me.

I was certain Jesus would run the intruders off and return our country to the way it should have been. But as the months passed, as they turned into years, I came to realize that Jesus had other ideas. He kept talking of His death and resurrection. He spoke of the forgiveness of sin. I didn't want to hear that. To make matters worse, He showed compassion to invaders, even healing the servant of a Roman centurion.[4] I knew He was off track. Somehow, He was missing His mission—at least as I saw it then.

I became fixated on that and decided to force His hand. I betrayed Jesus. I led a mob of soldiers, temple guards, and servants of religious leaders to the Garden of Gethsemane and betrayed Him with a kiss.[5] Only one of us was surprised, and it wasn't Jesus.

I believed Jesus would defend Himself with force; I believed He would become the conquering Messiah whom I and others wanted. He let the mob take Him. After Peter cut off the ear of one of the high priest's servants, Jesus even healed the man. Jesus not only refused to do what I expected, but He also showed love while being arrested.[6] Then the chain of trials, beatings, and crucifixion began.

I missed out on salvation by choice. To the very end, Jesus reached out to me.[7] I rejected Jesus because He didn't fit my expectations. My failure was more than I could take.[8]

145

Jesus

Can you surrender your salvation? Can you miss out by falling away? No! The Christian life is often an up-and-down existence. You are not perfect, and neither is anyone else you know or meet. That means you will have successes, and you will have times when you surrender to temptation or lose your focus on spiritual things. Some of the greatest names in the Bible wandered from their moorings, but I didn't give up on them.

God

When you give your life to Jesus, several things occur, and these changes last forever. Your standing before Me changes, and I adopt you. Believers become part of the family. The illustration in the Bible is the example of a slave who is adopted by his owner and becomes a full-fledged son with all the legal rights of those born into the family. "You are no longer a slave but a son, and if a son, then an heir of God through Christ."[9]

Before, you were a slave to sin, but not anymore.[10] Your faith also makes you a friend of My Son.[11] Your friendship with Jesus is eternal, and nothing can change it.

Your salvation also made you a citizen of My kingdom. You are familiar with citizenship. My kingdom is composed of My people. Because of your faith, I make you part of a kingdom that never ends. This, too, changes your standing.

You are no longer foreigners and aliens, but fellow citizens with My people and members of My household, built on the foundation of the apostles and prophets, with Christ Jesus Himself as the chief cornerstone. In Him the whole building is joined together and rises to become a holy temple in the Lord. And in Him you, too, are being built together to become a dwelling in which I live by My Spirit.[12]

Salvation is about belonging to My family and My kingdom. Jesus made it possible for you to be part of that. As mentioned before, you have been changed, and those changes will keep you close and fully grounded in the faith.

The closer you draw to Us, the more powerful the relationship becomes. There will be temptations and failures, but believers always fight their way back. That statement fits those who are true believers. History is filled with improper behavior done in My name that I never approved.

Although everything else may end, My love for you will never die. John the apostle said, "The world and the desires it causes are disappearing. But if we obey God, we will live forever."[13]

JESUS

Salvation and eternity are My gifts to you for your committed belief. You may stumble, and if you do, you will find Me standing by your side, pointing the way back to the road of righteousness.

You have seen those who claim to be Christians but live as if they've never met Me. I taught, "You will know them by their fruits."[14] My followers are known by the way they love, the sins they avoid, the worship they do, and the good they achieve.

Paul wrote this to a church leader named Titus: "God has shown us how kind he is by coming to save all people. He taught us to give up our wicked ways and our worldly desires and to live decent and honest lives in this world. We are filled with hope, as we wait for the glorious return of our great God and Savior Jesus Christ. He gave himself to rescue us from everything that is evil and to make our hearts pure. He wanted us to be his own people and to be eager to do right."[15]

If you did the saving, then you might have reason to be concerned, but don't. Your salvation is secure because I hold it in My hand.

*To what shall we liken the kingdom of God? Or
with what parable shall we picture it? It is like
a mustard seed which, when it is sown on the
ground, is smaller than all the seeds on earth;
but when it is sown, it grows up and becomes
greater than all herbs, and shoots out large
branches, so that the birds of the air
may nest under its shade.*

Mark 4:30–32 NKJV

KINGDOM OF GOD

The kingdom doesn't refer to place so much as it refers to authority. The kingdom of God is the keystone of New Testament teaching.

29
What is the kingdom of God?

David Livingstone and Leo Tolstoy were very different people, but there was one thing they shared: they held the kingdom of God in high regard. Livingstone, medical missionary to Africa in the late 1800s, said, "I will place no value on anything I have or possess unless it is in relationship to the kingdom of God." He died on the mission field. Tolstoy, the famous Russian author who wrote War and Peace *and* Anna Karenina, *said, "The only significance of life consists in helping to establish the kingdom of God."*

Today, the kingdom of God is a puzzle to many. What is it? What does it mean? These are important questions. Talk of the kingdom permeates the entire New Testament, which makes it important to know about and understand its meaning.

Q
Jesus, You spoke frequently of the "kingdom of God" and even included it in the model prayer, but I don't understand what it means. What is the kingdom of God?

JESUS

Kingdom concepts were central to My teaching and that of the early church. In fact, all My teaching is based on the truth that there is a kingdom of God. The term appears more than seventy times in the New Testament. As I went about teaching in the synagogues and preaching to the people, I did two things: I healed the sick, and I taught about the kingdom.[1]

As you read through the New Testament, notice that Matthew used the phrase "kingdom of heaven." He chose that expression about thirty times over "kingdom of God." Aside from the word choice, there is no real difference. The phrases are interchangeable.

People are used to living under the rule of a king, a queen, or an elected government here on earth. Citizens of the United States, for example, feel a strong patriotism for their government. Those in England feel the same for their country and their queen. Everyone lives within the laws of the land, just as you do. Through much of history, and still present in several countries, royalty reigned over the people. Citizens living under a king are subject to the king's leadership.

It is the same with the kingdom of God. When you choose to follow My Father, you are a subject of His kingdom. While the kingdom of God is similar to earthly kingdoms, it is also different.

Earthly kingdoms are led by imperfect people. The best, most beneficial, and most efficient form of government is the benevolent king. In such a system, a powerful but always loving king governs with the best interests of his people at heart. His agenda is their welfare. This is difficult to achieve since all leaders are subject to failure. The kingdom of God, however, is the very realization of this: God is King over all.

However, you don't yet see this working in the world. That's the first thing to know about the kingdom of God: it is both a present reality and a future fulfillment. There will come a time when My Father will rule without hindrance. This will happen after My second coming—when I return bodily to earth—and it will reach its pinnacle in the new heaven and the new earth.

The Pharisees, those religious leaders who gave Me so much trouble during My earthly ministry, were pressing Me for a date when the kingdom of God would come. I told them that the kingdom of God wouldn't be preceded by signs they could observe, or with a single event. Instead, I let them know that the kingdom of God was already in their midst.[2]

Unlike countries that have boundaries and borders, the kingdom of God is limitless. It occupies the hearts of God's followers. A Christian in London shares the same kingdom of God citizenship with a Christian in Bangladesh and with one in China and with one in Cairo, Egypt. Earthly boundaries do not define the borders of the kingdom. Wherever one of My followers lives, there is the kingdom of God. If you were to mark on a globe where the kingdom is, you would have to place millions upon millions of dots instead of lines and borders.

God

When I look at the world, I don't see edges marking My kingdom, I see individuals scattered over the surface of the world, living their lives, connected to Me through My Son. My kingdom is populated by believers of every nation, nationality, color, social class, and gender.

A believer's citizenship is in heaven. Certainly a believer might be a citizen of Canada or the United States or Argentina, but his or her spiritual citizenship is fixed in heaven.[3] For now, no living person experiences all that the kingdom will be, but he or she can sense the kingdom, My reign, in his or her heart.

JOHN THE BAPTIST

I was the first person in New Testament times to speak of the kingdom's arrival by name. My preaching was intended to alert people to the coming of Jesus and the kingdom. "Repent," I said countless times, "for the kingdom is at hand."[4]

The words meant a great deal to the people of my day because every one of my compatriots looked forward to the coming of the Messiah. They believed that He would set up an earthly kingdom, run off the Romans who occupied our land, and turn our country into a mighty nation. When I said, "The kingdom is at hand," they heard, "The Messiah is coming." And they were right about His arrival, although they were wrong about the purpose of His coming. It was my pleasure—my highest honor—to baptize Jesus.[5]

JESUS

The kingdom of God was the heart of My teaching and preaching. I taught it to crowds of thousands and to individuals. Nicodemus came to Me one evening with a question. He was a religious leader, and he came at night to avoid being seen. He said, "Rabbi, your miracles prove that You are sent by God." I knew he wasn't there just to praise Me. He had a deeper question lurking in his soul, so I said, "Unless you are born again, you will not see the kingdom of God."[6]

That puzzled him. He wanted to know how a grown man could be born again. Of course, he was thinking of physical birth, and I was speaking of spiritual birth. People become citizens by faith. You become part of the kingdom of God when you place your faith and trust in Me. Salvation is the same thing as entering the kingdom of God. One is the same as the other.

The concept is so important that I taught My disciples to pray for it. They asked Me to teach them to pray, and I gave them a model for prayer. Part of that model includes praying words like these: Our Father in heaven, holy is Your name. May Your kingdom come and Your will be done here on earth as it is in heaven.[7] How important is the kingdom of God? It is very important, and you should pray for its spread.

I taught people to pray for the coming of the kingdom; I also taught them to seek it. When I delivered a long lesson now called the Sermon on the Mount,[8] I told the crowds that they should search out God's kingdom and God's righteousness first before all other things. I wanted them to always keep the kingdom in the forefront of their minds.

The importance of entering the kingdom of God by faith remained a part of My teaching. I even emphasized its importance after My death and resurrection. I appeared to hundreds after I rose from the dead, and when I taught I always brought up the kingdom of God.[9]

I handed over the message that God's kingdom had come to My disciples, and they took it to the world as part of the early church's mission. It is impossible to separate teachings about the kingdom of God from the rest of My instructions. Kingdom matters remain central to My message.

The kingdom is another proof of how much My Father loves you and the rest of the world. He wants you to be part of the never-ending kingdom.

30
What makes the kingdom of
God important today?

> *There is no disputing the fact that the world in which Jesus walked was different from the one in which we live. Jesus taught in an agrarian society that had little technology. Today, cell phones enable people to call almost anywhere in the world. Satellites beam television shows into homes. In Jesus' day, few people traveled far from their homes. Now people travel across the country in a few hours.*
>
> *On the surface it seems as if everything has changed. But are the people of the twenty-first century all that different from the people of the first century? Even though tools and technologies have changed, is it likely that hearts and souls have changed as well?*

 I can understand how the kingdom of God might be important to first-century people, but that was two thousand years ago. What difference does it make to contemporary people like me?

GOD

Your world is changing fast. Technology has made the globe a much smaller place. Every generation sees more advances than the previous. By the nineteenth century, knowledge started doubling every fifty years; knowledge now doubles every year. In biblical times, knowledge advanced slowly. Today, it is impossible for you or anyone you know to keep up with all the rapid changes.

That seems to imply that twenty-first-century people are more advanced and sophisticated than the people who came before. In one sense, that is true. The people of Jesus' day couldn't fathom the technology you use routinely, nor could they imagine advances in medicine, government, and exploration. But even though things around you have changed, people have remained the same.

"Whatever is has already been, and what will be has been before," King Solomon concluded.[1] Technology changes, new discoveries are made faster than can be recorded, and yet some things are unchanging: a person's soul, the need for a vital spiritual life, the need for forgiveness, and much more. Humans are spiritual beings. You are more than mind and body. You are mind, body, and soul. The kingdom of God is as important to twenty-first-century people as it was to first-century people.

The world has changed, but humans have not. It is the twenty-first century, and there are still locks on the doors, still prisons, still divorces, still hatred, and still sin. My kingdom is still populated by people of faith. It represents My benevolent love and rule over their lives. They have become citizens by choice and by the work of My Son, Jesus.

The passing centuries have not diminished every person's need to be forgiven and accepted into the kingdom. I am immutable; I do not change.[2] My nature does not alter. The definitions of sin, forgiveness, hope, faith, and salvation have not changed. Consequently, the passing years do not change human spiritual need or My love for humankind. My Son's death on the cross is as important today as it was then. Neither the kingdom of God nor your need for it changes over time. My kingdom is spiritual and will be physical.

JESUS

My preaching centered on the kingdom of God for a reason. My Father reigns in the hearts and minds of all His believers. The kingdom of God will never pass away. Even after all is done and this heaven and this earth are replaced with a new creation, the kingdom of God will exist.

The kingdom of God is about relationship. Although My Father owns all things, His kingdom doesn't reside on any particular continent; His kingdom resides in the hearts and minds of His followers. Not even death changes that. Flesh and blood—your physical self—cannot inherit the kingdom of God, but your changed soul can.[3]

URBANUS

I lived in Rome and was a worker in the church there. The apostle Paul considered me a coworker.[4] I listened with great interest as the pastor read a letter Paul wrote to our church community. Many of us were Jews and grew up keeping religious laws and observing holidays and holy feasts. Paul reminded us that as Christians we belonged to a kingdom that went beyond our human country and observances. He told us that the kingdom of God isn't a matter of dietary law but of righteousness, peace, and joy in the Holy Spirit.[5] He went on to say that we Christians were part of a larger community, one established and overseen by God, which means we are to care for one another.

The kingdom of God is not something that is added to faith; it is the result of faith. When I gave my life to Jesus, I became part of a kingdom without borders. My fellow citizens live all over the world, and no matter where I go, I am at home with them.

JESUS

The world will never change so much that humankind won't need a living relationship with My Father the King. Governments may come and go, but the kingdom of God remains forever.

Unlike an earthly government you are born into, you are *born again* into the kingdom. I used several stories to illustrate how the kingdom expands. In one teaching, I said the kingdom of God is like a mustard seed. When planted, the tiny seed grows quickly and becomes the largest plant in the garden, large enough for birds to roost in.[6] The kingdom started small but quickly grew into a worldwide presence and is still growing. It has spread not only geographically but through time.

This is why the kingdom of God is relevant to the twenty-first-century-believer. The world has changed a hundred times over, but the human need hasn't. The kingdom is made available to everyone, and those who choose to accept it find joy, peace, and purpose. I taught that the kingdom was like a hidden treasure found by a man who, for the joy of the discovery, sold all he had and bought the field with the treasure.[7] He saw the value of the treasure. The kingdom is of more value.

People long for benevolent leadership. In fact, because the people I taught during My ministry were hungry for leadership that wasn't burdensome and legalistic. They had been suppressed by a string of undesirable kings, high priests, and the Roman government. Some who had witnessed My miracles and heard My messages decided I had come to set up an earthly kingdom. They were so convinced they made plans to force Me to be their ruler. People can become desperate for valid leadership. As you know by now, I came for a different reason. I withdrew to the mountains for a time just to be alone.[8]

What they didn't know was that My kingdom is not of this world. I told that to Pontius Pilate during My trial. I had been seized and delivered to Pilate. He was the Roman official ruling over the land. I told him that My realm was not from "this side," meaning this side of heaven. The word I used for *world* was *cosmos*. Today that term refers to the universe, but then it meant the order of the world. My kingdom had nothing to do with Rome or with Palestine or any other place on the planet. The kingdom is located in the hearts of believers.

Because the kingdom is spiritual in nature, it applies to all times, including the twenty-first century.

GOD

The kingdom is relevant to you because you have the same spiritual needs as first-century people. Like everyone else, you need a relationship with Me through Jesus. That relationship places you in the kingdom of God, and nothing can remove you. You become part of the same kingdom as the apostles and early believers. Those who come after you will experience the same change and citizenship.

You are part of a kingdom greater and longer lasting than any earthly government. You belong to something that will enable you to relate to other believers and give you purpose in your life. No matter how much the world changes, the kingdom of God remains unchanged. It goes beyond technology or human history, and it's closer than you realize.

31
God, do we have to die to be citizens of Your kingdom?

Humans have a desire not only to know the "what" of life, but also to know the "when" of life. People are creatures sailing on a river of time, "future-tense" people, so to speak, always wondering about the days ahead. Sometimes people stare at the future so much and for so long that they forget to live in the present.

What about the kingdom of God? Is it just a future thing, a by-and-by hope waiting someplace beyond time's horizon? Or is it possible that it's a right-here-right-now experience? The answers to these questions will have a huge impact on people's daily lives, people who are used to planning for and even living for the future—but what about living for today?

 Q **Is the kingdom of God just something for the future? When do I become a part of the kingdom?**

GOD

There is a tendency to think of spiritual matters as something either locked in the ancient past or waiting for you in the future. All My work is meant to bless you today. Just as salvation is past tense, present tense, and future tense, so, too, are other spiritual matters—and this is especially true of My kingdom.

It is important to have a broad view of the "when" of the kingdom. My kingdom has always been a part of My plan for humanity. That means the kingdom has existed from the beginning, exists in you now, and will continue to exist in the future.

It's tempting to confuse the kingdom of God with heaven. The two are closely connected, but they are not the same thing. Your eternal life in heaven waits in the future; your citizenship in the kingdom of God begins the moment you take Jesus as your Savior.

Think of the country where you live. When did you become a citizen? If you were born there, you became a citizen at birth. Did your country exist before your birth? Yes. Will the country continue to exist in your future? Yes, even if the country changes leadership and government.

It is the same with the kingdom of God. Just as your birth gave you citizenship, so your rebirth[1] makes you a citizen of the kingdom. As a follower of My Son, you live your kingdom life daily and will continue to do so until your earthly death or My Son's return.

You don't experience everything My kingdom has to offer until after death, but there is a great deal to experience today.

JESUS

Kingdom living affects every part of your life. It changes your attitude, your values, your worries, and the way you deal with other people.

In many ways, the kingdom of God is defined by contrasts. Kingdom people live differently from those outside the kingdom. That's not to say kingdom people are perfect. They're not; but they have a different set of values and behavior. They look at life differently.

During My ministry, I encountered falsely religious people. One group, the Pharisees, was especially troublesome. They were a group of deeply religious but spiritually shallow leaders. They loved to be noticed by others. They prayed on the street corners so they could be heard and seen.[2] I taught that a kingdom person prays in private.[3] Prayer is not a performance; it's a heartfelt conversation with My Father.

Kingdom people worry less in the present. You are not exempt from problems, but faith enables you to face them with the confidence that God is there to help you. I taught people to take note of nature, how the birds, which do not plant or reap crops, still live their lives because the Father feeds them.[4]

Kingdom living also lessens worry. Worry achieves nothing. No one can lengthen his or her life by worrying.[5] People who live as citizens judge less and are less critical of others, choosing to deal with their own faults instead of the faults of others.[6] Citizens of the kingdom treat others as they wish to be treated.[7]

The truth I want you to see is this: The kingdom of God affects your daily life, not just your future life.

ANDREW

As a disciple, I had opportunity to listen to Jesus' teachings. Each one moved my heart and soul, but the most majestic yet simple teaching was the one He gave from the side of a local mountain.

He said, "Be happy even if you're poor because yours is the kingdom of God."[8] He didn't say the people would be part of the kingdom in the future, but right now. Then He switched to the future tense. He said, "You are blessed even if you're hungry now, because you will be fed."[9] That's when I came to understand that the kingdom of God exists in my present and in my future.

JESUS

The kingdom of God is boundless in time and space. It is borderless and timeless, which means it exists in your future. Just as you do not have to die to enter the kingdom, death does not remove you from it.

Heaven and the kingdom both continue into the endless future, but they are different. Heaven is a place of eternal life, and it is where the Father lives and reigns. The kingdom is less about place and more about relationship. As long as God reigns, the kingdom will exist, and He will reign forever.

Death is your transition from this life to the next, but it does not change your status in the kingdom of God. My ministry and sacrifice opened the door for your spiritual rebirth and entrance into the kingdom. While you don't enter the kingdom by your death, you can say you enter it by My death.[10]

It is important to understand that the kingdom of God is a present reality. You are part of it, now and forever. Millions of people are citizens in the kingdom.

The kingdom also gives you a distinction. As one of My followers, you should consider yourself a citizen of the kingdom. Your standing in the kingdom makes you one of the chosen people, a member of a holy nation, one of God's people.[11]

Being part of the kingdom helps you in your day-to-day life. You are part of something wonderful and immeasurable.

32
Is there also a future kingdom
two kingdoms?

Galileo, the Italian physicist and astronomer, was one of the first to use a telescope in astronomy. Previously, astronomers could only gaze at the heavens and chart the movement of the known planets. Galileo wanted to do more: he wanted to see the heavens in detail. He turned his small telescope to the moon and saw lunar mountains and valleys; he pointed the device at Jupiter and observed four of the planet's largest satellites; he discovered sunspots, saw the phases of Venus, and learned the Milky Way is composed of stars. He made scientific history by looking farther than any other man in his age.

 So there is a present kingdom and a future kingdom. Are there really two separate kingdoms?

GOD

My kingdom has many facets. We've talked about the present nature of the kingdom and mentioned that it continues into the future. But that doesn't mean there are two kingdoms. There is only one kingdom of God. However, in the future you will experience the kingdom fully.

Remember, a person enters the kingdom of God by rebirth. That rebirth happens at the moment of salvation, that is, when a person accepts My Son as Lord and Savior. For that person, everything changes. His or her sins are forgiven, and he becomes My child.[1] I adopt you into My family. But you don't yet experience all the kingdom has to offer. The time is coming when all will be made known.

JESUS

Part of My Father's plan is to allow history to take its course, but a time is coming when a heavenly kingdom will replace the current worldly kingdom.

Two kingdoms operate in your world: the kingdom of the world and the kingdom of God. I told My detractors that they were from this world below; I was from the world above.[2] The two kingdoms—the two worlds—are at odds with each other and have been so through human history. It is important that you understand this. I made every effort to make certain My disciples knew they were no longer part of the worldly kingdom but were part of a heavenly one. I chose them for the kingdom of God.[3]

There is a tendency to think that heavenly means nonphysical. It doesn't. The kingdom of God is purely spiritual now. Human governments occupy and rule the physical world. My Father allows this for a time. In the future, My Father and I will rule not just the hearts and souls of Our followers but also the planet itself.[4]

This is not the introduction of a new kingdom but an expanding of the kingdom of God. The first chapter in this earthly reign is often called the *Millennium*. The word refers to My thousand-year reign on earth. A millennium is one thousand years.

JOHN

Late in my life, God gave me a vision of the future. I recorded the whole thing in the book of Revelation, the last book in the Bible. I saw many things that I was permitted to write down and other things I was commanded to keep secret.[5] One of the things I was permitted to record was the thousand-year reign of Christ. When you read Revelation, you immediately notice that it is symbolic, but those images and symbols represent real events to come.

Here's what I saw regarding the physical rule of Jesus over the earth: First, I saw an angel with a key descend from heaven and unlock the great abyss. Satan was thrown into the abyss and held captive for a thousand years so he could not deceive the nations during that time.[6]

I also saw the believers through the ages sitting on thrones and ruling the world with God and with our Savior, Jesus.[7]

It will be a great time of peace and unhindered, unpolluted spirituality. The laws of God will be written on every person's heart and mind. We will experience God as never before.[8] Imagine a world led by God, a world without evil influence, a world of true peace and happiness. That is what the kingdom of God will be like in the Millennium.

Jesus

Although a thousand years is a long time in human history, it is just a page in eternity's history book. The kingdom of God has no end. It encompasses all heaven and earth. There will be a time when the full reign of My Father will be complete. The Millennium will be just a taste of the perfection ahead. Each day that passes is another step closer to that time.

God

That time is kept secret. My Son ascended to heaven after His resurrection. He will remain in heaven until the time arrives for all things to be made anew.[9] Everything is on schedule. You will have to trust Me on that. I have not forgotten; I do not get distracted. It will be worth the wait. At the right time, I will bring all things in heaven and earth together under the rule of My Son.[10]

History is the record of humankind's effort to rule itself. Some countries have done well, creating good environments for their citizens. Others have shown how evil people in power can be. Even the best, the most noble of governments are infected with corruption and lose track of their real purpose.

I created humans to live in a theocracy—a society led and ruled by Me—but that ended with Adam and Eve. For a time, My chosen people lived in a theocracy led by priests and prophets, but soon they wanted a king.[11] Even the best kings of Israel made mistakes that hurt them and the people they served. Solomon, the wisest man to live and a great king, almost destroyed the people he dedicated himself to serve.

This shows that, although humankind has achieved much, it has had trouble governing itself and living with its neighbors. Can you imagine how much more could have been achieved under My benevolent leadership? That day is coming. First, the return of My Son, then His thousand-year reign on earth, followed by a world returned to the way I had originally designed it. I do this for you.

Have you wondered what this world will be like? There are hallmarks that will help you understand. It will be a place of security. Violence will be no more.[12] My kingdom will forever be a place of holiness, truth, comfort, and purpose. There will be no oppression.

It will be the restoring of unity among people and, more important, the restoring of the relationship between you and My Father. God's presence will be undiminished. Everything that puts distance between you and Me will be removed.

The future kingdom will be different from the one that exists today only in that it will be the culmination of all things. For now, you experience the kingdom of God spiritually. Soon, you will experience the kingdom of God in its fullness on earth.

There is one kingdom, spread over time, and with each passing day you move a little closer to seeing its fullness. You can look forward to it, pray for it, and live for it.

If God is on our side, can anyone be against us? God did not keep back his own Son, but he gave him for us. If God did this, won't he freely give us everything else? If God says his chosen ones are acceptable to him, can anyone bring charges against them? Or can anyone condemn them? No indeed! Christ died and was raised to life, and now he is at God's right side, speaking to him for us.

Romans 8:31–34 CEV

HEAVEN AND HELL

Eternal life, eternal punishment—both are nearly impossible for people to believe, but the Bible teaches both are real. The concept of eternal life, though difficult, can be understood in this present life.

33
Jesus, are You the only way to heaven?

In 1930, Michael J. Cullen opened the first true supermarket in the United States. Since then, this has become a supermarket society. People have grown accustomed to walking long, shiny aisles, grabbing what they want, and ignoring everything else. People are used to having choices about everything, from the kind of oranges to buy to the type of cars to drive. We've become a pick-and-keep people. That's a good thing in most areas of life, but does a consumer mind-set work with the spiritual?

Christians have said that Jesus is the only means of salvation, the only person who can forgive our sins and promise us eternal life. Others think such assertions are biased and narrow-minded.

Q **There are so many religions, and each says it's the only one that has things right. Is there just one way to heaven, or do they all work?**

GOD

There are nineteen major world religions and nearly three hundred religious groups. Each makes special and unique claims about representing the correct spiritual path. It is no wonder that many people are confused as to which is the right way, or even if there is a right way.

For centuries, critics have claimed that Christianity, the faith based on My Son Jesus' teaching, believes that Jesus is the only means to Me and to heaven. Surprising as this sounds, I agree with them. Christianity is narrow-minded. How can it not be? Christianity is not the only faith to teach that it is the one-and-only means to eternal life. Islam, one of the largest and fastest-growing religious groups, makes the same claim, and extremists in the group believe other faiths need to be eradicated.

I want to make a distinction between the Christian faith and religion. Every culture has an innate desire to connect to the divine. Notice how I phrased that. I didn't say they had an innate desire to connect to Me. Many have done their best to keep Me out of their religious systems. In My place they have substituted made-up gods like Baal or Molech. The Greeks had their pantheon of gods, and the Romans had a similar family of deities. Pagan cultures created systems that required human sacrifice to appease the gods and to bring rain and good crops. Some sacrificed adults; others sacrificed their own children.

Religion is a human creation in which people try to reach out to gods. Christianity is the opposite. I reached out to you in many ways and ultimately through My Son, Jesus. This is the difference between religion and Christianity. One begins with people; Christianity begins with Me.

There is only one means of salvation and that is through My Son. The claim that Jesus is the only path to Me is the truth and what you need to hear. Love is what motivates Me—My love for you. The most unloving thing I could do would be to let you believe that all paths lead to Me, when such is not the case. There is only one path to Me, and I want you on that path because that is what will bring eternal life and happiness to you.

Jesus

I made this claim several times in My ministry, and I made it as clear as possible. On several occasions, the disciples heard me say that I was the way, the truth, and the life, and that no one could come to the Father except through Me.[1] I am *the* path, not just one of the paths. I am the only path. I am the embodiment of spiritual truth, and I am the Giver of eternal life.

I said this a different way when I described Myself as a gate for the sheep.[2] Often at night, a shepherd would lead his flock into a pen with a stone wall around the perimeter so the animals would not wander off while the shepherd slept. In many cases, the pens didn't have gates, and so the shepherd would sleep in the opening. By doing so, he would know if any animal other than his sheep tried to sneak in or if his sheep tried to leave. He was a human gate. I am like that shepherd: I am the Gate.

Peter

This truth has been the cornerstone of the church from the beginning. I made a point of mentioning it in my early sermons. My preaching was often in front of unsupportive and even angry crowds. I ended up in jail many times, but I had to preach the truth as Jesus gave it to me, and that included saying there was salvation in no one else.[3] No matter what the reaction would be, I had to make it clear because so much depended on it. I wasn't talking about starting a rival religion. I was pointing people to the only One who could change their eternity. Religion cannot do what God has done in sending Jesus to be the sacrifice and Savior of the world.

It would have been easier on me and the other apostles to avoid the topic and simply preach warm and comfortable sermons. It would have saved us from imprisonment and beatings, but the world did not need that kind of message. To withhold that aspect of the truth would have been dishonest and selfish. So I, and the others, preached Jesus as the only means of gaining heaven.

GOD

There are many reasons why Jesus is the only Savior of the world.

Jesus is unique. He alone can claim to be My Son.[4] This means that He is unique in all history. As My Son, He could speak for Me. Strictly speaking, Jesus and I are One, not just in purpose but in deity. Jesus is God in the flesh.[5]

He also is sinless.[6] No other person can make that claim. This means He could do what no one else could: become the perfect sacrifice for the sin of the world.[7] He was the sinless One who died for sinners.[8]

Jesus preached, taught, healed, forgave, and more, but His primary purpose was to make it possible for sinners to be forgiven. Sin brings spiritual and physical death; Jesus' sacrifice brought eternal forgiveness and eternal life.[9]

My Son also did what no one else will ever do. He defeated death. His death on the cross defeated sin; His resurrection defeated death. Believers who die receive eternal life and will be resurrected in the future.[10]

My Son did what humankind could not. He made up for your sin. As a just God, I must judge sin; as a loving God, I long to forgive sin and reward My people in life and in eternal life. Jesus' self-sacrifice meant taking on your and everyone else's sin.[11] Jesus and His sacrifice made it possible for us to have an unhindered fellowship.

From the moment Adam and Eve sinned, it has been My goal to restore our relationship. Salvation began in heaven and came to earth in Jesus, so you can someday be in heaven.

JESUS

I am the means of salvation. Many religious leaders I dealt with did not like hearing that. On several occasions, they tried to take My life before I was ready to lay it down. They were angry because what I taught was different from what they proclaimed, but I could not let that change Me or My work. You are too important for that.

My message is for everyone who will listen. There is only one way to heaven, and that is through Me. There is no arrogance in that statement, just truth. Your eternal life is My motivation.

My life, My message, My sacrifice, My resurrection, and My continued involvement in the church and the lives of My followers are centered on you. All I did, I did for you. Other religions may rise, but faith in Me makes the eternal difference.

34
What will happen to people who don't believe?

Every culture has a god-image, and almost all come from the society in which they live. In the Western world, the temptation has been to cast God in the image of a kindly grandfather, someone who sits on a park bench and watches the children play. It's a comfortable image, but is it an accurate one? The God of the Bible seems to be different from the way artists portray Him.

Even a casual reading of the Bible shows a very different God. In a world that is approaching seven billion people, it is safe to say that many are not believers in the God of the Bible. What does the future look like for them?

 It's easy to see that not everyone believes in You, God, or in Jesus. What will happen to those people?

GOD

I am a just God as well as a loving God. Many times I've expressed My undying love and desire that everyone come to Me through My Son, Jesus.[1] The reality is, however, that many will not.

JESUS

My message has been a "whoever" message. Whoever calls upon My name shall have salvation, but those who reject the offer of eternal life will be judged.[2] Everything that can be done to open the doors to eternal life has been done, and countless millions have responded. Still, there are those who have not. Some have made God their enemy by denouncing Him and His existence. There have always been those who foolishly claim that God does not exist, as if they have a way of knowing such things.[3]

Some are too busy to think about such things, and they reject the offer of salvation by inaction. Salvation is like a gift offered by one person to another. The person offering the gift cannot force the other to accept it. The intended recipient can walk away, just as a person with a deadly disease can choose to reject treatment. That's how free will works. The choice has always rested with you.

God

It does no good for Me to soft-pedal the answer to your question. To do so would be dishonest and not fair to humanity. You have a right to know some of what lies ahead.

For the believer there waits the greatest joy. When a believer dies, he or she is ushered into My presence.[4] That, however, is not the end of things. I created humans to live forever in their bodies. Death strips the soul away from the body, which is not a natural state for humans. There is a myth that good people who die become angels. That is a misconception. Angels are a special class of creation. Angels never become humans, and humans never become angels. Adam was meant to live forever in his body; the same can be said of you.

Everyone will be resurrected. Those who have accepted Christ are resurrected to eternal life; those who have rejected Jesus are resurrected to judgment.

In the New Testament, the term *judge* means "to separate one thing from another." Originally, the word meant "to sieve," "to filter." There are several judgments. In fact, everyone stands in one kind of judgment or another.

The judgment for believers is different from all the rest. That's because followers of Christ are never judged for their sins or judged to see if they're good enough to be rewarded with heaven. The truth is, no one is good enough, but since Jesus paid the price for the sin of all believers, they are considered sinless. I know that no one other than My Son is sinless, but for the purposes of salvation, believers are considered pure and blameless. The biblical word for this is *sanctified*.

Sanctified means "to be set apart from the common." In the Old Testament days, certain items in the temple could be used only for worship. They were never used for anything but worship in the temple. Those items were considered holy and were set apart from everything else. Jesus, when He prayed in the Upper Room, said He sanctified Himself so that His followers could be set apart.[5] To be a follower of Christ means you have been set apart from those who reject Jesus. It also means that you never stand in judgment for your sins because Jesus did that for you. The works done in this life will be judged, but for rewards rather than condemnation.

GOD

Nonbelievers face a different kind of judgment; a judgment called the Great White Throne.

JOHN

In the revelation God gave me, I saw an extraordinarily large, white throne, with God seated upon it. Heaven and earth seemed to fly away, leaving just Him and the throne. In front of Him stood the dead from every walk of life. In front of the Father were books, one of which was the Book of Life, and He read from it. Every person was judged by his works. Since people can't work their way into heaven, their names were not written in the Book of Life, and they were condemned to the Lake of Fire.[6]

GOD

Resurrected to life or resurrected to a second death—the choice remains with the individual. At the judgment, no one will be asked why he sinned, only why he didn't repent.

I gave My only Son as a sacrifice so that not a single person would have to stand before Me at the judgment.[7] The Holy Spirit works in everyone's life, enabling them to understand their need for forgiveness and a lasting relationship with My Son. The Bible has been printed in nearly every language. Preachers and missionaries have sailed the seas and broadcast the message of Jesus all over the globe. Even the most hardened sinner can turn and come back to Me. That is what I long for.

My Son's work has changed everything for those who choose to follow Him. He made friendship with Me possible and exchanged people's eternal punishment for eternal life.[8] Nothing brings more joy to heaven than when someone exchanges disbelief for faith. Even the angels rejoice.[9]

35
What is heaven like?

For some, heaven is "pie-in-the-sky-by-and-by," an illusion, a fairy tale, a story to help us make sense of this life and give us something to hold on to. For people of faith, however, it is a home they have yet to visit. It is real, not imaginary. When Socrates was asked what country he came from, he said, "I am a citizen of the world." Christians see themselves as citizens of heaven.

If there is a heaven, then it must be a unique place and different from what is seen on earth. Heaven has been a part of the Christian thinking for thousands of years, and those who believe in it stake their hopes in a better life to come. Is heaven what they think it is?

 Christians speak of heaven frequently, but what goes on there? What will I see and experience?

GOD

Many details about heaven are not to be revealed now. The apostle Paul mentioned a man who was caught up to the third heaven; he saw and heard things there that he was not permitted to share with others.[1] There are things about heaven you will learn when you get there. There are reasons for this. Heaven exists in a realm that is impossible for humans to comprehend. There is more to it than what you experience in the world. Human constraints limit your ability to understand.

My revelation is reserved for the faithful, those who can appreciate it. I have given a great deal of information about Myself, My plans, and My desires, and this information is recorded in the Bible for all to read, but the Bible does not contain everything. John finished his gospel account by acknowledging that he had not included everything.[2] There is more to learn in the next life, and that's by design.

JESUS

Don't let the term *third heaven* confuse you. In the first century, Jews described their world as having three heavens: the first heaven was the atmosphere, the second heaven was the realm of stars and planets, and the third heaven was where the Father dwells. It is a universe all its own.

Heaven is more than an idea or a state of mind. Heaven is inhabited by My Father, angels, and the believers who have died. I described it to My apostles as being a place of many mansions, in which I would personally prepare a place for all believers.[3] Heaven is a livable place—you continue to live and operate in heaven.

Heaven is much more than someplace in the sky. At present, when a believer dies, he or she is immediately in heaven with all those who have gone before. There is great joy there. Paul spoke for millions when he said that as much as he loved his life and work, he longed for heaven.[4]

But that is not your permanent abode. In the future there will be a new heaven and a new earth, and a place called New Jerusalem—a place of righteousness and joy, which is a form of heaven where the communion between you and My Father and Me will reach its pinnacle.[5]

You will not live as a disembodied spirit. While it is true that at death your soul and body part, with your soul going to heaven and your body to the grave, a heavenly body waits for you.[6] Many believers yearn for this transition, and they are right to do so. What waits ahead is far better than what is.[7]

GOD

Heaven is a place of reward for all believers.[8] Some rewards are general and applied to every believer, for example, eternal life. But I reward all who serve Me according to their good works.[9] No one will be displeased with the rewards they receive.

You will be with Me. Anything that now separates us will be gone. Our relationship will continue without interruption, and nothing will diminish it. Heaven is My home, and it will be yours as well.[10]

Heaven is an eternal place populated by people to whom I've given eternal life. It is also a place of glory. Some have taken to calling the place itself *glory*. The early Christians used to recite a confession, a short, easy-to-remember statement of belief. One such confession said that Jesus revealed

God in flesh and on earth, that the Spirit confirmed His identity, that He was seen by the angels, that He was preached around the world, and that He went to heaven after His resurrection.[11]

Glory is more than another name for heaven; it is a state of sharing. In heaven, I share My glory with everyone there. The word *glory* refers to My radiance, splendor, and majesty. Heaven is a place of glory because I am, by nature, a person of glory. Heaven is a place of light, brilliant and beautiful. Glory is the absence of troubles, depression, and concerns.[12]

JESUS

You will fellowship with My Father, Me, and others in heaven. Interactions with others of faith will occur without hindrance. You will see those whom you've known, and those who lived and died long before. The love of God will bind you to others and to God Himself.

Heaven is your rest. The struggles of this life will be gone. There will be no more sadness, illness, or death. Everything you do will bring honor to God.

In heaven there is no sin, just pure holiness. No one, not even My Father, will remember your sins.[13] There will be no more guilt or regret.

Heaven is My Father's home, and it will be yours. Your life on earth, as glorious as it may seem, is so much less by comparison. The universe is majestic; it is even more majestic when seen from heaven and seen through new eyes.

GOD

Heaven is a promise and a hope for millions. Many want to leave behind the misery of a present life to take in the joy of the future life. Even the apostles looked forward to a time of reward. Still, heaven is more than a safe spot.

Heaven is a place of purity; holiness is everywhere and at all times. Those who have only read about Jesus will see Him face-to-face, and that memory will last forever.

36
What will we do for eternity?

The science-fiction author Issac Asimov said that since he did not believe in God, he did not have to fear the torment of hell or the boredom of heaven. Boredom? Daily challenges and opportunities make life interesting. Life is seldom boring, whether through good times or bad. But what about heaven? Could heaven be boring?

If heaven is a stress-free, pain-free, pressure-free zone, then will people who go there spend endless time wishing for something worthwhile to do, hoping for some worthwhile challenge? Or is heaven different from what people imagine?

 I have to admit, heaven sounds boring compared to the excitement of living on earth. Is it?

GOD

Your experience in heaven will be different from what you experience now, of course.

In heaven, you will not be encumbered by sin, doubt, or uncertainty. Your knowledge will be richer. You will have a deeper understanding of life—all of life. For now, your ability to understand all that God has done is limited. It is like looking at the world through a dirty window. You can see many things, but not clearly. In heaven, your spiritual understanding will be clear, and it will bring you unimaginable joy.[1] Questions you've harbored for years will have answers because you will be empowered to understand. Heaven will be a place of learning, and you will have a desire to know more than you do now. Think of it as an adventure in discovery, where the journey is as enjoyable as the destination.

Worship will be ideal. In heaven, nothing will distance us: not sin, time, worldly concerns, or confusion. You will worship Me and My Son face-to-face.[2] Imagine this clear, unhindered exchange of love.

Communion, which is based in relationship, is made personal in heaven.

It will be perfect. Part of worship is the joy I feel when I bless you for blessing Me. When worship moves into genuine communication and sharing, communion takes place. In heaven, that emotional bond grows forever. You will be with Me and I will be with you.[3]

In heaven, life is richer and more rewarding. Certainly, you can have a fulfilling life on earth. You might have a wonderful career in a field you love; your family may be stable and happy; you might make positive changes to the world through politics, science, business, ministry, missions, social work, or any of a thousand other noble professions. Even so, heaven will be richer and more satisfying. Or your life on earth might be filled with heartache, struggle, illness, rejection, poverty, and pain. Heaven will be even more amazing to you.[4]

JESUS

When I walked the earth, many thousands heard My messages and saw My miracles, but it was a small percentage of the population then. Since then, billions of people have entered the world, many of whom place their faith in Me. In heaven, I will be there with them. My promise to My followers was that I'd prepare a place for them and come again to take them with Me. Whether people enter heaven through death or at My second coming, the destination and result remain the same.[5]

Heaven is part of your reward. It will make you happy, but the joy and celebration go the other way too. Your arrival in heaven will give Me a joy that matches your own. We will live in mutual appreciation. My greatest happiness comes from knowing that you will be with Me forever.

You will also have meaningful work. Heaven does not change your design. Just as Adam had a purpose in the garden of Eden, so you will have purpose in heaven. Before his sin, Adam's work was not burdensome. He had been created for the garden, and he found joy and meaning in being its caretaker. Eve had a purpose just as Adam did. Every human, including you, has been given skills and talents. In heaven, you will also have skills that allow you to serve My Father.

Work helps define you. I worked as a carpenter before starting My three years of ministry. In heaven you will be involved in work that goes beyond your dreams.

PAUL

One of the things revealed to me by God is this: there are heavenly places. Heaven is not one place but many.[6] I used that phrase many times in my writing. To understand what we do in heaven, we need only to look at Jesus. He reigns over everything; we will reign wherever God places us, and the universe holds many heavenly realms.

Those heavenly places are not described in the Bible. God has chosen to keep them hidden until we enter heaven. In many ways, I was childish in my understanding. God revealed a great deal to me, but my knowledge was partial and incomplete, and I looked forward to that day when I would know everything completely, just as God knows me. Then the joy of my service would be be infinitely greater.[7]

GOD

The greatest work anyone can do is to be a servant. Even My Son became a servant to humanity when He went to the cross. That was an act of obedience. It was the greatest work the universe has seen.[8]

Relationships will be different in heaven, but they will still exist. You will recognize friends and family, and they will recognize you. The love you shared on earth will be shared in heaven.

Heaven is a place of abundance. You will spend your eternal life enjoying all you see, everyone you meet, and all you do. In heaven you will be more than you are, do more than you've done, and be freer than you've ever been. Relationships that were strained will be healed.

Heaven is a place where things are done. I have kept much of it secret. You will learn and be active. Worship, service, ruling with Christ, being with loved ones, learning, sharing are just a part of what you will be doing. Your creativity will thrive. You will do all these things without concern about sin, money, illness, or sadness. Free of those distractions, your life will soar unfettered.

Imagine living your life with no fear of death, never hindered by illness, and, most of all, in full fellowship with Me. You'll be sharing heaven with Me, and your worldview will become an eternal view with plenty to do.

37
What will we look like in heaven?

Children think they'll never grow up, and when they do, they wish they could slow their aging. Adults' bodies remind them of time's passing. Soon they face the fact that they won't live forever in their present bodies. Their thoughts turn toward heaven. If the Bible is true and accurate, believers will be spending a long time there. What does the Bible teach about people in heaven? Will people look different from the way they looked on earth?

If heaven is different from earth, then it must follow that existence there will be different—that people will be different. The question is, just how different?

 Since heaven is a unique place, will our future bodies be unique? Will people recognize me?

GOD

Heaven is a place populated by spiritual beings, often called angels. It is also the future home for all believers. The faithful who die now are immediately ushered into heaven, and they never will face death again. They exist and thrive in new physical bodies.

Those bodies are similar to what you have now, but they are no longer subject to sin, illness, or aging. You are a citizen of heaven, which means heaven is your home. I transform your earthly body into something greater.[1] Your body will be immortal.[2]

Either through death or at My Son's second coming, your earthly body will be exchanged for a new body suitable for eternal life. Your new body will be incorruptible, and it will bear the image of heaven.[3] You will look different from the way you appear now, but you will still be recognizable to those who knew you on earth.

JOHN

During my vision, I was taken to heaven where I saw things I recorded in the book of Revelation. I saw many strange things, witnessed the future, and saw people I knew on earth. I was the last of the apostles to die and the only one not to die as a martyr, although I suffered at the hands of persecutors. This means that at the time of my vision, my fellow apostles had been killed. I saw them sitting on thrones alongside the great patriarchs of the Old Testament. They looked different, but I knew each one.[4]

JESUS

People recognize one another by more than physical appearance. Your future body will be similar to Mine after the resurrection. There were moments when those close to Me did not recognize Me at first. On the day of My resurrection, Mary Magdalene assumed I was the gardener who took care of the garden that surrounded the borrowed tomb, but the moment I spoke her name she recognized Me.[5]

A similar event happened on the road to Emmaus. Emmaus was a small town near Jerusalem. Two of My followers were walking to the village and discussing the crucifixion. They were heartbroken, thinking that I was gone forever. I joined them on their journey and asked what they were discussing. The question surprised them, and they assumed I was the only one in the area who hadn't heard about the crucifixion. I helped them see that I had risen from the dead, and then I spent the rest of the trip explaining the need for the crucifixion and the resurrection.[6] In heaven (and then the new heaven and the new earth that follow), you will know and be known.

After My death and resurrection, I appeared somewhat different but not so much that My followers could not recognize Me. Your new, heavenly body will have parallels with My resurrected body. For example, I could be touched. My resurrection was not spiritual; it was physical. People touched Me, and I encouraged them to do so.[7]

I also ate.[8] So will you. While your body will be different in many respects, it will function the same. You will have a mouth with which to eat, eyes with which to see, hands and fingers with which to touch and work. What will be gone are disease and aging, the outside influences that work against your earthly body.

Three disciples had the unique experience of seeing the heavenly bodies of two men who died centuries before. I took Peter, James, and John on one of My retreats up a mountain. While there, I was transformed before their eyes. The word used in the original New Testament language is the root of *metamorphosis*, the same word used today to describe what happens to a caterpillar in its cocoon.

While the three disciples watched, Moses and Elijah, two men who lived centuries before, appeared.[9] Light surrounded us. It terrified the three men.

Moses lived 3,400 years before today, and 1,400 years before the transfiguration event. Elijah the prophet lived and died many centuries before. The disciples not only physically changed before their eyes but they saw and heard two men who had died and been buried hundreds of years. But they didn't see corpses; they saw two great men alive and recognizable. They saw Moses and Elijah in their heavenly bodies.

Moses and Elijah appeared alive and better than normal. They appeared human because they are human. Their heavenly bodies are material. Both men conversed with Me, showing their ability to think and communicate. Your heavenly body will be the same as those of Elijah and Moses.

One thing that stays the same is your distinctiveness. Creation is filled with diversity. Look around, and you will see variety in plants and animals. People are not meant to look the same. Diversity is the result of design. It will be the same in heaven. Everyone will share heavenly qualities, but everyone will appear unique. Your distinct identity will remain.

The positive qualities that make you who you are will remain. Your appearance is only part of what makes you unique. Your personality is as distinctive as your face. Your heavenly body will be different in many ways, but you will not lose your distinctiveness. You remain yourself but without the sin nature.

There will also be gender. I died on the cross as a male and rose from the dead as a male. At the Mount of Transfiguration, Moses and Elijah appeared as males. I designed the human race to have two genders. In heaven there are male and female.

But something will be different. There will be no need for marriage in heaven. That is not to say that you will not recognize and love your spouse through eternity. That remains the same. One of the purposes of marriage is procreation. In heaven, since everyone will be living an eternal life, procreation will be unnecessary.

The Sadducees often challenged Me. They were a group of religious teachers who did not believe in angels or the resurrection. I taught that there were angels and a future resurrection, and that angered them. They often brought questions to Me that seemed impossible to answer. Once they described a woman who had been widowed several times then asked, "Who will be her husband in the next life?"[10] I told them that there would be no giving and taking in marriage in the next life, but that people would be like the angels, who do not reproduce.[11]

GOD

Many things will be different about your new body. You will look different, but not so much that others cannot recognize you. Your body will be similar to Jesus' resurrected body. What differences there are will not keep you from being you.

Your body will be better than what you have now, and it will last through eternity. Those things that hinder you physically will be gone. You will not give up your human qualities, nor will you cease to be human. In fact, you will be a higher-level human, as will be those around you. No one will have trouble recognizing you; nor will you have trouble recognizing them.

38

Is there really such a place as hell?

One of the most famous men in nineteenth-century England was Charles Spurgeon. His sermons were so well received that they were reprinted in local newspapers. History records that he was a man who cared for the people in his congregation and people everywhere. He also had a great influence on generations of preachers to come. He advised his students that when they preached about hell, they should do so with tears in their eyes. Clearly, he believed in a literal hell. But was his belief misplaced? Hell is almost too much to believe.

There is nothing attractive about the topic of hell. The very idea of fiery punishments chafes our senses, so much so that some people avoid the topic altogether. How can hell be real, and how can a loving God send anyone there?

 The concept of hell is almost too much to believe. Can such a place really exist?

GOD

Just as there is a future judgment for those who have rejected My Son, there is a final destination. My overriding goal is for all to have salvation through My Son, Jesus, but the reality is that many choose to go their own way.

Hell is a place of eternal punishment and is mentioned in the Bible many times. My Son taught about hell in a straightforward way. He described the future judgment that takes place before My Great White Throne.[1] The judgment is for those who reject Jesus. At the end of the judgment, the wicked are sent to a place prepared for the devil and his angels.[2]

Hell was not created for humans. It was meant to be the final judgment for Satan and his followers. Those who reject My offer of salvation choose to reject heaven and its many blessings. At the judgment, every individual will know why he or she is there. No one goes to hell without knowing why.

JESUS

I taught as much about hell as I did about heaven. And I did not soft-pedal the description. The word I used for hell was *Gehenna*. Gehenna was a location near southeast Jerusalem. In previous centuries, certain pagan groups had made human sacrifices there, some even burning their children as an offering to their gods. When the Jews began to populate the area, they refused to build on a site of such hideous acts. The Valley of Hinnom, another name for Gehenna, became a trash dump. Dead animals and the bodies of criminals were tossed onto the trash heap. Fires burned there continuously. I used the image of that place to describe hell—the place of eternal punishment.

Like heaven, hell is a real place, not just a mental attitude or a myth meant to frighten people into making a spiritual decision. It isn't a fairy tale to make children behave. There is a place of future punishment just as there is a place of future life called heaven.

Hell is a physical place. In the future, everyone is resurrected. Those of faith are resurrected to life in heaven; those who have rejected Christ are resurrected to hell.[3] Hell is a place of fire, darkness, torment, and eternal destruction. It exists, but not in a place you can see.

In many ways, hell is the opposite of heaven. Heaven offers bliss; hell offers torment. In heaven you are forever in the presence of God; those in hell are absent from My Father's love. Those in heaven have purpose; those in hell don't. The list is long.

GOD

I created humans for continuous fellowship with Me. You have been designed for heaven, not for hell. The spiritual and moral condition of a person at death lasts for eternity.[4]

Although hell is a physical place, much of the suffering comes from the knowledge of what was sacrificed. There is loneliness in that. Before anyone is consigned to hell, he stands before Me. Every doubt he had about My existence will dissolve; every ounce of self-superiority will evaporate. He will be exposed to me, and hell for him will be knowing that will never happen again.

Everyone in hell will be there by choice. Without the power of choice, there could be no hell. No soul that seriously and constantly desires hell will miss it. Those who seek will find.[5]

Jesus

Not all punishment is the same. There are degrees of punishment based on deeds done during life and on how much light of understanding the person had.

I worked many miracles on earth. I traveled from town to town healing the sick and teaching about the kingdom of God. In some towns, I was well received, but others ignored the message. While I prefer to speak in love, I did speak in harsh and corrective terms when needed.

I told the towns of Chorazin and Bethsaida that if I had performed the same miracles in Tyre and Sidon—two ancient cities known for their terrible wickedness—they would have publicly repented and turned back to My Father. "On the judgment day, God will be more merciful to them than to you," I said to the people of Capernaum, comparing them to Tyre and Sidon.[6]

The two most sinful cities mentioned in the Bible were Sodom and Gomorrah. Both cities were destroyed for their wickedness, but they will fare better in the judgment than those people who had Me in their presence and turned from the truth. More had been revealed to them; therefore, more was required of them.

You don't have to be a theologian to know that those who have no respect for God have even less respect for other people.

There are two roads before everyone. Each road begins at a gate. The gate to heaven is narrow and the road is narrow; the gate to hell is broad and the road is wide. Still, you and everyone else get to choose the gate by which you will enter.[7]

In the next life, you will know more, especially about My Father's plans and His reasons. Everything you need to know about the place of eternal punishment has been revealed. Accept what you do know and avoid speculation that cannot be confirmed in this life. Let your mind dwell on Me and on heaven.[8]

39
Is Satan for real?

Satan is often portrayed as a cartoon character in modern society. Children's Halloween costumes feature horns, a red suit, pointed goatee, and trident-like pitchfork. The devil has appeared in newspaper comic strips, television programs, and movies. He has been reshaped, reformed, and restructured to appear as everything from a harmless imp to the headman in hell who torments those condemned to eternity there.

Is Satan the Bible's bogeyman? Is he a tool to frighten children and the gullible into good behavior? The twenty-first century has outgrown the need for a personal devil. So why do Christians still teach his existence?

 Is there really an evil being by the name of Satan who causes trouble in the world?

GOD

Satan has been around longer than humanity, and much of the trouble in the world is his doing. Not every problem or conflict should be laid at his feet since humans are able to create their own problems, but it would be wrong to dismiss Satan.

There is a tendency for humankind to blame others for mistakes and poor choices. However, there is a negative influence working in the world. He goes by different titles, but he is best known as Satan or the devil. He is real, active, and not to be underestimated.

It may seem ridiculous to believe in an entity like the devil, and it would be easy to dismiss him as a story meant to frighten children. But he is real. Jesus speaks of him as a real person.

The name Satan comes from a Hebrew word that means "adversary." It is more a title than a personal name. The name fits. In every way, Satan is My adversary, and he is yours.

Peter

My time was plagued with persecution. It started in Jerusalem and spread around most of the known world. Christians everywhere knew what it was to live in fear for their lives, to have their livelihood taken from them, to be forced from their homes, and to see their loved ones jailed or killed. They suffered at the hands of men, but I know who was behind it. I wrote to Christians who had been scattered by the persecution. I advised them to be alert and in control of themselves because the devil prowls the world looking for someone to devour.[1]

I take Satan's activity personally. One day Jesus took me aside and told me that Satan wanted to sift me like wheat.[2] I couldn't understand it then, but I would learn what that meant. After Jesus ascended to heaven, I became the first pastor of the church. My life would end on a cross—an upside-down cross. At every turn, we met with resistance, some of which I believe came from Satan.

Jesus

Satan is a tempter. He'll tempt anyone, including Me. After My baptism, I spent time alone in the wilderness. There, Satan tried to tempt Me.[3] His motive was clear: he wanted Me to depart from the path of My mission. I had been fasting forty days and was severely hungry. Satan appeared and tempted Me to use My power to turn stones into bread. I was capable of that, but I refused. He took me to the top of the temple overlooking a deep valley and encouraged Me to jump off, knowing that angels would not allow Me to fall to My death. That would be seen by people around the temple, and they would have made me a king when I had come to be a suffering Savior.

With the temptation to turn stones into bread, he used Scripture to justify his actions. He did the same when he suggested I jump. In the last temptation, Satan showed me all the cities of the world and offered to give them to Me. They weren't his to give, and I had come for a different purpose.[4]

Satan tried to take advantage of My physical weakness. He had a plan to thwart My mission, but he failed.

God

There is a misconception about Satan. He is not the opposite of Me. He is not the anti-god. He is powerful, highly intelligent, and knowledgeable, but he has limits. While I am all powerful, his power is limited; while I know all things, his knowledge, vast as it is, is limited; I am everywhere present at all times; Satan can be in only one place at a time.

Despite his limitations he is, in those areas and more, superior to humans. He moves over the earth and through the spiritual realms without hindrance. He has been working against My purposes since his fall from heaven.

At one time he lived in heaven. Satan is a fallen angel—not just any angel, but one of the highest-ranking angels. Pride brought him down. He was not satisfied with his position, and he wanted to be more and to have more. Like humans, angels have free will. They can choose to serve Me or to rebel against Me. Satan chose the latter.

When he did, he made several "I will" statements. Each shows his heart and the evil he allowed to grow in him.[5] He said he would ascend to heaven and raise his throne above the angels of God. He wanted authority that only I possess. He wanted to be the supreme angel, but he was just beginning.

He proclaimed that he wanted to supplant me. The desire for things he didn't have—including power—was at the heart of his sin. He said that he would lift himself above all of creation, something he was not capable of doing, and something he didn't deserve. He followed that with the most grievous statement, that he would make himself like God.[6] He set out to replace Me.

He enlisted other angels to help him. About a third followed him.[7] His rebellion failed, as he should have known it would, and I cast him from heaven.[8] He has been working against My plans for your redemption. He hates you because he hates Me. Since he cannot trouble Me directly, he can trouble those I love.

Hell was created for him and his followers. The day is coming when he will be bound, never to trouble the world again.

JESUS

Everything Satan does, he does to lead people astray, to distract them from the forgiveness and salvation that come through My sacrifice on the cross. Satan is the father of lies.[9] There is no truth in him.

Satan is the accuser. He has accused the most faithful of My servants.[10] If you imagine a courtroom with My Father as judge, I would be the defense attorney, and Satan would be the prosecutor.[11]

There is good news: Satan has no power over the believer. I have enabled every believer to resist him.[12] My Father has equipped you with spiritual armor to protect you.[13] The mission of the church is to turn people from darkness to the light and from Satan's power to My Father.[14]

Believers have no need to fear Satan. No matter what accusations he brings, I am there to declare you innocent.[15] He may trouble the nations, and his kingdom will try to make life difficult for everyone, but he is powerless against your faith.

Satan is real. He is powerful. He is cunning. But he can do nothing to you that you don't allow. Resist him, and know that his judgment is not far away. If you walk in the light, you will never need to fear his darkness.

40
Who really rules this earth,
God—You or Satan?

We've all seen a tug-of-war: two teams, each at the opposite end of a long rope, pulling with all their might. The goal is to drag the other side over a line. The team with the most strength, technique, and endurance wins. Is that how it is with earth? God's team facing off against Satan's team, each hoping to have the most pull?

A person could be forgiven for watching the evening news and concluding that this world is in the hands of someone other than God. Crime, war, poverty, cruelty, dishonesty, and greed are everywhere. Does this mean that God is no longer paying attention, or that some evil personality has taken over?

 Q **Every night the television news reminds me how much evil there is in the world. It's as though Satan is in charge. Is he?**

GOD

You have every right to be confused. Even a quick glance at current events and history reveals so much trouble, pain, despair, confusion, evil, and hatred that it appears as if I have no control over events. The wars, crimes, immorality, lying, violence, cheating, and hatred may make it appear that Satan is in control of everything. He's not. To understand this, let's go back to the beginning.

I created the world and the universe and declared it good,[1] and it was good. There was peace, harmony, and fellowship among Adam, Eve, and Me. During that time, there was no spiritual war, no sin, just perfection. But then sin came along.

The Serpent, another name for Satan, tempted Eve; Eve tempted Adam; and disobedience and sin were born. Humankind was cursed, and so was the earth. Everything changed. Perfection had become forever marred. I did

193

not lose control over the earth. The earth and everything in it is Mine.[2] What was lost that day was innocence.

There is a spiritual battle going on. The battle is not one of flesh and blood; it is a battle between the darkness of the world and spiritual good.[3]

This battle is over influence. As a person of free will, you can make your own decisions. Good decisions, bad decisions, and even indecisions are your prerogative. The spiritual war is over your mind, over whom you will follow. That decision affects the face of eternity.

JESUS

Your question about who rules the earth implies that there is one ruler and one ruler only. That was true and that will be true again, but since the battle is not over the physical planet but over the hearts and minds of the people who live there, the supposition needs to be changed.

The territories are the kingdom of God and the kingdom of Satan. Those who are My followers belong to the kingdom of God. That kingdom has no boundaries. Wherever there is a person with faith, there is the kingdom. Those who choose to remain outside the faith are part of Satan's kingdom by default.

You can enter the kingdom of God only by choice; but anyone can remain in Satan's kingdom simply by doing nothing at all. Think of a man standing at the shoreline with his toes at the waterline. Is he in the water? No. He must choose to take one more step. Once he does, he's no longer on dry ground.

My followers are those who have chosen to be part of the kingdom of God. Those who avoid the choice remain where they are. As people come to faith, the kingdom of God grows. Satan's goal is to keep that from happening. Since he cannot attack My Father directly, he attacks Him through you.

So in a sense Satan is *a* ruler of the world (not *the* ruler). He has influence over many people. Three times in My ministry I called him the prince of this world. The first time I was teaching about Satan's demise, saying that at the judgment he would be driven out.[4] I also referred to him by that title shortly before My betrayal and execution,[5] and again in the Upper Room when I was teaching My disciples about the coming of the Holy Spirit.[6]

Satan is the ruler, the prince, of everything outside the kingdom of God. When one becomes a believer, everything changes.

PAUL

Like our Lord, I called Satan by terms that revealed his influence on earth. I reminded the church in Ephesus that they had once been dead in their sins because they followed the course of the world, and the prince of the power of the air—Satan—had worked in them. Now, because of Christ, they were free of that bondage.[7]

I taught the troubled church in Corinth that Satan is capable of blinding the minds of those who reject belief, and I taught that he continues to work through people and societies.[8] Through my many missions, I battled Satan. He is more active with those who are threats to him. My ministry brought many to Christ, which meant he lost some of his unwitting followers. Satan stood in my way many times, keeping me from doing what I wanted.[9]

Satan was my enemy, and he continues to fight against godliness everywhere. I had a physical affliction I lived with my entire life; I called it a messenger of Satan.[10] Satan can cause believers trouble, but he cannot force his will on them.

Satan is a schemer. He has plans that he's honed over centuries.[11] He has no power over the Christian, but his kingdom is one of influence. He does not deceive through fear, but by pretending to offer something better. He and his servants often appear as angels of light.[12] Tricky as he is, we have guidance from God.

GOD

You have something available to you that Satan and his fallen angels don't. You have forgiveness and salvation. Those who have read the Bible have noticed that the forgiveness offered to you is offered only to humans, and not to any other living thing. Satan is in a hopeless situation. He sealed his fate when he rebelled. He wouldn't repent if he could, so he does his best to keep as many out of the kingdom as he can. I'm determined to keep the door of salvation open for anyone who chooses to embrace My Son, Jesus.

Satan manipulates people away from faith because he doesn't want to be alone in his rebellion. I call people to salvation. My love for you and all of humanity is so great I sent My Son to die for you.

Satan works against the church. He knows that the church has a great influence in the world, greater than his. The church is filled with people who once belonged in Satan's camp, even if they didn't know it, but they have been forgiven and empowered. The more that Christians pray and worship, the less influence Satan has in the world.

Satan will continue his activity, spreading his kingdom through deception and temptation until I end it all. That day will come. I am a God of peace, but I will crush Satan under your feet.[13] It is fitting that the victory be yours.

I remain the owner of the world, but a malevolent being who competes for your soul has invaded the world. For now, it can be said that Satan is the prince of the world, but I am the King of the universe. His time is drawing to a close.

Love comes from God, and when we love each other, it shows that we have been given new life. We are now God's children, and we know him. God is love, and anyone who doesn't love others has never known him. God showed his love for us when he sent his only Son into the world to give us life. Real love isn't our love for God, but his love for us. God sent his Son to be the sacrifice by which our sins are forgiven. Dear friends, since God loved us this much, we must love each other.

1 John 4:7–11 CEV

HUMANITY

> *The book of Genesis shows God taking a hands-on approach in creating Adam and Eve, something He didn't do with the rest of creation. God designed people to be different from the other animals.*

Are we unique?

No one knows how many animal species exist. Estimates run from three million to thirty million individual species. The variety is amazing. Spineless jellyfish share the ocean with 100-foot-long and 190-ton blue whales. Land animals are no less remarkable. However, the most unusual creature of all is the human being. Even though humans are not the strongest, the fastest, or even the longest lived, they interact with the world differently than any other creature.

Mark Twain noted, "Man is the only animal that blushes. Or needs to." There is something in that quip. Many animals can bond with their own kind or even bond with other species, like pet dogs with their owners. Humans seem to be unique.

God, some people say that we aren't that different from the world's other animals. Are they right? Are we nothing but higher-thinking animals? Or are we different?

GOD

You definitely are different! I designed you to be different. You aren't unique physiologically, because some animals are more powerful. A 90-pound chimpanzee is several times stronger than a 200-pound man. Some animals are much faster than you. Of course, the reverse is also true. But I created you to be unique in many ways. You are the result of direct, hands-on creation. I created Adam from the elements of the ground, and he became a living soul.[1] He was the result of direct creation, as was Eve.

I created everything.[2] I planned, designed, and created the world and the animal kingdom by the power of My voice alone.[3] With people, however, I took a different approach because you are special to Me.[4] I did more than call Adam and Eve into existence. I formed Adam from the ground and Eve from Adam's rib, and I breathed life into them.

Adam was a composite of oxygen, carbon, hydrogen, nitrogen, calcium, phosphorus, potassium, sulfur, sodium, magnesium, copper, zinc, water—about 70 percent water—and many other things. I used those lifeless elements to make human life. I used them to make you. With Adam, I turned inanimate material into a living, breathing, talking, thinking person.

Your creation makes you special. You have 100 trillion individual cells, 206 bones, 600 muscles, 22 internal organs, and a brain capable of holding 1,000 terabytes of information. But you needed more. You also needed a soul. I made Adam a living soul when I breathed life into him.[5] I made him in My image. He knew from the beginning that he was different from the animals I made. That's why he needed Eve, because she, too, had a soul. He needed someone who had the same kind of soul I had given him. You have a soul. Because of this, you are greater than your bones, muscles, internal organs, and brain—you have a spiritual element.

I made you, and consequently every human, in My image. You may wonder how physical humans can be made in the image of a Creator who is spirit.[6] The thing to remember is that you are more than just a body. You have an immaterial part of you that can be felt but not seen. When I made Adam, I made a physical body, but he didn't become alive until I breathed into him, making him both a physical creature and a spiritual one. You have that in common with Adam.

Every human not only *has* an immortal soul, but *is* an immortal soul. You would not be you without a soul. That immaterial part of you is what is created in My image. That is one of the key differences between humans and animals.

Jesus

You and every living thing have a type of soul. The Hebrews called this *nephesh*, and the Greeks called it *psuche*. Both mean "breath" or "spirit." The word *nephesh*, which emphasizes life, was used for both humans and animals. But the soul God placed in Adam was more than earthly life. Adam's soul lived on even after death, and your soul will too. You have an imperishable, indestructible, eternal soul. The body can die, but the soul cannot.

God

I also designed you with the ability to think in the abstract. The very fact that you can wonder about your uniqueness is proof that you are unique. High-level abstract thinking—the ability to imagine what isn't in existence—is something you can do that animals can't. I gave you this ability so you can plan buildings, design bridges, create medicines, write books, and understand the intricacies of the world around you. You wonder, you ponder, you think about things beyond your experience. That is something special.

David

And you can appreciate beauty. The ability to view something like a sunset and see more than a setting sun is unique to people. We compose poetry and music. I wrote many psalms and felt closer to heaven with each one. As king of Israel, I faced many hardships, made many mistakes, and achieved many things, but making music and writing the psalms allowed me to feel God's presence even more. Imagine life if you had no sense of beauty. It would seem empty.

God

Communication is another distinction. Some animals use a form of communication. Whales and dolphins have sophisticated means of communicating, for instance, and some monkeys and apes can communicate. A few great apes have even learned sign language. But what distinguishes you is your ability to communicate in depth, explain complex and abstract ideas, and create ideas from nothing. You are an amazing creation.

Think of the ways you can communicate. You can converse with words or write letters, books, and poetry. You can communicate volumes with just an expression. Many of the most important inventions have been related to improving communications among humans. You communicate on many levels.

Jesus

Have you considered your ability to feel and express emotion? Think of all the emotions you have felt: love, hope, joy, and contentment. Even emotions like sadness, anger, and fear have their place. You know what it feels like when someone says, "I love you." You know how to love others. These are not simple things. Managing your emotions takes a great deal of intelligence and wisdom. Emotion is not unique to humans, but the range, depth, and complexity of emotion are.

God

You have a great capacity for spirituality. Over the centuries people have gotten much of it wrong and have invented religions, but even that points to the truth of your spirituality. There is within you a longing for the spiritual. Not everyone pays attention to it, but that spiritual longing exists. You not only wonder about eternity, you long for it. I created you to be that way.

David

I wondered about our place in the universe and wrote a psalm that expressed this. I had spent part of the night on the palace roof looking at the stars. The more I looked at them, the more insignificant I felt. Soon I asked, "Why does God bother with humans? We are insignificant when compared to the vastness of creation."[7] You see, God crowned me—and you—with glory and honor.[8]

God

When I created Adam, I gave him and everyone who came after him a mandate that included the command to be fruitful and multiply.[9] Since there are seven billion people on the planet now, that part was a success. But there was more than that. I commanded him and everyone following to subdue the earth and rule over the fish, birds, and every land animal. I gave you a high level of intelligence so you could make the most and the best of the planet. That awareness is another way you are distinct from any other creature.

One of My desires is for you to use the opportunities and skills I gave you. You are the only creature who can design tools and machines, make medical instruments, transmit images and words through space, and engineer spacecraft. I designed you to achieve.

Jesus

You have a sense of morality, of right and wrong. That is a gift from God. When one animal steals food from another, it doesn't feel guilty. You are unique because such things matter to you.

42
Is being unique good or bad?

> Dictionaries give several definitions for the word unique. It can mean "sole," as in one of a kind, or it can mean "unequaled" and "unrivaled." God not only uniquely created people, but He created people to be unique. People have qualities and abilities not shared by animals, and they are more developed than any other creature.
>
> People are also the only creation that has a sense of history. George Santayana, U.S. philosopher and poet, said, "Those who cannot remember the past are condemned to repeat it."[1] History matters to people because it forces them to consider which is their measure, success or failure.

 God, since You created us to be unique, I have to ask: Have we humans lived up to our uniqueness? Have we made the right choices? Does uniqueness bring responsibility?

GOD

One of the many qualities and abilities that make you unique is the power of choice. Everybody has the power to choose his or her values and behavior. Your history has been the result of a long chain of choices. Your future will be the result of decisions you make today. Many of your choices have been well thought-out and motivated by good; other choices have been poorly considered and motivated by greed and selfishness. I am proud of what you have done with the intelligence, wisdom, and guidance I've given you. I'm also grieved by what you have done with these same gifts. What grieves Me even more is that many selfish actions have been done in My name. Choice is a remarkable power for good or bad. Choice is a blessing; it can also be a curse.

DAVID

Looking back at my life, I did a great many things right: I established Jerusalem, gathered material for the temple, and defended the people under my charge, but I also made a mess of some things—more than a mess. For instance, in the case of my attraction to Bathsheba,[2] I let lust and desire ruin my choices. I created a scenario in which Bathsheba's husband would die in battle. I did this to cover my sin. I am responsible for the death of a good and innocent man. One selfish choice led to another, which led to another. Tragedy followed. It was a hard cycle to break. A child died, and that was my fault. In some ways, my life reflected human history: great achievement marred by great failure.

GOD

David wasn't the first. That distinction will always be Adam's. He bore the burden of allowing sin to contaminate the human race.[3] Eve and he were the first to sin. Their actions affected your children and every man and woman since. Sin has exacted a terrible price from history and from the lives of individuals.

That is the price of choice. I gave you minds sophisticated enough to weigh the consequences of your actions, although you often fail to do so. But you have achieved great things just as I designed you to do. The gospel has been preached throughout the world. Heaven is filled with believers because so many people recognize their connection to Me. Some people think I sit in heaven waiting for people to make mistakes so I can judge them, but that's not the case. I love watching you succeed at the right things, and I take no joy in seeing someone fail.

I want a loving, respectful relationship with you. All the qualities that separate you from the animal kingdom are meant to draw you closer to Me. Millions of people have drawn closer, and millions more will. The story isn't over yet. There is still time for you to do good, but to do lasting good, you must return to our original, loving, respectful relationship. I never meant for you to work and live apart from Me. It goes against My design.

JESUS

The good man brings good things out of the good stored in him, and the evil man brings evil things out of the evil stored in him.[4] What you allow to live in your mind and heart will come out in action eventually. Your unique creation allows you to choose what is important and avoid what is sinful. Unlike animals, you are not driven by instinct but by your special mind and abilities—and your spiritual nature.

Being created in God's image means that you share some of His divine attributes. You know how to love, you know how to weigh decisions, you have the ability to learn facts, and you have the wisdom to know what to do with them. Choice is a powerful gift, and a great many people have made choices that have improved life, eased pain, and brought emotional relief to others.

I lived, worked, and taught among people. True, I encountered many selfish and self-centered individuals out to make their lives better no matter how much it hurt others, but I also encountered the finest minds and most sincere hearts: people willing to sacrifice everything for Me, for God, and for the world. History is marred by some of the things humanity has done; it is also filled with examples of how good people can be.

GOD

Have humans lived up to the uniqueness I gave them? Not completely, but opportunities still exist. You can make a difference in your life and the lives of those around you. You can be a solution to many problems. Because there is sin in the world, humanity will never live up to its full potential, but that doesn't mean all is lost. Your ability to do good in the world is enormous. Yes, it comes with responsibility, but isn't that a good thing?

The world is filled with both evil people and good people. History is proof of that. But I am always here to help you. You have time to live up to your unique potential, and I want to help you do that. Appreciate and use your uniqueness.

How do you do that? First and foremost, we must have relationship. I sent My Son to point the way, to teach by word, deed, and example—and to die on the cross for the sins of all humankind. Your relationship to Me through Jesus opens a different future for you.

But this is an individual choice. I do not force My way into anyone's life. I go where I've been invited. Together we make a difference in the world. Your power of choice cannot change the past, but it can help change the future.

JESUS

Because of sin, there will always be failures; because of forgiveness, you and everyone like you can start afresh. Living a good life is not easy. Sin is all around. So is temptation. I want you to know that you don't go through life alone. Let Me repeat what I told My disciples shortly before My ascension:

"Go therefore and make disciples of all the nations, baptizing them in the name of the Father and of the Son and of the Holy Spirit, teaching them to observe all things that I have commanded you; and lo, I am with you always, even to the end of the age."[5]

They did just that. They went into the world teaching everything that I taught, and they turned the world upside down. The good they did was immeasurable. Did I send out perfect people? No. They all had personal challenges, but they didn't let past failure disqualify them from future success. The apostle Paul became a follower sometime after My earthly ministry, but before his conversion, he persecuted My church. People died because of him. Many more were thrown into prison. I picked someone no one else would have chosen to be the greatest disciple of all. He preached, taught, and wrote. He penned half the New Testament. I didn't disqualify him because of his horrible past, and I won't disqualify you for your past.

It's never too late to make a difference. Learn from the past, but work for the God-led future.

GOD

Being endowed with unique abilities sets humans apart. Using those qualities in daily life sets the individual apart. Yes, being unique is good.

43
Why are there two sexes?

*Have you ever seen a one-handed clock? It seems a ridiculous con-
cept, doesn't it? But in the 1700s they were common. Clockmakers
made grandfather timepieces with just an hour hand. Perhaps it
was because life was slower-paced then and a minute wasn't considered important. Today, things are different. A one-handed clock
looks incomplete and is close to useless. Some things were designed
to work in pairs. It's true in most of the animal kingdom, and it is
certainly true with humans.*

*A clock has a minute hand, an hour hand, and often a second hand.
Their purpose is the same—to tell time—but they do so in slightly
differently ways. Together, they do what they could not do apart.*

 **Even as children we know there is a difference
between males and females; but why? Perhaps this is
a silly question, but in the beginning wasn't there
just Adam?**

GOD

There is nothing silly about the question. Often those things we take for
granted contain great but overlooked meaning. The first human was a male.
For a while he lived alone, a one-of-a-kind creation. From his flesh and
bone, I made a female. I had reasons for doing things that way, and those
reasons will help you understand why there are genders.

After his creation, Adam worked in the garden of Eden. He had responsibilities and tasks. Early on, I gave him the task of naming the animals. On
the surface, that may seem unusual. I am certainly capable of naming animals
Myself and revealing those names to Adam. But I had a goal in mind: I wanted
him to feel alone,[1] which was the best thing I could have done for him.

Day after day, Adam encountered new animals and assigned names
to them. As he did, he noticed that they came in pairs and that they dif-
fered from each other. There were male and female deer, male and female

birds, even male and female fish. It didn't take long for Adam to realize he was unique and alone. There was no companion for him. That realization brought a new set of powerful emotions to the surface. Adam was alone. I was there, of course, but humans need human companionship.

After he expressed his loneliness and need to me, I created Eve. I created Eve when Adam was ready. It was one thing for him to be exposed to initial creation and to see all that I had made; it was another thing for him to long for someone like him.

I made woman in a similar fashion to the way I made Adam: hands-on. She was a direct creation. I made Adam from the dust of the ground, but I made Eve from the flesh and bone of Adam.[2] This meant they shared a common creation, something Adam recognized from the beginning. When I showed Eve to Adam he said, "She is made from my bones and flesh. She shall be called Woman because she came out of man." The second human was created from the first. Do you remember what Adam was doing when he began to sense his emptiness? He was naming the animals. He called her *woman* to correspond to his designation as *man*. He later named her Eve.[3]

There are still places where the naming of children is an important process. In many countries, parents name children after family members. In ancient times, names carried great meaning. *Adam* means "earth," and his name refers to his creation from the dust of the ground. *Eve* means "living," and she was so named because she would become the mother of all living.

They became humanity's first couple. Ever since, men and women have left their homes to live as life-companions and to have families of their own. Physically Adam and Eve were separate flesh; emotionally and through marriage they became one flesh. From their union, children would be born—from flesh comes flesh. It has been that way from the beginning.[4]

JESUS

Men and women were designed to be together, but they were not designed to be identical. The most obvious difference is their bodies. Men are usually larger and physically stronger; women, while generally smaller, are stronger in many other ways. They need to be able to face the emotional and physical challenges of motherhood.

Men and women need each other for companionship; they also need each other to reproduce. In most of the animal kingdom, although some exceptions exist, animals reproduce without emotional involvement. Human emotions are complicated things. In an ideal relationship, the emotions of the man and the woman work together to strengthen the bond formed between them. The entrance of sin into the world has affected this and every area of life, but love, commitment, and dedication continue to be the strongest forces in a marriage.

All of creation is about relationship. When My Father created the world and the people who would populate it, He did so with the desire of establishing eternal relationships. Through all of human history He has been working to restore the relationship that was damaged long ago. As a man and a woman love each other and make sacrifices for each other, so My Father has loved you and the rest of the world. My ministry, death, and resurrection were the sacrifice that makes reconciliation possible.[5]

Did you notice that I used the word *reconciliation*? Marriage is used in the Bible to illustrate the importance and connection between Us and you. My ministry and that of the apostles is one of reconciliation.[6]

The relationship between the church and Me—and remember, the church is made of people, not buildings—is described as a marriage. The church is My bride, and I am the Groom.[7] Men are to love their wives as I loved the church and gave myself for it;[8] wives are to love and respect their husbands.[9]

There are two sexes, not only for procreation but to illustrate the need you have for Us and Our longing for you. You are not complete without a relationship to God; His love compels Him to reach out to you. I came to bring *reconciliation*, a term commonly used in connection with marriage.

Eve

Adam and I lived and worked in the garden. It was a glorious existence until I allowed myself to be deceived by the Serpent and ate of the only tree God said not to eat of. This was the only prohibition He gave, and I disobeyed it.[10] I enticed Adam to do the same thing, and he did.

That changed everything for everyone. I regret my actions. I've repented, and God has forgiven me, but the damage remains. Have you ever wondered why Adam chose to follow me in my crime? Imagine what our lives would have been like had he refused; we would have been separated.

Men and women are meant to bond for life. We lived many centuries together and endured a great deal of pain. I was the world's first mother and grandmother, but I was also the first mother to have a child die, murdered by one of my other children.[11] I could not have faced those agonies without the help of God and without the husband He gave me.

Jesus

The two sexes are meant to complement each other, but not everyone marries. That is no sin. I did not marry. To do so would have been unfair to a wife. I came to teach and to die on the cross. No woman should have to see her husband die that way. It was a Roman custom of the day to force the family to watch their loved one's crucifixion. The apostle Paul was single during his ministry, and he saw it as an advantage.[12] His ministry was difficult, and he endured many beatings and traveled much of the known world. Peter was married.[13] As important as marriage is, the unmarried are just as important and loved in God's eyes.

God

So why are there two sexes? I created two sexes for companionship, for reproduction, for encouragement, to represent the relationship of My Son to the church He established, to represent the love I have for you, and to build a thriving society.

44
What is our biggest problem?

In 1966, the singing duo of Simon and Garfunkel recorded "7 O'Clock News/Silent Night." It is a unique piece in which the musicians sang a simple version of the Christmas hymn superimposed over a simulated newscast highlighting turbulent events from August 1966. During the piece, the words to "Silent Night" grew fainter as the volume of a newscaster's words about death and war increased. That bit of musical art is a reminder of human longing for security and peace in the ongoing problems of the day.

The world is filled with many good things, but it is also troubled by compounding problems that the passing of time has not been able to end. What is the source of such trouble?

Q **The world is filled with troubles, heartaches, dangers, violence, and so much more. What is our problem?**

GOD

Philosophers, politicians, scientists, and others have wondered about the question you ask. Your news programs are packed with accounts of violence, corruption, greed, conflict, and death. From My perspective, since I see all things, humanity's reality is grim. War follows war. Even in the most advanced societies such troubles exist.

Humanity has struggled from the beginning. I created Adam and Eve in perfection, but one of their children became a murderer and killed his brother.[1] Murder came to be in one generation. Lying and deception, for some, is an expected part of human behavior. Humankind's biggest challenge, its tallest obstacle, is itself.

The shortest answer to your question is one word: *sin*. But sin is not the cause; sin is a symptom. When you are ill, you don't notice the organism causing the illness, but you do notice the symptoms it brings. Colds and flu are caused by viruses too small to see, but the aches, pains, and congestion they cause receive the attention. Sin is the result of selfishness, a deep, seldom considered problem.

Selfishness is the desire to please oneself even if it costs others pain or destroys relationships. Selfishness is evil and inappropriate because selfishness leads to sin. Something spiritually inappropriate tempts a person, and the individual responds to the temptation. That desire leads to sin.[2]

The Serpent was in the garden with Adam and Eve.[3] He was the instigator of the first human sin, and he achieved that by playing on basic human desire. Humans have certain desires given by God. The Serpent twisted those to his liking.[4] For example, humans have a desire to enjoy good things: food, drink, sex, anything that brings physical gratification. I intended those things for good, but the Serpent manipulated those desires. The need for food can become gluttony, drink can be intoxication, and the desire for sex can lead to a whole host of sins. This is what is called the "lust of the flesh."

You also want to obtain things even though you are getting what you need for survival, comfort, and provision for your family. Selfishness inflates those needs and makes you want more than what others have. Envy and jealousy are part of the selfishness that leads to sin. The striving for material possessions has ruined many people. Possessions are not the problem, but the unquenchable desire for them is. This is what is called the "lust of the eyes."

Most people have a high sense of entitlement, and they think they have a right to anything they desire. This belief is centered in selfishness. The uncontrolled desire to possess things leads to being possessed by the desire.

Adam and Eve had all anyone could want: safety, comfort, loving relationships with each other and with God, and meaningful work. Yet they failed; they succumbed to sin because the Serpent introduced selfishness.

The Serpent began with a question to Eve: "God told you that you could eat from any tree in the garden, didn't He?"[5] Eve corrected him and said, "Any tree but the one in the middle of the garden."[6] The Serpent then took the next step and played on her human nature: "You won't die. God only said that because He's afraid you'll become like Him."[7]

She looked at the forbidden fruit and saw that it looked good for food and was pleasing to her eye and that it would give her wisdom; she took it, ate it, and gave some to Adam.[8] Her sin began when she let herself get in the way of obedience. Adam was quick to follow.

JESUS

Throughout the centuries, My Father has provided guidance that would cause people to think of others first and themselves second. When you think of others first, you are less likely to get lost in selfishness. The Ten Commandments are examples of how you should treat God and treat others. The Old Testament prophets called for justice for all people. My Father listed His requirements by calling people to do justice, to love, to be kind, and to walk humbly with Him.[9]

During my ministry, I called upon people to treat others as they themselves wanted to be treated.[10] If we took all the teaching of the Bible and reduced it to a single sentence, it would be this: "Love God with all your heart, mind, and soul, and treat others the same way you want to be treated."[11] Everything hinges on this. To do those things requires love and concern that extend to others, including God.

Humankind's biggest problem is the loss of spiritual sight. Since the world is not looking out, it is reduced to looking inward. There is nothing wrong with caring for yourself and your family, but you were designed to think of others as well.

If there is only inward thinking, then your heavenly Father is cut out of your thinking and planning. That makes people ingrown, desiring to please themselves first and foremost. Sin enters when pleasing self becomes more important than pleasing God. Sin is the result, not the cause.

One of the purposes for My ministry was to open the eyes of the blind. I did so physically, but I also did so spiritually. Once you begin to see the world through spiritual eyes again, then you will understand your purpose. You learn to love God and to love others. That is life changing, which in turn is world changing.

GOD

Part of humanity's problem is that it no longer thinks that the spiritual matters, or in some cases, that it even exists. There are two types of atheists in the world: those who deny I exist and those who live as if I don't exist.

You were designed for fellowship with Me. Without that fellowship, you are incomplete and incapable of living a godly life. This is where the real problem rests. Selfishness has led to sin, which has driven us apart. The whole purpose of Jesus' ministry and sacrifice was to bridge that gap.

The world will never be free of inward, spiritless thinking, but the rift between us can be healed. The world needs to broaden its vision again to see and think about things of the soul. Once you do that, then you will be better able to live the kind of life you were designed to live.

You live in a spiritual realm as well as a physical realm. You have needs and concerns. You should think about physical life, but don't overlook the spiritual. It is not an either/or situation. To be complete, both body and soul need to be nurtured.

Think beyond yourself. Think of others and their hopes and dreams. Love your neighbor—and in the twenty-first century, everyone is your neighbor. Turn your eyes to heaven, and you will see more of earth.

Humanity's biggest problem began in the garden of Eden, but through My love and the work of My Son, that problem can be done away with—one person at a time.

45
Why does sin still plague us?

There are at least eight Old Testament words for sin and at least twelve such words in the New Testament. Twenty different words! On the one hand, sin is an easy concept to grasp; but maybe it is more complex than most realize. One thing is certain: few people would claim to be sinless. Not even the greatest prophets or apostles claimed that. Is sin part of human nature? Why is it so prevalent; so persistent?

Misbehavior that violates basic human morals is seen everywhere, and this is after thousands of years of human development. Call it sin, selfish behavior, evil, or anything else, but no one can argue the fact that it affects everyone.

 I try to be good. I never set out to sin. I live a good life. Many people do. So why do we still struggle with sin?

God

Being a Christian does not make a person sinless. It may seem like a paradox, but the more spiritually in tune a person is, the more aware he or she is of personal sin. Perhaps you've encountered someone who says that he is no longer a sinner. There is some irony in that. That statement is a sin in and of itself.[1] The Bible is My inspired word. From beginning to end, it shows that every person has sinned. It began with Adam and Eve and continues on. Every time you look at a person, you see a sinner. Pastors, priests, theologians, missionaries, the rich, the poor—everyone is a sinner. It is part of the human condition. Sin is mentioned more than five hundred times in the Bible. It's that important.

Science can treat many disorders. Think of the many diseases, such as smallpox, that have been eradicated. Once-deadly diseases can now be treated with antibiotics and antivirals. However, there is no cure for sin.

Paul

I struggled with sin my whole life. I left all I had—my career, my home, my friends—to be an apostle for Jesus. I would do it all over again even though I suffered greatly for my decisions. Nothing mattered more to me than serving Jesus and spreading His Word, even though that meant imprisonment, beatings, and becoming an outcast. I lived for Jesus; I died for Jesus. Yet despite my zeal and my constant study, I struggled with sin. My old ways of self-righteousness and legalism were my biggest problems. I grew so frustrated that I wrote of my struggle, and emotion took over. I felt like a wretched man stuck in the middle of an inner war. It seemed that no matter how hard I tried to do right, sooner or later I would do wrong.[2]

While there is no cure for sin, there is a cure for its effects—Jesus.[3]

JESUS

Sin affects everything: your desires, your thinking, and your decision-making. Some theologians coined the term *total depravity* for this, which simply means that everyone sins and that sin is universal.[4]

The fact that Paul wrestled with his old nature shows that doing right mattered to him. It is the same for you. Because you ask this question, it means that the problem of sin is important to you. That means a lot.

What you must always remember is that people of faith are not alone in this. I carried your sins to the cross so that punishment for sin would not fall on you. My sacrifice took away your sins.[5] When you do sin, I make it possible for you to be forgiven.[6]

Don't get the idea that sinning is okay because everyone does it, or that the more you sin, the more forgiveness you receive. That's upside-down thinking. Believers do not sin so they can enjoy being forgiven.[7] It is the goal of every Christian to avoid sin and to live righteously.

There is help to do that. First is the Bible. The Bible gives you the information you need to recognize sin and to avoid it.[8] The Bible defines sin, shows the problems sin creates, and makes clear the remedy for sin, which is faith in Me. It is the obligation of every Christian to avoid sin, but when you do sin, I am your Advocate with the Father.[9] I stand up for you in the same way a defense attorney speaks for his client.

The Holy Spirit is involved in your life as well. Part of His work includes convicting people about sin and leading believers on the path of right living.[10] This is a good thing. In some ways, the Holy Spirit acts like an alarm, alerting you to potential problems or letting you know when you've sinned. He convicts people of sin, not to crush their spirits or to make them feel worthless, but to prompt them to deal with the matter and to seek forgiveness.

GOD

Sin will remain a problem until Jesus comes again. Part of the Christian life is facing personal sin and sin in the world. It is the price of your free will. For you to be fully human, you must have the right to make your own decisions. I have given this world to you and the rest of humankind. Humans have performed great acts of love and sacrifice and have accomplished great things. Humans also have carried out despicable acts of selfishness and have committed horrible atrocities. Free will is a two-edged sword. It can do good, and it can do harm.

Jesus told a parable about a man who planted wheat in his fields.[11] At night, an enemy came by and sowed tares in the wheat. Tares look very much like wheat during its early growth stage. Only when the plants reach maturity can the farmer tell the difference. In the story, the farmer's workers asked if they should rip out the tares, but the owner said no. He didn't want to uproot the good plants while removing the bad.

Could I remove every sinner from the face of the planet? Yes, but that would mean removing everyone. Could I remove the unrepentant sinners? Yes, but every believer, at some time, has been unrepentant. Many of the people around you will, in the future, come to Me. Paul helped instigate the first wave of persecution against the church, but then he had a dramatic meeting with Jesus while on the road to enlarge the persecution to another city. He became a great preacher and theologian. From sinner to saint, he is proof that people do make dramatic spiritual changes.

JESUS

My followers are salt and light. I called them salt because their presence in the world acts like a preservative.[12] Imagine a world with no people of faith. The presence of believers keeps the world from completely deteriorating. During the first century, salt was very valuable. At times, Roman soldiers were paid with salt, hence the phrase "worth his salt." Believers, just by being believers, are the world's preservatives.

I also called my followers light.[13] The only way to expel darkness is by introducing light. You can't sweep darkness away; you can't drain it from a room. But even a small candle can push back darkness, and darkness is powerless to do anything about it. Your presence in the world keeps darkness at bay. It's still there, but faith keeps it from dominating the world.

Matthew, also called Levi, was a tax collector. In his day, cheating was rampant in the tax collection process. Matthew and others in his business were allowed to keep whatever they collected in excess of the taxes due. Yet Matthew left that behind to follow Me.

Sinners can become saints, given time.

*Make a joyful shout to the LORD, all you lands!
Serve the LORD with gladness; come before His
presence with singing. Know that the LORD, He
is God; it is He who has made us, and not we
ourselves; we are His people and the sheep of
His pasture. Enter into His gates with thanksgiving, and into His courts with praise. Be
thankful to Him, and bless His name. For the
LORD is good; His mercy is everlasting, and His
truth endures to all generations.*

Psalm 100 NKJV

CHRISTIAN LIVING

All people have a limited amount of time on the planet. Everyone dies. What people do before that day is their legacy—that is their mark on the world.

46
How can we experience peace?

Peace is a lovely word. We speak of peace among nations, a peaceful spirit, and being at peace. During the sixties, the peace sign could be seen everywhere, and it's making a comeback in recent years. During those years, two fingers raised to form a V came to signify peace instead of victory. Today, there is still a lot of talk about peace: world peace, personal peace, mental peace, social peace, and just plain peace and quiet.

Most people hunger for peace of one kind or another. It's not new. The most famous city in the world—Jerusalem—got its name from the Hebrew word for peace: shalom. Jerusalem *means "foundation of peace." Yet there is little peace in that city. Even back then, people longed for peace.*

 The word *peace* seems to be almost everywhere in the Bible. How can I experience peace when I'm in such turmoil?

GOD

You have emotional needs. You want to love and be loved; you want a sense of purpose; you want to know that your life matters; you want a sense of security; and you hunger for inner peace.

People know intrinsically that the world needs peace. Individuals need peace. The wealthy have discovered that money cannot bring inner peace; philosophers have learned that wise sayings will not comfort a distraught heart; busyness can, for a while, mask the discomfort of missing peace, but it cannot eradicate it.

Part of the answer to your question rests in understanding what peace is. There are different forms of peace. When countries agree to get along and to avoid international friction, they are said to be at peace. For them, peace is the absence of disputes and war. Cooperation is a type of peace, and it is a wonderful thing, but those searching for peace are not looking for cooperation among countries.

Some assume peace is a life with no turmoil, no family arguments, no stressful situations at work, no destructive inner dialogue. Freedom from such things is certainly desirable, but it isn't the peace you yearn for.

Peace is quiet in the midst of turmoil. It is facing difficulty with a confident and calm spirit. This quality is rare and difficult to maintain. Peace is so powerful that it affects the body and extends life.[1]

Personal peace is life changing, but many miss it because they do not understand its origins or its nature.

JESUS

Peace has always been a gift of God. My Father is the Author of peace. Without Him, there would be no peace. The topic was central to My ministry, and I spoke of peace many times.

Peace is a choice. You cannot control all that happens around you, but you can control your response to it; you can control how it affects you. Don't worry over anything, but lay every concern on God through prayer, and He will grant you a peace that goes beyond your ability to understand, and that peace will protect your mind and heart.[2]

Like many things in your life, peace is a choice, but there is more to it than that. It is God's desire for you to have peace. This is not a small thing. He longs for you to have inward peace in every circumstance.[3] Peace is one of His many gifts to you.

Peace is also part of My ministry. One of the best-known prophecies of My incarnation calls Me the Prince of Peace.[4] Granting peace was part of what I did during My earthly ministry. For example, an ill woman came to Me, touched My cloak, and was healed of her sickness. Since she had sneaked up on me, she was concerned that I would be angry with her. Imagine the joy she felt over her healing, and then imagine her fear at being caught. I told her to go in peace.[5] I did this many times. Being healed of long-held afflictions could not bring peace, but people's knowledge of the fact that I loved them did.

When I sent the disciples out to the towns in the region, I said, "Anytime you enter a house, say, 'Peace to this house.'"[6] That was more than just a Jewish custom. True, the people of that day greeted one another with "*Shalom*," which means "peace," but My motive was more than social compliance. I want people to have spiritual peace and peace in every earthly circumstance.

Shortly before My arrest and crucifixion, I met with My disciples in the Upper Room. It was a rented room provided for us by friends. We were there to celebrate Passover. It was My last such celebration. In a few hours, I would be left to die on the cross. I spent that time with the men who had given the last three years of their lives to My ministry. They would be the ones to start the church after My ascension.

ANDREW

My brother Peter and I were in that room. We knew there was something special going on. Jesus had been clear about His betrayal and death, but it was hard to believe. Jesus was teaching us many things. Then He told us that one of us—one of the Twelve—would betray Him. We couldn't believe that. He also told us of His departure. It was unsettling, and I didn't know what to think. Then He said, "I'm going away, but I will leave you peace, not the world's kind of peace, but My peace." He told us not to let our hearts be troubled.[7]

He knew our concern, our fear, and our uncertainty. When He said He was giving us His peace, it made all the difference. I have observed Jesus' reactions in every possible situation, from laughter to weeping over unresponsive towns. I've seen Him attacked by His critics, and not once have I seen Him without inner peace.

To think that the same peace Jesus possessed could be mine was almost too much to believe. That's the thing about this kind of peace. We choose it, but we must first choose Jesus. I learned to allow the peace of Christ to rule in my heart. That is our responsibility and privilege.[8] It isn't always easy, but it is always beneficial.

GOD

The world is chaotic. The contemporary world is filled with concerns and troubles, and it would be understandable if you thought your age is the most pressure filled ever, but every generation has lived in uncertain times. And in every generation, there are those who have found peace for their souls. Peace is like a bird nestled in the crevice of a cliff face, safe from the raging wind and driving rain. I am that shelter. The storms will rage in your life, just as they do in everyone's, but you can choose the kind of peace that comforts you in the storm.

Jesus

In that same Upper Room, I told my disciples that in Me they could have peace. In the world, they—like you—faced tribulations, but they could take courage because I have overcome the world.[9]

Peace comes from knowing that you never face any problem alone. I am with you always, even to the end of the age.[10]

The keys to peace are these: Have faith in God, who knows all things and can do all things. Study the Bible to open your mind to the moving of God in your life and to provide the wisdom you need in times of trouble. And pray. Peace comes from regular prayer. Let your concerns be known to God.

Peace is your choice, and I long to give you the peace that passes understanding.

47
Why should we pray?

Prayer is one of the most talked-about subjects, and yet it is so little understood. Some have made it a ritual, while others have all but forgotten it. In the middle are those for whom prayer is a part of daily life. But a question arises: If God knows everything, why does anyone need to pray? It seems redundant.

Surely God isn't dependent on people to let Him know their needs and the needs of the world. If He is, then how can He be omniscient—all-knowing? Is there another purpose for prayer, something everyone has overlooked?

 If You know all things, God, then don't You know what I'm going to pray for before I pray?

GOD

I know what you're going to ask before you ask it. I know what you're going to confess before you confess it.

Prayer is, at its basic level, a conversation with Me. The Bible records more than 650 prayers. Those prayers are there to show that prayer is part of every follower's life. From those examples, you can learn a great deal about prayer. Every great person of the Bible was a person of prayer who desired to know Me better and who cared about what I wanted them to do. Prayer helped make those people great. Prayer saw them through difficulties and gave them wisdom. Prayer kept us close.

Prayer isn't meant to inform Me; it is meant to bring us closer together. Remember, you are made in My image. I don't need to hear your prayers to know what's going on; I need your prayers because I want to hear your voice.

Your prayers are a joy for Me. You are My creation, the object of My love. Every time you pray, we grow closer. Whether you are seeking wisdom, facing a crushing problem, confessing sin, or offering prayers on the behalf of others, we are drawn a little closer together. Prayer often brings unexpected benefits that go well beyond your imagination.[1] You may come with one set of needs, and I may meet needs you did not know you had—and I may do so in an unexpected way.

Silas

I can attest to that. I was a frequent traveler with Paul and one of the early leaders of the church. While in the city of Philippi, Paul and I were imprisoned for our ministry. This wasn't unusual. Anytime we were jailed for the gospel, we spent our time singing hymns and praying.[2] An earthquake freed us, by not only opening the prison doors but also freeing us from our chains. I did not pray for an earthquake. Paul and I prayed, not to tell God of our troubles, but to spend those difficult hours with Him.

Prayer raises my soul to heaven. It does the same for anyone who takes the time to pray. When I was a boy, I learned all the great stories from the Scriptures. One of my favorites is the story of how the face of Moses changed when he went up the mountain to receive the Commandments from God. When he came down, Moses' face shone with the glory of God.[3] Prayer makes me feel that way. I feel God moving within my mind and heart, and it changes me. This is why I made no complaints about being arrested for doing nothing more than talking about Jesus. Prayer is what gave me strength to face the trials. Prayer will do the same for you.

Jesus

Prayer was part of My ministry. I often slipped away from the crowds so I could have time alone just to pray.[4] I knew all that My Father intended, and He knew My every need. My longing for prayer had nothing to do with the exchange of information; it had everything to do with fellowship.

Prayer humbles the heart of the one doing the praying. It is impossible for anyone who understands what prayer is to be arrogant about it. However, not everyone understands. I once pointed out a Pharisee—one of the religious leaders who opposed Me on every front—praying on a street corner. He was praying publicly to gain the attention of those around him. His prayer had nothing to do with communicating with God.[5]

Prayer is always personal. It is you in conversation with the Father. Imagine standing in His throne room laying out all that is on your heart, all your concerns and needs. Do you know what He does? He leans closer to hear every word. Of course, you cannot see the Father, but His interest is just as real as what I described.

Prayer humbles, but it also encourages. Here is another reason to pray even if the Father already knows what you're going to say: Prayer excites your soul. Silas told you how prayer made him feel. You can feel the same. Your world is filled with so many distractions that prayer is easy to overlook, but the opportunity to pray is always there.

How often should you pray? Prayer can be done at any time; it should be done without ceasing.[6] Prayer can be a lifelong dialogue with God.

One of My disciples recorded what many call the High Priestly Prayer.[7] In the Upper Room I celebrated the Last Supper and delivered My final message to the disciples before My crucifixion. I prayed for God's will to be done. I prayed for My disciples and the troubles they would face. I prayed for those who would follow in their footsteps. I prayed for many things.

Prayer helped Me during My earthly work.

GOD

While I don't need you to inform Me of your needs and desires and praise, you do need Me to inform you of My desires. It is during prayer that you learn about My direction in your life. It is during prayer that I impress upon you My desire.

Prayer is not a substitute for personal responsibility. Through your prayers, I can provide encouragement, enlightenment, and even wisdom.[8] There is even a kind of prayer without words. It happens with the help of the Holy Spirit. In times of great stress or weakness, when life is too much and you don't know what to pray for or how to form the words, the Holy Spirit intercedes for you. He searches your heart, knows your pain and doubt, and helps you express your emotions.

Prayer shouldn't be relegated just to bad times. Prayer is our conversation. Prayer in good times is just as meaningful. In good times and bad, pray.

Come to Me openly, honestly. I long to hear from you.

48
God, should we pray to You or Jesus?

A reporter asked the president of a large Protestant denomination, "Does God speak to you?" He answered, "Yes, He does." The reporter, thinking he had trapped the man of faith, then asked, "So He speaks to you in an audible voice?" The man shook his head. "Oh, no, of course not. God speaks a whole lot louder than that." That's a clever answer, but it raises the question of just how God speaks to people.

Communication with God must somehow be different from communication with other people. While most human communication is through spoken or written words, there are also other ways: body language, facial expression, and even actions. Could this mean that God communicates with us in ways other than words?

 Do You and Jesus really talk to us in prayer? If prayer is dialogue, then doesn't that mean I should hear You when I pray? And should all my prayers be directed to You?

GOD

When you pray, I listen intently. You can approach Me with the confidence that I will be attentive to you and your needs, and that I will grant anything you ask according to My will.[1] But I'm not a passive participant in the conversation. As you've noted, you need to hear from Me.

Communication is not a human invention. I created the concept and the mechanism. I made your brain in such a way that it understands the world around you, makes judgments and decisions, feels emotion, and expresses ideas and feelings to others. There are many forms of communication in creation. Ants communicate by scent, birds by song, whales and porpoise by clicks and tones, and humans by words.

Over the course of human history, I have taken the initiative to communicate with humans. Some communication is active; some is passive. By active,

I mean direct communication that is objective and unambiguous. For example, I spoke to Abraham, Moses, and many of the prophets verbally. They heard My voice. When I spoke to Moses, I spoke to him face-to-face, as a man would speak to a friend.[2] But that was unusual. Moses served Me in an unusual time.

I have spoken to others in visions. A vision is more than a dream; it is something in which the visionary participates. The great prophet Isaiah received My call through a vision. In the vision he was standing in the Holy of Holies, a place in the temple only the high priest could enter and then only once a year. He saw an image of Me and of angels. When I asked, "Who will go for us?" he begged to be chosen.[3]

I also speak through the Bible. This is known as *illumination*. Illumination is My enabling you to understand the Scriptures. By using the Bible, I can communicate to the world in written form, but I also guide and enlighten minds. The more you study My Word, the more you know about Me and My plans. I have provided specific guidelines. The Bible is My lasting communication with the world.[4]

The Holy Spirit is another way I communicate information and My desires. When Peter delivered his first sermons to hostile crowds, I gave him the words he needed.[5]

I can speak to My people audibly and have done so many times, but it is not the norm. As your God, I want to guide you, but I also want you to make careful, prayerful decisions. I've given you many freedoms, one of which is the freedom to make your own choices. I have provided the Bible to give your life direction, to point out the evils that threaten to entrap you, and to provide information about Me, Jesus, the Holy Spirit, and the history of Our work with humankind.

At times, My direction will come in quiet leading; at other times, I will be more direct.

JESUS

To whom should you pray? The confusion is understandable. After all, the Father and I are One.[6] The Holy Spirit is also part of the Trinity. This confuses some people, who wonder if it's right to pray to Me instead of the Father. In one sense, it is the same thing, but while we are One in deity, we are individual persons.

There is no sin in praying to Me. In fact, I told the disciples they could ask anything in My name and I would do it. Although praying to Me is permissible, it is not the pattern of Scripture. One of the best ways to understand such concepts is to look at how biblical people handled the situation. Remember, I taught the people the model prayer; an outline of the basic elements of prayer. The first thing I said was, "Pray this way," then I started the example prayer with the words "Our Father in heaven." I taught that prayer should be directed to My Father in heaven.[7] This was the pattern followed by all the New Testament leaders. While it is not wrong to pray to Me, it is best to direct your prayers to the Father.

When I prayed in the Upper Room, I addressed My Father six times. Prayer is based on the idea of "sonship." That is, every believer has the rights of a son. Gender doesn't matter here, only your standing. When you pray to the Father, you do so as His adopted child.[8]

Prayer is directed to the Father, but it is done in My name. Near the end of My earthly ministry, I taught this to My disciples: "So far, you haven't asked anything in My name. Do so from now on."[9] It is not unusual to hear Christians ending their prayers with "In Jesus' name." When they do so, they are being obedient to My teaching. However, those words are often said without thought. Each time you utter those words, you should be reminded that My sacrifice has made it possible for you to approach God at all. There is no requirement to end every prayer with the phrase "In Jesus' name," but it does show that prayer involves both My Father and Me. While I am mentioned in almost every prayer recorded in the New Testament, the phrase "in Jesus' name" never appears. This doesn't make it wrong; it is just something you should know.

It is easy to fall into the trap of praying to God through others. I am the only intermediary between you and God.[10] Direct your prayer to the Father, but remember that I make prayer possible.

Did you know that the Father has obligated Himself to hear the prayers of His followers? He is under no obligation to hear the prayers of those who reject Him, but He is always ready to hear from those who follow Him.[11]

JAMES

I followed Peter as pastor of the Jerusalem church. It was a difficult time for us. The early persecutions had begun. Many of the congregation endured rough treatment, many lost their jobs, and many more had to leave the city. The Romans considered us a sect of Judaism and misrepresented our beliefs. A short distance into the future, they would begin a deadly persecution. The first wave of persecution came from some of the religious leaders. It seemed that every day brought a new challenge. At times, the pressures seemed too much to bear. We never felt that God had abandoned us. We prayed daily, and it brought us great strength, wisdom, and comfort.

When the world turns against you, there is comfort in prayer. Knowing that God our Father is listening and that Jesus is speaking on our behalf made it possible for me to get through dark times. It gave me the courage to face my death. I became a martyr. Prayer and the knowledge that my words were being heard was what kept me strong during those awful times.

During my ministry, I encouraged everyone to be people of prayer. In good times and in bad, and in health and in illness, I taught people to pray for themselves and for others. In prayer, I could feel the presence of God and the strength of Jesus.

I never heard the audible voice of God, but I never missed His presence. Jesus opened the door for me, just as He has opened the door for you.

49
God, how do You want to be worshipped?

"To believe God," Martin Luther said, "is to worship God." Christians assert that worship is the key activity of every believer. Everything else a man or a woman of faith does is connected to the private and public act of worship. This is an interesting concept. If correct, then God must want or need worship.

A river that flows both directions at the same time—water from the north makes its way south, while water from the south makes its way north—is impossible. Is this the way worship works? Does it flow both directions? If worship is as important as some say, then shouldn't we know what God wants in worship?

 Worship is all about You. I get that. But what is essential? What moves You? What do You want us to do?

DAVID

The whole earth should shout for joy! Let everyone worship God with gladness; let us bring songs of joy to Him. We should know that the Lord is our God. He created us, and we belong to Him. We are like the sheep in His pasture. Let us be thankful and full of praise because our God is good and faithful and His love will last forever.[1]

I've been a warrior and I've been a king, but the one thing I loved the most was worship. I danced before the Lord,[2] and I wrote many praise songs. In my good days, and in days spent in danger and fear of my life, I continued to worship God and encourage everyone around me to do so.

The Hebrew word for *worship* means "to bow down" or "to kneel down." In one of my psalms, I wrote that we should bow down in worship and kneel before our Maker.[3] Worship was my greatest joy. It can be your greatest joy too.

GOD

Two words describe the essence of worship. As David said, the Old Testament word for *worship* means to take a humble position, such

236

as bowing or kneeling. The Jews used to pray in one of three positions: standing with hands raised and palms turned heavenward; kneeling with outstretched hands; or lying prone on the floor but hands still turned palms up. Do you see the symbolism? It shows the two-way flow in worship. The worshipper gives, and the worshipper receives.

The New Testament word for *worship* means "to kiss." Kissing expresses love, admiration, and even respect. Worship contains all those elements and more.

Your question is a joy for Me. Not many people ask what is important to Me in worship, even though worship is central to belief. If there is no worship, there is no belief.

Worship has changed over the years and varies from culture to culture. Some people worship in large buildings designed by internationally known architects; others worship in tiny structures or even in huts. Through the centuries, magnificent cathedrals have been built in My name, often for all the right reasons; but the size of the building or its grandeur isn't what moves Me. I look for something more personal.

JESUS

For many years, the temple stood as the ultimate place of worship. In My day, the temple was a magnificent structure that gleamed with gold. It was a remarkable thing to see. Many people who went there, however, went through the motions of worship but weren't truly worshipping.

I illustrated this with a story of two men. One was a religious leader who had all the outward signs of righteousness. The other was a tax collector hated by everyone around him. Both went to the temple to worship. The religious leader thanked God that he was not like "other people," by which he meant the tax collector. The tax collector had a different prayer. He asked God for mercy.[4]

Do you see the difference? One appeared religious but then went to the temple to tell God how righteous he was, while the other went to seek mercy and forgiveness. The tax collector came to worship the God who could forgive him. The key to worship is to understand, on a regular basis, the goodness and mercy of God.

God

Church buildings, while often built to honor Me, are not part of worship. I don't see structures; I see people. I see hearts. Worship began in the garden of Eden. There were no churches, just Adam, Eve, and Me. The worship was pure and unhindered. It wasn't confined to a day or a time; they worshipped constantly. Thousands of years later, I still desire that kind of worship above all.

You ask what matters to Me and what moves Me? It's simple, really. Worship is not complex. What I long for is a simple expression of love. David gave several elements that should be part of worship.

Worship is emotional. That doesn't mean chaos—uncontrolled emotion is the antithesis of what I desire. Worship causes joy, not just for you but for Me as well. Nothing brings greater joy to Me than hearing the praise and prayers of My children. I return the joy to My worshippers.

Thanksgiving is another element of worship.[5] This is important to note: I enjoy receiving thanks from My people, not because I'm an egotist in need of praise but because your giving of thanks reminds you of Me and our connection through Jesus. Giving thanks is as much a benefit to you as it is a pleasure for Me.

Praise is a form of thanksgiving, but where expressing gratitude centers on what I've done, praise centers on who I am.[6] Here is the irony in this: the one doing the praising is as blessed as I am receiving the praise. In worship, I always give back more than I receive. I grant encouragement, wisdom, knowledge, love, and respect to anyone who worships Me.

Remember the tax collector My Son mentioned? Worship can bring purposeful sorrow. In the tax collector's case, he was concerned about his sin. Jesus didn't say what that sin was. He told you only that the man was repentant. His sin is no one's business but Mine and his. The same is true for you or anyone else who worships. It brings to mind sin. Does that sound bad? Regret is not a pleasant emotion, but it can lead to positive outcomes. The tax collector repented. His openness allowed him to reconnect with Me. Repentance is part of worship, and it can be one of the most meaningful aspects of your life.[7]

It is part of My plan, My desire, that all believers gather in churches for public worship.[8] Worshipping together allows you to strengthen one another, to share the same joy and love. My Son founded only one institution—the church—and He did so for many reasons, one of which was to provide a place for corporate worship.

However, there is also private worship. Just as you can pray without ceasing, you can also be worshipful throughout the day. In fact, prayer is part of worship. Expressing your gratitude, your praise, your joy, and keeping your mind fixed on Me is worship.

What moves Me most is relationship. Worship brings us together, binds us in love, allows Me to hear from you, and meets some of your spiritual needs.

Open your heart to Me on a regular basis. Do this privately, but also do so in church. Worship outside in nature, but also worship inside with fellow believers. Worship is important to you and to every person of faith.

JESUS

My Father deserves worship just for being who He is, but He also deserves your worship because of what He's done. The best worship is simple, daily, and heartfelt.

50
How can we love the unlovable?

> *Some people are easy to love. They're kind, courteous, and seem more interested in other people than they are in themselves. They are quick to help, slow to blame, and willing listeners. Then there are the other folks: self-centered, domineering, quick with a complaint, and looking for someone to argue with. Those people are difficult to love and less fun to hug than a cactus.*
>
> *There's another group that is difficult to love—the outcasts, the people who don't fit in, the people with problems that make us uncomfortable. Loving them is easier said than done.*

 God, it's hard enough to love the lovable. Must I also love the unlovable?

GOD

Love is My strongest emotion. Love is also the strongest human emotion, but at the same time it is the most misunderstood emotion. For the majority of people, love is a feeling of affection that can come and go. Married couples considering divorce often speak of "falling out of love." By that they mean they don't feel the same way about their spouse as they once did. The wife thinks of her husband but no longer feels that inner urge to see him; the husband grows busy and forgets to nurture the love he has for his wife. Soon the love of their lives becomes unlovable, and they begin looking for affection in other places.

Frightened and unconfident people often turn on those around them. They can become cruel and hateful. They can't love others because they can't love themselves.

Then there are those people who don't fit in. Something has set them apart. It might be a tragedy that isolates them from others; it might be an illness or a handicap; or it might be simply that their behavior clashes with your own.

You are nevertheless to love these people, even though it isn't easy. Many things in the Christian life are difficult and counterintuitive to what society now expects. The world needs love, My love expressed through you.

Jesus

Society has a limited idea of what love is. For you to know the answer to your question, you must first understand the types of love available to you. English has only one word for love, but the ancient Greek in which the New Testament was written has three terms that each describe a type of love.

Eros is the root of *erotic*, and it describes physical attraction and sexual love. It isn't part of the New Testament.

Philos refers to affection and brotherly love. It was the most commonly used word for *love* in New Testament times.

Agape is the most meaningful and the most powerful. It describes love that goes beyond emotion. It is deliberate love; chosen love. It has nothing to do with physical attraction or the good feeling you might have for a friend. *Agape* is the kind of love I expressed. I used the term in a new way, so much so that it confused Peter when I appeared to him after My resurrection. I asked him, "Peter, do you love Me?"[1] And he was quick to say yes, but when he answered, he used a different word. I asked, "Peter, do you [*agapao*] Me?" he said, "Yes, Lord, I [*phileo*] You."[2]

Agape love is God-love. It originates with My Father and is poured into the world. A Christian will love with both agape and philos—with God-love and human affection. The love that is the hallmark of Christianity is not an emotion; it is a choice. While it can be felt, that love is an act done for the benefit of another even if it is unpleasant.

The most famous verse in the Bible describes My Father's agape love as the reason He sent Me into the world to die for it. That kind of sacrifice requires more than simple human love. It comes from a love that values others enough to sacrifice for them.

Love can also be direct and, if necessary, confrontational. Many things in the Bible are direct and harsh. Some people want to believe that it is a feel-good book, but its purpose is to help you and others lead a life that changes you for the better. Everything in the Bible grows from the love of My Father.

God

When Jesus was on earth, lepers lived harsh lives. They had a skin disease that required them to live away from other people. The only ones they could approach or touch were other lepers. If a person approached them, they had to move away and shout, "Unclean, unclean!" They couldn't touch members of their own families or any objects without making them ceremonially unclean. Then Jesus came along.[3]

One leper approached Him, which was a crime in his society. He said, "You can heal me if You are willing." Jesus smiled and then did something the man never expected: Jesus touched him. He didn't have to. Jesus could have healed without touching the leper's diseased skin. Yet Jesus touched him anyway.

A moment later, the man was well. He could return to a normal life. He was unlovable because of disease, but Jesus loved him anyway; not because he was pleasant but because He loved him despite his appearance.

Jesus

Once, while dining with a Pharisee, an outsider came into the house and poured expensive perfume on My feet. To understand this you need to know that washing another person's feet was considered demeaning. Yet she did this in full view of everyone in the room.[4] The religious leader saw this and questioned My willingness to let this woman anoint My feet.[5] He had two complaints. First, a woman was not allowed to touch any man other than her husband, and yet there she was, pouring perfume on My feet and wiping them with her hair. Second, she was a sinner—a prostitute. That was all he could see, but I saw a repentant woman. She was unlovable and untouchable except by the men who used her. Yet her touch honored Me. I expressed My love by forgiving her.

It might surprise you to learn that the disciples could be unlovable at times. They could be argumentative and competitive. And of course there was Judas Iscariot, the traitor. In the Upper Room, during the Passover meal, I announced that one of the disciples would betray Me. During that meal, I held out a sop to Judas.[6] A sop was bread dipped into the meat juice, and the custom of the day was for the host to offer it to an honored guest. I did that even though I knew that Judas would soon leave and lead a mob of men to arrest Me in the Garden of Gethsemane.

At that moment, no one could have been more unlovable than Judas, but I still reached out to him, even then, in those last moments before his betrayal.

GOD

Love makes a difference. Every day, I see people come to faith because someone has expressed My love to them. Someone who is unlovable today can become a new and different person because of Jesus. Christian love can change lives for eternity. Paul is an example of this. He called himself a blasphemer and a violent man.[7] Yet he changed himself and then helped change the world.

My Son died for all humanity, not just the nice, polite, and pleasant people. He died for the unpleasant, the rude, the selfish, the outcast, and those who don't fit in.

JESUS

One of the most frequent criticisms leveled by My critics was that I ate with sinners. I spent time with the sinners, the marginal, and the outcasts. I touched lepers and ministered to beggars because they needed Me. No one is beyond My love. My followers share that love with everyone they encounter, lovable or not.

You know what sort of times we live in, and so you should live properly. It is time to wake up. You know that the day when we will be saved is nearer now than when we first put our faith in the Lord. Night is almost over, and day will soon appear. We must stop behaving as people do in the dark and be ready to live in the light. So behave properly, as people do in the day. Don't go to wild parties or get drunk or be vulgar or indecent. Don't quarrel or be jealous. Let the Lord Jesus Christ be as near to you as the clothes you wear.

Romans 13:11–14 CEV

TODAY'S WORLD

God is all-knowing and all-seeing. His perspective on the world may be just what people expect—or it may surprise them.

51
God, are we confused about what You want?

Nothing is more frustrating than trying to please someone who refuses to be pleased. Some see God that way. They envision Him not as a heavenly Father but as a heavenly grouch who commands, "Thou shalt not have fun."

What does God want from His people? It can be frustrating to try to figure out exactly what God wants. Is it possible to please Him in thoughts and actions? Or are the usual efforts just too far away from His desires?

 None of us is perfect. I know that. But are we really off the mark from what You want?

GOD

Much of the world is off the mark and has little understanding of what I want. Some are afraid to ask what I want for fear that I will issue a long, impossible-to-keep list of requirements designed to crush a person's spirit and make him or her feel spiritually hopeless. I have no desire to do that. I have a simple set of wants, and each desire is as much for your benefit as it is for Mine.

People have gone astray from the beginning, and the Bible reminds us of that several times. Shepherds spend their lives caring for sheep. Sometimes one of the flock would wander off and the shepherd would go looking for the animal and bring the creature back into the fold. People are much smarter than sheep, but they, too, can wander away.[1] In fact, all of humanity has wandered from the basic principles of faith and a relationship with Me. Like an attentive shepherd, Jesus goes looking for them.[2]

What I want is not complicated. It doesn't require following a rigid set of rules. I want a relationship with you, and everything else flows from that. And when I say a relationship, I mean a family relationship.

Jesus

Rules and regulations can be burdensome. The people I ministered to in the first century lived under crushing rules. They had been taught that My Father required their obedience to the rules, but what He has always wanted is to be involved in people's lives. Early in My ministry, I encouraged people to come to Me because, unlike the religious laws of the day that weighed them down, My teaching was easy and light.[3]

I came to free people from legalism. I came so that you could have an abundant life,[4] not one weighed down by crushing rules and regulations.

Everything My Father wants comes from His love for you.[5]

Micah

I was a prophet of God seven centuries before Jesus. Then, as in all generations, people wondered what God expected of them. He spoke through me to the people, and I told them God requires us to be just in how we deal with others, that we love kindness, and that we humbly walk with Him.[6]

When I taught that truth, I was reminded it was nothing new. Moses, who lived even centuries before me, taught the same thing. He said that God required worship, love, and obedience.[7]

The years have not changed God's heart or His desires. What He wanted from the people of old, He continues to desire today.

God

I want you to have faith in My Son. Faith means believing in Him and what He has achieved. But it goes beyond simply believing that He lived and died. Faith is the result of your choosing to accept the salvation that comes from Him. It means putting your trust in Him and choosing to follow His teaching. This is what I want because it changes your present and your future.

I also want you to have forgiveness, and this comes through My Son.[8] Jesus' sacrifice made it possible for us to have a relationship. My heart's desire has always been the forgiveness of everyone. I have done everything for you to make that possible.[9]

You and all humans are as much spiritual beings as you are physical. My desire is for you to recognize your own soul, for you to live a complete existence and not merely a physical one.[10]

I want you to strive for perfection.[11] You already know that only Jesus can claim perfection, but you can aim for perfection. Aim for spiritual excellence.

I also want you to pray and to worship. I long to hear from you in prayer, and I find great pleasure in your worship.

Your happiness brings Me joy. My desire is to see your happiness.[12]

Avoid hypocrisy. In Jesus' day it was the religious leaders who inflicted their views on the people while living godless lives themselves. There must be a match between claims and actions.

Avoid legalism. Salvation comes by faith and not works. Works are important, but salvation comes by your giving your life to Jesus. Works are the outcome, not the cause of salvation. Christianity is simple. You believe in Christ, and you give yourself to Him. That changes you, and you change your life.

Be spiritually honest. This means facing yourself and your actions openly. Everyone has a spiritual need. Much good comes from being open to My leading. To acknowledge your sins may take courage, but it will open doors you have yet to imagine.

JESUS

All the things My Father just mentioned have to do with the internal spiritual life, but Micah reminded us that that doing good for others is also part of the Father's desire. Be just with others. Be only not kind, but love kindness. Make that a part of your life. Then walk humbly with God.

Notice the word *walk*. Two people walking together show trust and acceptance. Your life is like an ongoing stroll with My Father. God is with you at all times and in every place.[13]

All this can be reduced to a single answer about what God wants: He wants what is best for you.

52

What should our political role be?

Noah Webster stated, "The moral principles and precepts contained in the Scriptures ought to form the basis of all our civil constitutions and laws." Thomas Jefferson said, "The reason that Christianity is the best friend of government is because Christianity is the only religion that changes the heart." Jefferson penned the Declaration of Independence, served as the third president of the United States, governor of Virginia, member of Congress, and secretary of state, and he was minister to France. If anyone understood government, it was Thomas Jefferson.

Politics has always been a hot-button subject. Ironically, the more free the speech, the more heat surrounds political discussions. How much involvement should Christians have in government? What is the proper balance?

Q **Politics is a hot topic. Many churches and nonprofits have become involved in politics. Is that okay?**

GOD

Government is my gift to humanity.[1] At times it might seem more of a curse than a gift, but in general, governments are good things. There are 196 countries in the world, and each has its own form of government. Most governments are good and serve their people well. Some abuse their powers.

Christians live under every form of government. Some live in freedom, others under harsh suppression and persecution. In some countries, Christians take an active role in politics. Those believers need to know how fortunate they are. They have freedoms their brothers and sisters in some other countries do not.

You already know that no government is perfect. Imperfect people run governments, but that simply makes government human.

JESUS

I was born into a land run by two governments. When I was born, Herod the Great sat on the throne. He was the Jewish king, although most people did not consider him Jewish. He was evil, self-centered, and paranoid. He was the one who ordered the death of all children two years old and younger living in Bethlehem.[2] Mary and Joseph took Me and fled to Egypt. We could not return until Herod was dead. His kingdom was divided among family members after his death.

The real governmental ruler throughout My earthly life was Rome. Israel was an occupied land, run by the most powerful nation on earth. Yet as cruel as Rome was, it also kept the peace, built roads, and—at least in the first years of the church—protected My followers. It is ironic that I died on a Roman cross but that the Romans made it possible for the gospel to spread around the world so quickly. Later, Rome would persecute My followers in the most horrible ways. And yet people continued to come to faith. I ministered in an oppressed society.

Whether you live under a good government or an oppressive one, My Father is still in control.

GOD

Political involvement is a noble thing, but it must be done correctly. Christians live by a different standard than other people. Their first loyalty should be to the kingdom of God. You are a citizen of the kingdom before you are a citizen of anything else. Your loyalty belongs to Me first. When you become a Christian, you become a citizen of the kingdom. That never changes. Christians are kingdom people who think kingdom thoughts and who commit themselves to kingdom ideals.

Nevertheless, you still have to live in the world and live under your government. Being involved is part of your responsibility as a Christian and a citizen. The way you express your desires is important. When a Christian speaks for a Christian cause, the person must remember that he or she represents Jesus. There is too much angry speech and name-calling. In some circles, angry Christians have driven people away from the very person they should be leading others to—My Son.

This is not just a twenty-first-century behavior. Three times in the New Testament, Christians are encouraged to treat their government with respect. Everyone must submit to the governing authorities,[3] for several reasons. To rebel against an authority is to rebel against Me.[4]

251

Submission to government authority is, in some ways, submission to Me. Yes, there are cases when a government is so corrupt that it might require its people to transgress My laws. In those cases, your first obedience is to My teaching.

JESUS

During My ministry several enemies came to trick me. They wanted to know if it was proper for good Jews to pay tax to Caesar. I asked for a coin, and they handed over one with a picture of Caesar on it. I asked whose image was on the coin. They said Caesar's, so I told them to give to Caesar what was his and give to God what belonged to God.[5]

My Father deserves our attention, love, and worship, and He deserves our hearts and our minds. We owe Him our allegiance and dedication. What you give to your government is important but secondary to what you give to God. Give honor to whom honor is due; pay taxes to whom taxes are due.[6]

I know it is hard to understand that My Father allows governments to exist even when they are led by evil men. It is nonetheless true. Many times, even godless leaders are used to meet My Father's purposes. I stood before Pontius Pilate, who allowed My crucifixion. He asked Me questions, which I refused to answer. Frustrated, he reminded Me that he had the authority to release Me or crucify Me. I broke My silence and told him that the only authority he had over Me had been given to him by God.[7]

TITUS

On one of the missionary journeys I took with the apostle Paul, I was left behind in Crete to finish the work started there and to educate future leaders of the church. I received a letter from Paul advising me about many things. He not only gave me a list of qualifications for church elders, but also directed me to teach the people about their responsibility to government. They were to be peaceable, gentle, show consideration for everyone, and malign no one.[8]

GOD

Many politically active Christians have ignored that advice. I encourage you and believers everywhere to be a positive influence in society, to seek justice, and to look out for the helpless. Christians should speak to moral issues and to injustice. But it matters how they go about it. Peaceable methods coupled with the ability to convey important ideas in a reasoned tone is important. Legislation is not achieved by shouting. It has become commonplace to attack the person you disagree with instead of the idea or policy. More and more, people speak out of hatred and not love, out of anger and not reason. This saddens Me. In the end, damage is done to Our cause.

Should Christians try to influence policy? In those countries where people have a say in such matters, the answer is yes. But do so by bringing truth to the conversation, by showing that love motivates your actions. Elect qualified believers to office; those who are strong in the faith and knowledgeable in the affairs of government.

My Son was tried three times, once by the Jewish court, once by the high priest, and finally by the Roman governor. He did not lash out at them. He told the truth with conviction and courage. That's what you must do.

Christians involved in politics, policy, and government have a dual challenge: they must struggle to do what is best and moral for the country, and they must represent Jesus to the world. It's hard to do both, but it makes a difference.

Speak up. Be involved. Share your wisdom. Fight for justice. Do so in the strength of your convictions but as a person of peace and dignity. Take Jesus as your model, and speak the truth in love.

53
Does choice extend to abortion?

> *Isaac Bashevis Singer, the Polish-born author who won the 1978 Nobel Prize in literature, once quipped, "We have to believe in free will. We've got no choice." People have many abilities. They can think and feel, appreciate beauty, love and hate, reason, communicate, and design complicated machines and electronics.*
>
> *People make scores of choices every day. Most are mundane, such as deciding what time to get out of bed or what to have for lunch. However, there are also choices to be made about very important matters, some of them life changing. Are all choices the same as far as God is concerned? Does God care about the choices people make?*

 Q **Since You created me as an individual with the power of choice, am I free to make whatever choices I want?**

GOD

Choice is your most powerful ability. For you to be complete, you must be able to make decisions about your life. If you had no choice, you wouldn't be truly human. I created you to make choices about your life. This shows My love for you and My trust.

Choice is based in the idea of free will. I made you a free moral agent. You can choose the good; you can also choose the bad. There is the problem. You may make whatever choices you want, but every decision has a price.

I did more than give you the ability to make personal choices. I equipped you and all of humankind with a reasoning mind and a moral consciousness. It wasn't enough to free you to make choices; I also wanted to give you the tools necessary to make good and proper choices. The Bible is a guide to help you choose what is good over what is bad. The Holy Spirit also is a guide for you. He reminds you what is sinful and what is godly.[1]

All this came with a price. By giving you free will, I gave you the option of not only accepting Me but also rejecting Me. You are free to reject sin or embrace it. Without such freedom, you would be something less than you are now.

You are free to make whatever choices you please, but keep in mind that your choices affect not only you but those around you. I am here to guide you, to encourage you, and to make your path easier to determine.[2]

JESUS

I visited My friends Mary, Martha, and Lazarus at their Bethany home. Many people came to hear My teaching. Martha felt compelled to be the perfect host, and she worked herself into a frenzy. Her sister, Mary, chose to sit at My feet and learn. When Martha complained that her sister wasn't helping and asked Me to order her to help, I refused. I told Martha that she had chosen worry and trouble, while Mary had chosen a better course.[3]

Martha's choice was hurting her and damaging her relationship with her sister. By comparison, however, that choice was minor. But choice extends to bigger issues. If you're free to make choices, then can you choose something like abortion? Yes, you can, but should you? Having the ability to make choices comes with tremendous responsibility. Choice can be and is abused.

JOSHUA

I served as Moses' right-hand man. I was his military leader. After his death, it became my responsibility to lead the people. Moses led them from Egypt to the borders of the promised land. He could have lived a life of ease in Pharaoh's palace, but he chose instead to identify with his people.[4] Moses made his choices, and many benefited, but it was time for the people to make their choice. Would they follow God's command to enter the promised land?

I stood before them and asked the question: "Whom will you follow, the pagan gods you left behind? I and my family choose to follow the Lord."[5] The choice was theirs, but there was only one right choice.

GOD

I want you to make good choices, right choices, but most of all I want you to make spiritual choices.[6] There are choices that seem right but end badly.[7] The freedom of choice can be a curse if you do not have a spiritual foundation. One thing humans are very good at is rationalizing. That's why I established a moral code called the Ten Commandments. Those statements can keep you on the right track in your decision-making.

Let me share some guidelines to help you in your decision-making. When facing an important, life-changing decision, ask yourself, *Will my decision move me away from God? Will my decision damage our relationship? Will it put distance between us that wasn't there before?* Keep Me involved in your choices.

Also ask yourself this: *Is there anything in the Bible that prohibits this choice?* Besides the Ten Commandments, the Bible provides other guidelines to what is and isn't appropriate for proper spiritual living. Jesus' teaching gives you everything you need to know about how to live a godly life. The rest of the New Testament builds on that.

Will your decision hurt you? The number of people who choose actions that hurt themselves might surprise you. You may ask, Does abortion hurt the one undergoing the procedure? Yes, it does. In many cases, that decision follows the parents and haunts them for the rest of their lives.

Does your choice hurt others? A choice to be greedy, or hurtful, or to steal, or any of a hundred other misbehaviors hurts more than the decision-maker. A drunk who decides to drive home can cause an accident. His decision can destroy lives, something he or she cannot undo. Does abortion hurt others? Yes. It takes the life of the unborn. I know every person even before they are born.[8] I see them in the womb.[9] The choice of an abortion not only ends a life of the child but damages family and friends.

Does the choice stem from greed or love? It is easy to choose and justify the greedy path. Love provides a different motivation for the choices you make. Choices based on love are not always easier, but they are always more gratifying.

Ask yourself who will pay the price for your choice. You do not live in isolation. What you say does and will impact people around you and sometimes linger for years or even generations.

Does your choice support or break the golden rule? My Son taught that you should treat others the same way you wish to be treated.[10] When you make a choice, consider whether it is beneficial for others as well as you. If someone near you made the same decision, would you be pleased or bothered?

Does your decision break any of the Ten Commandments? The Ten Commandments still outline My idea of proper and godly living. Does your choice cause you to consider other things more valuable than your relationship with Me? Have you made an idol out of money, or success, or fame, or anything else? Does your choice put distance between you and your neighbors?

JESUS

Your first choice is a spiritual one. Joshua asked the people of his day whom they would serve. The question is valid today. Whom will you serve? The answer to that will make a difference in all your future decisions.

You are free to make any choice you wish, but every choice has a consequence. Freedom to choose is not freedom to do wrong. Freedom to choose gives you the opportunity to show your love and commitment to God, just as He chooses to show His love and commitment to you.

54
God, do You love or hate homosexuals?

Few things have generated as much animosity and anger as the topic of homosexuality, and much of the heat has come from Christians. It is easy to see the chasm widening. Some have held up signs that say God hates homosexuals. Is that true? Does God really despise homosexuals?

The Bible speaks about homosexuality. That can't be denied. Some estimate that as many as 17 percent of males are homosexuals and about half that percentage are for women. The percentages may seem small, but the number of people is remarkable. Just what does God think of homosexuals and the Christian reaction to them?

 Q **Every day I hear more and more about homosexuality, and I know the Bible prohibits it. Why do You hate homosexuals?**

GOD

I do not hate homosexuals. I do hate sin, all sin. Here is where the contemporary problem exists. Many have responded to homosexuals with hatred. That includes some in the church. Hatred is not an option.

My Son made it clear that judgment leads to judgment. That is not to say you are to walk around blind to the sin that surrounds you; it means you must always remember that you, too, have sins that need to be addressed. The goal is not to hate, but to change yourself and the world with the love of Christ.

My goal has always been the salvation and forgiveness of everyone. If I can forgive those like Paul who persecuted the church, then I can forgive a homosexual or an immoral heterosexual. The gospel message is one of love expressed to all people;[1] and not just some people, but all people.

I am not saying I approve of homosexual behavior. I've made it clear in the Bible that I don't, but I don't single out the homosexual for greater punishment than the heterosexual fornicator or adulterer.

JESUS

Some have noticed that I never mentioned homosexual behavior during My time on earth. My audience was limited to Jews and a few Romans. In the Jewish culture, homosexuality was not tolerated. When the church spread into the world and entered countries with pagan backgrounds, things changed. That's why the topic comes up only in the letters of Paul. However, My silence on the topic is not the same as condoning the behavior.

I did deal with sexual sin. In one case, I had returned from the Mount of Olives to the temple courts. A group of religious leaders brought to me a woman caught in adultery.[2] They did this in full view of everyone rather than privately. They wanted an audience. I noticed they didn't bring the man with whom she was accused of comitting adultery. This was not the first time they tried to trap me. Under the law of Moses, the poor woman could be stoned to death. I suggested that any one of them without sin could cast the first stone.[3] Instead of throwing stones, they left, one by one. But that still left me with the adulterous woman. There was no one left to condemn her. I told her I wouldn't condemn her either and that she should go and sin no more.

That last part is what mattered. Yes, she was an adulterer, but she could change. She could be forgiven. She could begin a new life. The same is true for anyone guilty of sexual sin, including the homosexual. I didn't praise the woman for her adultery, and I don't praise the homosexual for his or her practices. The same command applies to all: Go and sin no more.

I am interested in repentance, not retribution. As long as there is life, there is hope. There is more joy in heaven over one sinner who repents than over ninety-nine righteous people who don't need repentance.[4]

Sexual sin is not always physical. It can occur in the mind. The example I gave was a man who looked at a woman with lust; he had committed adultery with her in his heart.[5] This sin is true for heterosexuals and homosexuals.

GOD

My design was heterosexual.[6] One man married to one woman in a lifetime commitment of mutual love and support. I created sex as a means of procreation and enjoyment between husband and wife. Humankind has drifted from that design and undermined it with a wide range of sexual misconduct. This behavior has at a minimum harmed many, destroyed lives, and broken homes. I want you to know that all forms of sexual sin have done this and not just homosexual behavior.

Everyone has sexual leanings. Even the great King David surrendered to sexual temptation, an act that forever changed his life and kingdom. I made you sexual beings, but the person's leaning isn't sin, it's the action. There is a difference between desire and action. Sex is a powerful force in human life. Keeping sex pure is a choice. Departing from My design is also a choice. There is a difference between homosexual desire and homosexual behavior.

Paul

One verse that is cited frequently on this matter states that no homosexual shall inherit the kingdom of God.[7] The statement is found in my letter to the church at Corinth. Corinth was an immoral city filled with pagan temple prostitutes and so much promiscuity that the name of the city became a derogatory term. To say that someone was acting like a Corinthian was the most degrading of insults.

I started a church there, and that meant reaching out to the kind of people I never met in Jerusalem. When I wrote to the Corinthian church, I knew the congregation was filled with sexually immoral people, idolaters, adulterers, male prostitutes, homosexuals, thieves, greedy people, drunkards, revilers, and extortionists. While in the city, I worked with these people. I reminded them that those who continued such practices would miss the kingdom of God.

But I added a simple phrase: "Such were many of you." In that church there were former idolaters, adulterers, thieves, and homosexuals who now were part of God's family. Jesus had changed them.[8] They were different because of Jesus. Some had to battle urges and old lifestyle habits, but they succeeded. God never allows anyone to be tempted beyond his or her strength to resist.[9]

God

What is missed all too often is what Paul just explained: the church is filled with used-to-be's. The first-century church firmly taught that homo-sexuality was contrary to My design and My will, but at the same time, the church was open and supportive of anyone who wanted to change, and that included not just the homosexuals but anyone with any sin problem, from greed to drunkenness.

I never meant for the church to be a country club. I always meant it to be a spiritual hospital, a place filled not with perfect people, but with people on the mend from sin.

I want the church to reach out in love to see the person behind the sin and not just the sin. My Son called to task those who pointed out the sins of others while they had larger sins of their own to deal with.[10] Such behavior comes from hypocrisy, not love. More can be done through love than through hatred.

No one has been shouted into heaven, but millions have been led there by those showing My love for all people. That is the work I want My church to be doing. No good comes from pointing an accusing finger, but great good can be done by using that same finger to point the way to Jesus.

I want people to come to Me in love, not terror; to seek Me because they long for spiritual healing, not because they fear judgment. I know everyone's past, but My mind is fixed on their future—on your future.

55
Is taking care of our planet spiritual or political?

> *The great church Reformer Martin Luther said, "The power of God is present at all places, even in the tiniest leaf. God is currently and personally present in the wilderness, in the garden, and in the field." The beauty of nature moves people.*
>
> *A closer look reveals something else: human presence is altering our world. Over the past few decades, concern has moved from the health effects of smog to environmental pollution and now to global warming. As with many other issues, people take sides. Global warming is one such divisive topic—not its reality, but its cause. Is it natural or caused by humans? Is earth stewardship nothing more than a political football or is it part of godly thinking?*

 Everywhere I turn I hear someone talking about the environment. Is taking care of the planet part of a Christian's duty?

God

Earth is your home. I designed it to support life in general and human life specifically. Taking care of your home is important, not only because it affects the lives of more than six billion people but because it reveals your thinking about My creation.

Earth is yours to live upon, but it does not belong to you. Humans are possessive and often think they can own things. No one can truly own anything. Think of something you believe is yours: a house, a car, a television, or even something as small as a book. You might be tempted to say, "I spent good money on this, and now it belongs to me." But does it? One hundred years from now, everything you "own" will belong to someone else. What isn't tossed away in future years as outdated or useless will be held in the name of someone else. Property may be passed down to family members for generations, but your personal ownership ends at death.

On the other hand, I truly own everything. Every cubic inch of space is Mine. That means the earth and the heavens and everything in them are Mine.[1] I have given them to you for your use and pleasure, but their ownership remains Mine.

That is important because, in one sense, you live your life as a renter, not an owner. People came before you; people will follow you. Humanity has a responsibility to future generations. The next generation will live in whatever you leave behind.

An erroneous idea resurfaces from time to time: The planet is so big, humanity cannot dramatically change it. It has. I gave Adam and Eve a directive:[2]

First, they were to be fruitful. I wanted them to make use of the garden I gave them and draw from it the things they needed. This they did, and humanity is still doing so. I approve of this.

Second, I told them to multiply. I did not design the earth for two people. I designed it to support billions. This, too, humanity has succeeded in. Two became several; several became hundreds; hundreds grew to billions. This is also a good thing, although misuse of resources, war, and political fighting have allowed many to be pushed to the side and left to live in poverty. This is unacceptable, and Christians need to address the problem. Many have, but more needs to be done.

I also told humanity's first couple to subdue the earth—not abuse it but subdue it, make use of its resources, and enjoy its beauty and pleasures. Humans are My ultimate creation and the ones for whom I made earth, but the planet is home to more than one million species of animals and insects, and that's just what is known to your scientists. Hundreds of thousands more species exist. I created plants for food to nourish animals and humans.[3]

When I was finished creating the earth, I pronounced everything good.[4] I'm not sure I can pronounce it good today. Seven hundred man-made toxins can be found in human tissue. Those toxins come from the air you breathe, the water you drink, the food you eat, and the medications you take. Humans can and do have an impact on the environment.

This is not a political issue—it is a stewardship issue. *Stewardship* is the

263

biblical term for management. A steward was someone who managed the affairs of another. A steward might oversee money, property, a large home, a farm, or even a business. To be called "a good steward" was a high honor. When I created Adam and Eve, I also created the garden of Eden and made them stewards over it. As humanity grew in numbers, it also took on more land and became stewards of that too. The earth needs good stewardship, and you are one of My stewards.

The way you treat My creation reflects the way you think of Me.[5] The world around you is designed to reveal My existence and My presence. By studying creation, you can learn a great deal about Me.[6] It was My intent to place you in a world filled with such wonder that the world would convince you of My existence and love. Such messages are being overlooked or explained away. To lose an appreciation for the world is to lose appreciation for Me.

Christians are not meant to live in isolation. The world cannot be changed by withdrawing from it. My followers are meant to make a difference according to their skills and abilities. The loudest and clearest sermon preached is the way you live your life. When people see what matters to you, they are drawn to genuine belief. If the world sees that the children of the Creator have no interest in preserving creation, then they will assume that things do not matter to Me or to the church. Everything matters.

No one holds in high regard a renter who destroys the home he rents. The earth is your home and the home of all humanity. It is all you have.

I am pleased that many have chosen to speak out about the environment, not because some political party says they should but because they want to take responsibility for where they live. Christians should lead in this effort. There are many reasons to fight for the health of the planet, but people of faith do so for reasons just as important: they know to whom the world belongs, and they know that showing concern for the environment shows Christian love for those living and those to come in future generations.

Taking care of the environment is part of the Christian duty. The first command I gave was for Adam and Eve to take care of the place I had given them. Humanity has outgrown the garden of Eden, but the world is still My gift. I want you to enjoy all I've given, but I also want people everywhere to show respect for the gift.

You can do this by first remembering that all you see is Mine. A person can claim ownership for only a short time. I own everything but give it to you for your benefit. I've created the grass that feeds the cattle you eat, the plants that produce food and energy, and so much more.[7] Your appreciation of that is important.

I uniquely designed the earth for you. Any closer to the sun, and life could not exist. The same would be true if the planet were any farther away. The atmosphere provides oxygen, rain, and protection against harmful rays from the sun. Everything you see—wind, soil, fresh water, the abundance of animal life—is part of a system designed to support you. Everything from the earth's magnetic field to the presence of the moon makes your existence possible. This did not happen by accident. It happened because I made it that way.

Do you value this gift? If so, then you know why caring for the environment is a spiritual issue that goes back to the garden of Eden. For the person of faith, politics has nothing to do with being a good steward of My creation. Caring about what you leave behind for the generations to come is the driving factor.

NOTES

Chapter 1: God, who are You? What are You?

1. J. I. Packer, *Knowing God* (Downers Grove, IL: InterVarsity Press, 1979), 29.
2. No one is like you, O LORD; you are great, and your name is mighty in power. (Jeremiah 10:6 NIV)
3. God created man in His own image, in the image of God He created him; male and female He created them. (Genesis 1:27 NASB)
4. To the King eternal, immortal, invisible, to God who alone is wise, be honor and glory forever and ever. Amen. (1 Timothy 1:17 NKJV)
5. Did any of you measure the ocean by yourself or stretch out the sky with your own hands? Did you put the soil of the earth in a bucket or weigh the hills and mountains on balance scales? Has anyone told the LORD what he must do or given him advice? Did the LORD ask anyone to teach him wisdom and justice? Who gave him knowledge and understanding? (Isaiah 40:12–14 CEV)
6. One called to another and said: "Holy, holy, holy is the LORD of hosts; the whole earth is full of his glory." (Isaiah 6:2 NRSV)
7. John 4:24 NASB. The account begins with verse 7 of chapter 4.
8. Amos 9:3.
9. John 6:46 NIV.
10. Jeremiah 29:13 NASB.

Chapter 2: God, how can we believe that You created us?

1. God said, "Now we will make humans, and they will be like us." (Genesis 1:26 CEV)
2. You formed my inward parts; You covered me in my mother's womb. I will praise You, for I am fearfully and wonderfully made. (Psalm 139:13–14 NJKV)
3. The heavens keep telling the wonders of God, and the skies declare what he has done. (Psalm 19:1 CEV)
4. Romans 1:25 NIV.
5. 1 Kings 4:29–31 NASB.
6. Ecclesiastes 12:1 NKJV.
7. Psalm 139:14 NRSV.
8. Know that the LORD is God. It is he who made us, and we are his; we are his people, the sheep of his pasture. (Psalm 100:3 NIV)

Chapter 3: God, who are we to You?

1. Job 7:17 NIV.

2. Psalm 8:4 NASB.

3. Psalm 144:3 CEV.

4. Hebrews 2:6–8 NASB.

5. All things have been committed to me by my Father. No one knows who the Son is except the Father, and no one knows who the Father is except the Son and those to whom the Son chooses to reveal him. (Luke 10:22 NIV)

6. God so loved the world that he gave his only Son, so that everyone who believes in him may not perish but may have eternal life. Indeed, God did not send the Son into the world to condemn the world, but in order that the world might be saved through him. (John 3:16–17 NRSV)

7. Jeremiah 31:3 NLT.

8. Jeremiah 29:11 NIV.

9. It happened just as the Scriptures say: "Abraham believed God, and God counted him as righteous because of his faith." He was even called the friend of God. (James 2:23 NLT)

10. John 15:14–15 NIV.

11. Matthew 6:9 NKJV.

12. In Antioch the Lord's followers were first called Christians. (Acts 11:26 CEV)

13. To all who are beloved of God in Rome, called as saints. (Romans 1:7 NASB)

Chapter 4: God, what does it mean that You are love?

1. 1 John 4:7–8 NLT.

2. I have loved you, my people, with an everlasting love. With unfailing love I have drawn you to myself. (Jeremiah 31:3 NLT)

3. I am the good shepherd. The good shepherd lays down his life for the sheep. The hired hand is not the shepherd who owns the sheep. So when he sees the wolf coming, he abandons the sheep and runs away. Then the wolf attacks the flock and scatters it. The man runs away because he is a hired hand and cares nothing for the sheep. (John 10:11–13 NIV)

4. I am the good shepherd. I know My own sheep, and they know Me, as the Father knows Me, and I know the Father. I lay down My life for the sheep. (John 10:14–15 HCSB)

5. John 15:13 NKJV.

6. This is real love—not that we loved God, but that he loved us and sent his Son as a sacrifice to take away our sins. (1 John 4:10 NLT)

7. Job 19:27 CEV.

8. I am convinced that neither death nor life, neither angels nor demons, neither the present nor the future, nor any powers, neither height nor depth, nor anything else in all creation, will be able to separate us from the love of God that is in Christ Jesus our Lord. (Romans 8:38–39 NIV)

Chapter 5: God, is Jesus really Your Son?

1. He who has seen Me has seen the Father. (John 14:9 NASB)

2. I tell you the truth, a time is coming and has now come when the dead will hear the voice of the Son of God and those who hear will live. For as the Father has life in himself, so he has granted the Son to have life in himself. And he has given him authority to judge because he is the Son of Man. (John 5:25–27 NIV)

3. John 1:1–2 NKJV.

4. In the sixth month the angel Gabriel was sent by God to a city of Galilee named Nazareth, to a virgin betrothed to a man whose name was Joseph, of the house of David. The virgin's name was Mary. And having come in, the angel said to her, "Rejoice, highly favored one, the Lord is with you; blessed are you among women!" But when she saw him, she was troubled at his saying, and considered what manner of greeting this was. Then the angel said to her, "Do not be afraid, Mary, for you have found favor with God. And behold, you will conceive in your womb and bring forth a Son, and shall call His name JESUS. He will be great, and will be called the Son of the Highest; and the Lord God will give Him the throne of His father David. And He will reign over the house of Jacob forever, and of His kingdom there will be no end." Then Mary said to the angel, "How can this be, since I do not know a man?" And the angel answered and said to her, "The Holy Spirit will come upon you, and the power of the Highest will overshadow you; therefore, also, that Holy One who is to be born will be called the Son of God. Now indeed, Elizabeth your relative has also conceived a son in her old age; and this is now the sixth month for her who was called barren. For with God nothing will be impossible." Then Mary said, "Behold the maidservant of the Lord! Let it be to me according to your word." And the angel departed from her. (Luke 1:26–38 NKJV)

5. An angel of the Lord appeared to him in a dream. "Joseph, son of David," the angel said, "do not be afraid to take Mary as your wife. For the child within her was conceived by the Holy Spirit. And she will have a son, and you are to name him Jesus, for he will save his people from their sins." (Matthew 1:20–21 NLT)

6. John 1:15 NKJV.

7. John 8:58 NIV.

8. John 1:14 NKJV.

9. When the time was right, God sent his Son, and a woman gave birth to him. His Son obeyed the Law, so he could set us free from the Law, and we could become God's children. (Galatians 4:4–5 NRSV)

10. See Matthew 12:50 and John 8:19 as examples.

11. The account can be found in Matthew chapter 4 and Luke chapter 4.

12. Hebrews 1:6 NLT.

13. The Father wants all people to honor the Son as much as they honor him. When anyone refuses to honor the Son, that is the same as refusing to honor the Father who sent him. (John 5:23 NRSV)

14. 1 John 4:9 NRSV.

15. John 11:27 NASB.
16. Matthew 16:16 NIV.

Chapter 6: How do we know the Bible is accurate?

1. The days are surely coming, says the LORD, when I will make a new covenant with the house of Israel and the house of Judah. It will not be like the covenant that I made with their ancestors when I took them by the hand to bring them out of the land of Egypt—a covenant that they broke, though I was their husband, says the LORD. But this is the covenant that I will make with the house of Israel after those days, says the LORD: I will put my law within them, and I will write it on their hearts; and I will be their God, and they shall be my people. No longer shall they teach one another, or say to each other, "Know the LORD," for they shall all know me, from the least of them to the greatest, says the LORD; for I will forgive their iniquity, and remember their sin no more. (Jeremiah 31:31–34 NRSV)

2. When you come, bring the cloak that I left with Carpus at Troas, and my scrolls, especially the parchments. (2 Timothy 4:13 NIV)

3. 2 Timothy 3:16–17 NIV.

4. Above all, you must understand that no prophecy of Scripture came about by the prophet's own interpretation. For prophecy never had its origin in the will of man, but men spoke from God as they were carried along by the Holy Spirit. (2 Peter 1:20–21 NIV)

5. See Exodus 4:22; 2 Samuel 7:5; Isaiah 43:14 as examples.

6. Exodus 4:12 NKJV.

7. 2 Samuel 23:2 NLT.

8. Jeremiah 1:9 NIV.

9. All the rivers flow into the sea, yet the sea is not full. To the place where the rivers flow, there they flow again. (Ecclesiastes 1:7 NASB)

10. Isaiah 40:22 NASB.

11. Job 26:7 NLT.

12. As the stars of the sky cannot be counted and the sand on the seashore cannot be measured, so I will multiply the descendants of my servant David and the Levites who minister before me. (Jeremiah 33:22 NLT)

13. Micah 5:2 NLT.

14. The Lord himself will give you a sign: The virgin will be with child and will give birth to a son, and will call him Immanuel. (Isaiah 7:14 NIV)

15. Psalm 22.

16. See Isaiah 53:3–12.

17. Hebrews 4:12 NASB.

Chapter 7: How do we know if we understand the Bible correctly?

1. Long ago God spoke many times and in many ways to our ancestors through the prophets. (Hebrews 1:1 NLT)

2.   No one knows how many words are in the English language. The number changes yearly as new words are added and some become obsolete. Even defining *word* is difficult. The word *dog* can be a noun referring to some species of canine, but it can also be a verb meaning to follow or annoy someone.

3.   Those prophets were moved by the Holy Spirit, and they spoke from God. (2 Peter 1:21 NLT)

4.   Ephesians 1:17–18 CEV.

5.   John 5:39 NKJV.

6.   Jesus said to them, "Have you come out with swords and clubs, as though I were a criminal, to capture Me? Every day I was among you, teaching in the temple complex, and you didn't arrest Me. But the Scriptures must be fulfilled." Then they all deserted Him and ran away. (Mark 14:48–50 HCSB); Jesus said to them, "Have you never read in the Scriptures: The stone that the builders rejected has become the cornerstone. This came from the Lord and is wonderful in our eyes?" (Matthew 21:42 HCSB)

7.   Beginning with Moses and all the prophets, he interpreted to them the things about himself in all the scriptures. (Luke 24:27 NRSV)

8.   Psalm 36:7 NIV.

9.   Our LORD, you are the one who gives me strength and protects me like a fortress when I am in trouble. (Jeremiah 16:19 CEV)

Chapter 8: God, why were You different in the Old Testament?

1.   Psalm 103:13 CEV.

2.   The LORD has appeared of old to me, saying: "Yes, I have loved you with an everlasting love; therefore with lovingkindness I have drawn you." (Jeremiah 31:3 NKJV)

3.   See Romans 1:18; 2 Thessalonians 1:6–9; and Revelation 6:15–17 as examples.

4.   Read the entire story in the small Old Testament book of Jonah.

5.   Jonah 3:4 NRSV.

6.   "Nineveh has more than a hundred and twenty thousand people who cannot tell their right hand from their left, and many cattle as well. Should I not be concerned about that great city?" (Jonah 4:11 NIV)

7.   God is not a man, that he should lie, nor a son of man, that he should change his mind. Does he speak and then not act? Does he promise and not fulfill? (Numbers 23:19 NIV) See also 1 Samuel 15:29.

8.   Jesus Christ is the same yesterday and today and forever. (Hebrews 13:8 NIV)

9.   Such knowledge is too wonderful for me; it is high, I cannot attain it. (Psalm 139:6 NKJV)

10.   Galatians 3:24 NKJV.

11.   The Law was given by Moses, but Jesus Christ brought us undeserved kindness and truth. (John 1:17 CEV)

12. Do not think that I came to abolish the Law or the Prophets; I did not come to abolish but to fulfill. (Matthew 5:17 NASB)

Chapter 9: Why weren't all early writings included in the Bible?

1. J. I. Packer, *God Speaks to Man* (Philadelphia: Westminster Press, 1965), 81.

2. John Baillie, *The Idea of Revelation in Recent Thought* (New York: Columbia University Press, 1956), 24.

3. When Moses had finished writing this entire body of instruction in a book, he gave this command to the Levites who carried the Ark of the LORD's Covenant: "Take this Book of Instruction and place it beside the Ark of the Covenant of the LORD your God, so it may remain there as a witness against the people of Israel." (Deuteronomy 31:24–26 NLT)

4. Deuteronomy 17:18–19 NASB.

5. Joshua 1:8 NRSV.

6. Deuteronomy 18:18 NRSV.

7. Deuteronomy 18:21–22 NLT.

8. When Jesus had called the Twelve together, he gave them power and authority to drive out all demons and to cure diseases, and he sent them out to preach the kingdom of God and to heal the sick. (Luke 9:1–2 NIV)

9. The signs of a true apostle were performed among you with utmost patience, signs and wonders and mighty works. (2 Corinthians 12:12 NRSV)

10. Hebrews 4:12 NLT.

11. 1 Thessalonians 2:13 NKJV.

Chapter 10: Is nature the sixty-seventh book of the Bible?

1. Romans 1:19–20 NKJV.

2. C. S. Lewis, *Surprised by Joy* (London: G. Bles, 1955), 266.

3. C. S. Lewis, *Mere Christianity* (New York: Macmillan, 1943), 17.

4. William Paley, *Natural Theology* (Boston: Gould and Lincoln, 1860), 5.

5. Psalm 111:2 NIV.

6. By faith we understand that the worlds were framed by the word of God, so that the things which are seen were not made of things which are visible. (Hebrews 11:3 NKJV)

7. John 21:25 NIV.

8. Now all we can see of God is like a cloudy picture in a mirror. Later we will see him face to face. We don't know everything, but then we will, just as God completely understands us. (1 Corinthians 13:12 CEV)

9. Psalm 19:1–4 CEV.

Chapter 11: Are we living in the end times now?

1.   Dear friends, don't forget that for the Lord one day is the same as a thousand years, and a thousand years is the same as one day. (2 Peter 3:8 CEV).
2.   Concerning that day and hour no one knows—neither the angels in heaven, nor the Son—except the Father only. (Matthew 24:36 HCSB)
3.   The day of the Lord will come as unexpectedly as a thief. (2 Peter 3:10 NLT)
4.   Acts 1:7 NRSV.
5.   Many false prophets will appear and will deceive many people. (Matthew 24:11 NLT)
6.   Brethren, concerning the coming of our Lord Jesus Christ and our gathering together to Him, we ask you, not to be soon shaken in mind or troubled, either by spirit or by word or by letter, as if from us, as though the day of Christ had come. Let no one deceive you by any means. (2 Thessalonians 2:1–3 NKJV)
7.   The account can be found in Luke 2:25–35.
8.   Luke 2:29–32 NLT.
9.   2 Peter 3:3–4 NASB.
10.   Even so, come, Lord Jesus! (Revelation 22:20 NKJV)

Chapter 12: Why and when is the earth going to end?

1.   2 Peter 3:10 NLT.
2.   In him all things hold together. (Colossians 1:17 NRSV)
3.   He sustains all things by his powerful word. (Hebrews 1:3 NRSV)
4.   According to His promise we are looking for new heavens and a new earth, in which righteousness dwells. (2 Peter 3:13 NASB)
5.   Isaiah 34:4 NIV.
6.   Romans 8:21–22 NKJV.
7.   Isaiah 65:17–18 NIV.
8.   Revelation 21:1–5 NKJV.
9.   John 14:1–3 NLT.

Chapter 13: What's ahead for us in the future?

1.   Matthew 24:6–8 NRSV.
2.   Matthew 24:9–14 NKJV.
3.   The account can be found in Acts 7.
4.   We should be cheerful, because we would rather leave these bodies and be at home with the Lord. (2 Corinthians 5:8 CEV)
5.   1 Thessalonians 4:16–18 NIV.
6.   1 Corinthians 15:51–53 NIV.
7.   2 Thessalonians 2:7–9 NLT.
8.   Matthew 24:23–27 NASB.
9.   I saw an angel coming down from heaven with the key to the bottomless pit and a heavy chain in his hand. He seized the dragon—that old serpent, who is

the devil, Satan—and bound him in chains for a thousand years. The angel threw him into the bottomless pit, which he then shut and locked so Satan could not deceive the nations anymore until the thousand years were finished. Afterward he must be released for a little while. (Revelation 20:1–3 NLT)

10.   Revelation 20:11–12 NASB.

11.   If any man builds on this foundation using gold, silver, costly stones, wood, hay or straw, his work will be shown for what it is, because the Day will bring it to light. It will be revealed with fire, and the fire will test the quality of each man's work. If what he has built survives, he will receive his reward. If it is burned up, he will suffer loss; he himself will be saved, but only as one escaping through the flames. (1 Corinthians 3:12–15 NIV)

12.   From the Lord you will receive the reward of the inheritance; for you serve the Lord Christ. (Colossians 3:24 NKJV)

Chapter 14: Why should we work if the world is going to end?

1.   Ecclesiastes 3:1 NIV.

2.   We must quickly carry out the tasks assigned us by the one who sent us. The night is coming, and then no one can work. (John 9:4 NLT)

3.   2 Thessalonians 3:6–9 NKJV.

4.   Greet Tryphaena and Tryphosa, workers in the Lord. Greet Persis the beloved, who has worked hard in the Lord. (Romans 16:12 NASB)

5.   1 Timothy 6:13–15 NRSV.

6.   Adapted from Matthew 4:18–20 NIV: As Jesus was walking beside the Sea of Galilee, he saw two brothers, Simon called Peter and his brother Andrew. They were casting a net into the lake, for they were fishermen. "Come, follow me," Jesus said, "and I will make you fishers of men." At once they left their nets and followed him.

7.   Matthew 9:37–38 NASB.

8.   Based on Colossians 3:23–25 NKJV: And whatever you do, do it heartily, as to the Lord and not to men, knowing that from the Lord you will receive the reward of the inheritance; for you serve the Lord Christ.

Chapter 15: How should we prepare for the end of the world?

1.   Dorothy Sayers, *Creed or Chaos* (New York: Harcourt Brace, 1949). 59.

2.   Mark 13:33 NIV.

3.   1 Thessalonians 5:6 NKJV.

4.   Romans 13:11–14 NASB.

5.   Matthew 28:18–20 NRSV.

6.   They prayed and said, "You, Lord, who know the hearts of all men, show which one of these two You have chosen to occupy this ministry and apostleship from which Judas turned aside to go to his own place." And they drew lots for them, and the lot fell to Matthias; and he was added to the eleven apostles. (Acts 1:24–26 NASB)

7. Luke 19:10 <small>NKJV</small>.
8. James 1:27 <small>NLT</small>.
9. He wanted to justify himself, so he asked Jesus, "And who is my neighbor?" (Luke 10:29 <small>NIV</small>)
10. Luke 10:37 <small>NIV</small>.
11. Ephesians 4:13 <small>NIV</small>.
12. Brothers and sisters, I could not speak to you as spiritual people, but rather as people of the flesh, as infants in Christ. I fed you with milk, not solid food, for you were not ready for solid food. (1 Corinthians 3:1–2 <small>NRSV</small>)
13. Luke 4:16 <small>NKJV</small>.
14. Some people have gotten out of the habit of meeting for worship, but we must not do that. We should keep on encouraging each other, especially since you know that the day of the Lord's coming is getting closer. (Hebrews 10:25 <small>CEV</small>)

Chapter 16: God, why do You allow natural calamities to kill so many people?

1. Even the very hairs of your head are all numbered. (Matthew 10:30 <small>NIV</small>)
2. Job 42:3 <small>NIV</small>.
3. Luke 13:4 <small>NASB</small>.
4. Enoch had faith and did not die. He pleased God, and God took him up to heaven. That's why his body was never found. (Hebrews 11:5 <small>CEV</small>)
5. As they were going along and talking, behold, there appeared a chariot of fire and horses of fire which separated the two of them. And Elijah went up by a whirlwind to heaven. (2 Kings 2:11 <small>NASB</small>)
6. Just as man is destined to die once, and after that to face judgment, so Christ was sacrificed once to take away the sins of many people; and he will appear a second time, not to bear sin, but to bring salvation to those who are waiting for him. (Hebrews 9:27–28 <small>NIV</small>)
7. Deuteronomy 11:17 <small>NLT</small>.
8. Job 19:25–27 <small>NKJV</small>.
9. Adapted from Hebrews 11:13–14 <small>NLT</small>: All these people died still believing what God had promised them. They did not receive what was promised, but they saw it all from a distance and welcomed it. They agreed that they were foreigners and nomads here on earth. Obviously people who say such things are looking forward to a country they can call their own.
10. Habakkuk 3:17–18 <small>NIV</small>.
11. We know that all things work together for good for those who love God, who are called according to his purpose. (Romans 8:28 <small>NRSV</small>)

Chapter 17: Why is there so much suffering?

1. Genesis 2:8–9 <small>NIV</small>.
2. Revelation 22:1–3 <small>NIV</small>.

3. Matthew 2:6 NKJV.

4. Jesus began a tour of the nearby towns and villages, preaching and announcing the Good News about the Kingdom of God. He took his twelve disciples with him, along with some women he had healed and from whom he had cast out evil spirits. Among them were Mary Magdalene, from whom he had cast out seven demons. (Luke 8:1–2 NLT)

5. 1 Peter 4:12–16 NIV.

6. James 5:10–11 CEV.

7. 2 Timothy 3:12 NLT.

8. When you reap the harvest of your land, moreover, you shall not reap to the very corners of your field nor gather the gleaning of your harvest; you are to leave them for the needy and the alien. I am the LORD your God. (Leviticus 23:22 NASB)

9. The LORD said to the man, "You listened to your wife and ate fruit from that tree. And so, the ground will be under a curse because of what you did. As long as you live, you will have to struggle to grow enough food. Your food will be plants, but the ground will produce thorns and thistles. You will have to sweat to earn a living; you were made out of soil, and you will once again turn into soil." (Genesis 3:17–19 CEV)

10. Romans 8:18 NASB.

Chapter 18: God, why are some people rich and others poor?

1. Matthew 5:45 CEV.

2. Psalm 73:3–5 NIV.

3. Ecclesiastes 5:10 NASB.

4. Matthew 13:22 NKJV.

5. Based on Matthew 19:20–22 NRSV: The young man said to him, "I have kept all these; what do I still lack?" Jesus said to him, "If you wish to be perfect, go, sell your possessions, and give the money to the poor, and you will have treasure in heaven; then come, follow me." When the young man heard this word, he went away grieving, for he had many possessions.

6. 1 Timothy 6:17–19 NLT.

7. 1 Timothy 6:10 NASB.

8. Matthew 6:19–21 NIV.

Chapter 19: God, do You truly care for everyone?

1. Genesis 15:5 NIV.

2. Matthew 24:14 NKJV.

3. John 4:42 NLT.

4. John 1:9 NASB.

5. John 6:33 NIV.

6. John 5:24 NIV.

7. Joel 2:32 NKJV.

8. See Acts 2:21.
9. See Romans 10:13.
10. Luke 15:4–7 NLT.
11. Luke 15:8–10 NLT.
12. Acts 10:34–35 NIV.
13. Colossians 3:11 NLT.

Chapter 20: Why is there disease?

1. Centers of Disease Control and Prevention (www.cdc.gov).
2. Adam's life lasted 930 years; then he died. (Genesis 5:5 HCSB)
3. Seth's life lasted 912 years; then he died. (Genesis 5:8 HCSB)
4. Methuselah lived 969 years, and then he died. (Genesis 5:27 NIV)
5. As for the days of our life, they contain seventy years, or if due to strength, eighty years. (Psalm 90:10 NASB)
6. The last enemy that will be destroyed is death. (1 Corinthians 15:26 NKJV)
7. 2 Corinthians 12:7–9 NASB.
8. The crowds found out where he was going, and they followed him. And He welcomed them and taught them about the Kingdom of God, and he healed those who were sick. (Luke 9:11 NLT)
9. See Leviticus 13–14.

Chapter 21: Jesus, how did You live knowing how You would die?

1. See Isaiah 53; Psalm 22.
2. Matthew 20:18–19 NIV.
3. Matthew 26:2 NKJV.
4. Judas then, having received the Roman cohort and officers from the chief priests and the Pharisees, came there with lanterns and torches and weapons. (John 18:3 NASB)
5. Pilate released Barabbas to them. He ordered Jesus flogged with a lead-tipped whip, then turned him over to the Roman soldiers to be crucified. (Matthew 27:26 NLT)
6. 1 Peter 2:24–25 NRSV.
7. Mark 14:36 NIV.
8. The account is found in Mark 14:26–50.
9. John 15:13 CEV.
10. Matthew 9:36 CEV.
11. God loved us so much that he made us alive with Christ, and God's wonderful kindness is what saves you. (Ephesians 2:4–5 CEV)
12. Adapted from Romans 5:6-8 NIV: When we were still powerless, Christ died for the ungodly. Very rarely will anyone die for a righteous man, though for a good man someone might possibly dare to die. But God demonstrates his own love for us in this: While we were still sinners, Christ died for us.

13. It is not possible that the blood of bulls and goats could take away sins. (Hebrews 10:4 NKJV)

14. 1 Peter 3:18 NLT.

Chapter 22: Jesus, where did Your soul go after You died?

1. Death ruled like a king because Adam had sinned. But that cannot compare with what Jesus Christ has done. God has been so kind to us, and he has accepted us because of Jesus. And so we will live and rule like kings. (Romans 5:17 CEV)

2. The full account can be found in John 11:1–44.

3. The full account can be found in Luke 16:19–31 NASB.

4. 1 Peter 4:5–6 NIV.

5. Ephesians 4:9-10 CEV.

6. We are confident, yes, well pleased rather to be absent from the body and to be present with the Lord. (2 Corinthians 5:8 NKJV)

7. Adapted from 1 Timothy 2:4 NIV: Who wants all men to be saved and to come to a knowledge of the truth.

Chapter 23: Just what is salvation?

1. Based on 2 Corinthians 11:24–28 NIV: Five times I received from the Jews the forty lashes minus one. Three times I was beaten with rods, once I was stoned, three times I was shipwrecked, I spent a night and a day in the open sea, I have been constantly on the move. I have been in danger from rivers, in danger from bandits, in danger from my own countrymen, in danger from Gentiles; in danger in the city, in danger in the country, in danger at sea; and in danger from false brothers. I have labored and toiled and have often gone without sleep; I have known hunger and thirst and have often gone without food; I have been cold and naked. Besides everything else, I face daily the pressure of my concern for all the churches.

2. 1 Timothy 1:15 NKJV.

3. Ecclesiastes 7:20 NASB.

4. Galatians 3:22 NLT.

5. 1 John 1:8 CEV.

6. 1 John 1:9 NRSV.

7. I wipe away your sins because of who I am. And so, I will forget the wrongs you have done. (Isaiah 43:25 CEV)

8. The thief's purpose is to steal and kill and destroy. My purpose is to give them a rich and satisfying life. (John 10:10 NLT)

9. Ephesians 2:5 NIV.

10. 1 Corinthians 1:18 NIV.

11. Ephesians 2:8–10 NKJV.

Chapter 24: How do we know if we are saved?

1. 1 Peter 1:8–9 NIV.
2. 2 Timothy 1:12 NKJV.
3. Adapted from Romans 6:23 NIV: The wages of sin is death, but the gift of God is eternal life in Christ Jesus our Lord.
4. Read about the account in Acts 9:1–22.
5. Romans 10:9–11 NLT.
6. Based on 2 Corinthians 5:17 NLT: This means that anyone who belongs to Christ has become a new person. The old life is gone; a new life has begun!
7. Can any of you prove me guilty of sin? If I am telling the truth, why don't you believe me? (John 8:46 NIV)
8. When He has come, He will convict the world of sin, and of righteousness, and of judgment: of sin, because they do not believe in Me; of righteousness, because I go to My Father and you see Me no more; of judgment, because the ruler of this world is judged. (John 16:8–11 NKJV)
9. 1 Corinthians 2:14–15 CEV.

Chapter 25: Jesus, what is Your role in salvation?

1. Isaiah 1:11 NIV.
2. Based on Hebrews 10:3–4 NKJV.
3. John 1:29 NASB.
4. Ephesians 2:14–15 CEV.
5. Adapted from Colossians 1:19–20 NKJV: It pleased the Father that in Him all the fullness should dwell, and by Him to reconcile all things to Himself, by Him, whether things on earth or things in heaven, having made peace through the blood of His cross.
6. You are a chosen people. You are royal priests, a holy nation, God's very own possession. As a result, you can show others the goodness of God, for he called you out of the darkness into his wonderful light. (1 Peter 2:9 NLT)
7. 1 Peter 1:18–19 CEV.
8. Read the account in Genesis 22:1–18.
9. He considered God to be able even to raise someone from the dead, from which he also got him back as an illustration. (Hebrews 11:19 HCSB)
10. The account is found in Acts 16:19–34. Quoted portions are from the NIV translation.

Chapter 26: Can we go to heaven without forgiveness?

1. The wages of sin is death, but the gift of God is eternal life in Christ Jesus our Lord. (Romans 6:23 HCSB)
2. Isaiah 53:6 NKJV.

3. The Lord God took the man and put him into the garden of Eden to cultivate it and keep it. The Lord God commanded the man, saying, "From any tree of the garden you may eat freely; but from the tree of the knowledge of good and evil you shall not eat, for in the day that you eat from it you will surely die." (Genesis 2:15–17 NASB)

4. Based on Exodus 20:1–17 NKJV. The material has been trimmed, and the full text should be read.

5. One day, after Moses had grown up, he went out to where his own people were and watched them at their hard labor. He saw an Egyptian beating a Hebrew, one of his own people. Glancing this way and that and seeing no one, he killed the Egyptian and hid him in the sand. (Exodus 2:11–12 NIV)

6. John 13:34 NRSV.

7. Matthew 6:14 NLT.

8. Romans 3:22–26 NIV.

Chapter 27: Jesus, were You really raised from the dead?

1. 1 Corinthians 15:23 CEV.

2. Elijah took the child and brought him down from the upper room into the house and gave him to his mother; and Elijah said, "See, your son is alive." (1 Kings 17:23 NASB)

3. Read the full account in John 11:1–44.

4. There was a young man named Eutychus sitting on the window sill, sinking into a deep sleep; and as Paul kept on talking, he was overcome by sleep and fell down from the third floor and was picked up dead. But Paul went down and fell upon him, and after embracing him, he said, "Do not be troubled, for his life is in him." When he had gone back up and had broken the bread and eaten, he talked with them a long while until daybreak, and then left. They took away the boy alive, and were greatly comforted. (Acts 20:9–12 NASB)

5. When the Roman officer saw what had happened, he praised God and said, "Jesus must really have been a good man!" (Luke 23:47 CEV)

6. Joseph of Arimathea, being a disciple of Jesus, but secretly, for fear of the Jews, asked Pilate that he might take away the body of Jesus; and Pilate gave him permission. So he came and took the body of Jesus. And Nicodemus, who at first came to Jesus by night, also came, bringing a mixture of myrrh and aloes, about a hundred pounds. Then they took the body of Jesus, and bound it in strips of linen with the spices, as the custom of the Jews is to bury. Now in the place where He was crucified there was a garden, and in the garden a new tomb in which no one had yet been laid. So there they laid Jesus, because of the Jews' Preparation Day, for the tomb was nearby. (John 19:38–42 NKJV)

7. Nicodemus (who had previously come to Him at night) also came, bringing a mixture of about 75 pounds of myrrh and aloes. (John 19:39 HCSB)

8. One of the soldiers pierced His side with a spear, and immediately blood and water came out. (John 19:34 NKJV)

9. Joseph put the body in his own tomb that had been cut into solid rock and had never been used. He rolled a big stone against the entrance to the tomb and went away. (Matthew 27:60 CEV)

10. They sealed it tight and placed soldiers there to guard it. (Matthew 27:66 CEV)

11. When Jesus saw his mother there, and the disciple whom he loved standing nearby, he said to his mother, "Dear woman, here is your son," and to the disciple, "Here is your mother." From that time on, this disciple took her into his home. (John 19:26–27 NIV)

12. Acts 2:22–24 CEV.

13. 1 Corinthians 15:3–9 NLT.

14. Thomas, who is called the Twin, said to his fellow disciples, "Let us also go, that we may die with Him." (John 11:16 NKJV)

15. John 20:25 CEV.

16. John 20:28 CEV.

17. 1 Corinthians 15:12–19 NLT.

Chapter 28: Can I lose my salvation?

1. John 3:36 NIV.

2. He who hears My word and believes in Him who sent Me has everlasting life, and shall not come into judgment, but has passed from death into life. (John 5:24 NKJV)

3. He called the twelve to Himself, and began to send them out two by two, and gave them power over unclean spirits. (Mark 6:7 NKJV)

4. The account is found in Matthew 8:5–13.

5. Jesus said to him, "Judas, are you betraying the Son of Man with a kiss?" (Luke 22:48 NKJV)

6. When those around Him saw what was going to happen, they said to Him, "Lord, shall we strike with the sword?" And one of them struck the servant of the high priest and cut off his right ear. But Jesus answered and said, "Permit even this." And He touched his ear and healed him. (Luke 22:49–51 NKJV)

7. The account is found in John 13:21–27.

8. Judas threw the money into the temple and left. Then he went away and hanged himself. (Matthew 27:5 NIV)

9. Galatians 4:7 NKJV.

10. Sin is no longer your master, for you no longer live under the requirements of the law. Instead, you live under the freedom of God's grace. (Romans 6:14 NLT)

11. I no longer call you servants, because a servant does not know his master's business. Instead, I have called you friends, for everything that I learned from my Father I have made known to you. (John 15:15 NIV)

12. Adapted from Ephesians 2:19–22 NIV: Consequently, you are no longer foreigners and aliens, but fellow citizens with God's people and members of God's household, built on the foundation of the apostles and prophets, with

Christ Jesus himself as the chief cornerstone. In him the whole building is joined together and rises to become a holy temple in the Lord. And in him you too are being built together to become a dwelling in which God lives by his Spirit.

13.   1 John 2:17 CEV.

14.   Matthew 7:16 NASB.

15.   Titus 2:11–14 CEV.

Chapter 29: What is the kingdom of God?

1.   Jesus went about all Galilee, teaching in their synagogues, preaching the gospel of the kingdom, and healing all kinds of sickness and all kinds of disease among the people. (Matthew 4:23 NKJV)

2.   Having been questioned by the Pharisees as to when the kingdom of God was coming, He answered them and said, "The kingdom of God is not coming with signs to be observed; nor will they say, 'Look, here it is!' or, 'There it is!' For behold, the kingdom of God is in your midst." (Luke 17:20–21 NASB)

3.   Our citizenship is in heaven. And we eagerly await a Savior from there, the Lord Jesus Christ, who, by the power that enables him to bring everything under his control, will transform our lowly bodies so that they will be like his glorious body. (Philippians 3:20–21 NIV)

4.   In those days John the Baptist came, preaching in the wilderness of Judea, saying, "Repent, for the kingdom of heaven is at hand." (Matthew 3:1–2 NASB)

5.   Jesus went from Galilee to the Jordan River to be baptized by John. But John tried to talk him out of it. "I am the one who needs to be baptized by you," he said, "so why are you coming to me?" But Jesus said, "It should be done, for we must carry out all that God requires." So John agreed to baptize him. (Matthew 3:13–15 NLT)

6.   Based on John 3:1–3 CEV: There was a man named Nicodemus who was a Pharisee and a Jewish leader. One night he went to Jesus and said, "Sir, we know that God has sent you to teach us. You could not work these miracles, unless God were with you." Jesus replied, "I tell you for certain that you must be born from above before you can see God's kingdom!"

7.   Based on Matthew 6:9–10 NIV: This, then, is how you should pray: "Our Father in heaven, hallowed be your name, your kingdom come, your will be done on earth as it is in heaven.)

8.   The Sermon on the Mount is recorded in Matthew 5–7.

9.   During the forty days after his crucifixion, he appeared to the apostles from time to time, and he proved to them in many ways that he was actually alive. And he talked to them about the Kingdom of God. (Acts 1:3 NLT)

Chapter 30: What makes the kingdom of God important today?

1.   Whatever is has already been, and what will be has been before; and God will call the past to account. (Ecclesiastes 3:15 NIV)

2.   I am the LORD All-Powerful, and I never change. (Malachi 3:6 CEV)

3. I say this, brethren, that flesh and blood cannot inherit the Kingdom of God; nor does the perishable inherit the imperishable. (1 Corinthians 15:50 NASB)

4. Greet Urbanus, our co-worker in Christ, and my beloved Stachys. (Romans 16:9 NRSV)

5. The Kingdom of God is not a matter of what we eat or drink, but of living a life of goodness and peace and joy in the Holy Spirit. If you serve Christ with this attitude, you will please God, and others will approve of you, too. So then, let us aim for harmony in the church and try to build each other up. (Romans 14:17–19 NLT)

6. What shall we say the kingdom of God is like, or what parable shall we use to describe it? It is like a mustard seed, which is the smallest seed you plant in the ground. Yet when planted, it grows and becomes the largest of all garden plants, with such big branches that the birds of the air can perch in its shade. (Mark 4:30–32 NIV)

7. The kingdom of heaven is like treasure hidden in a field. When a man found it, he hid it again, and then in his joy went and sold all he had and bought that field. (Matthew 13:44 NIV)

8. When Jesus perceived that they were about to come and take Him by force to make Him king, He departed again to the mountain by Himself alone. (John 6:15 NKJV)

Chapter 31: God, do we have to die to be citizens of Your kingdom?

1. You have been born again, not of perishable seed, but of imperishable, through the living and enduring word of God. (1 Peter 1:23 NIV)

2. When you pray, you shall not be like the hypocrites. For they love to pray standing in the synagogues and on the corners of the streets, that they may be seen by men. Assuredly, I say to you, they have their reward. (Matthew 6:5 NKJV)

3. When you pray, go into your inner room, close your door and pray to your Father who is in secret, and your Father who sees what is done in secret will reward you. (Matthew 6:6 NASB)

4. I tell you not to worry about everyday life—whether you have enough food and drink, or enough clothes to wear. Isn't life more than food, and your body more than clothing? Look at the birds. They don't plant or harvest or store food in barns, for your heavenly Father feeds them. And aren't you far more valuable to him than they are? (Matthew 6:25–26 NLT)

5. Can any of you by worrying add a single hour to your span of life? (Matthew 6:27 NRSV)

6. Do not judge, or you too will be judged. For in the same way you judge others, you will be judged, and with the measure you use, it will be measured to you. (Matthew 7:1–2 NIV)

7. In everything, therefore, treat people the same way you want them to treat you, for this is the Law and the Prophets. (Matthew 7:12 NASB)

8. Based on Luke 6:20 NKJV: Blessed are you poor, for yours is the kingdom of God.

9. Based on Luke 6:21 NKJV: Blessed are you who hunger now, for you shall be satisfied. Blessed are you who weep now, for you shall laugh.

10. Jesus said to him, "I am the way, and the truth, and the life; no one comes to the Father but through Me." (John 14:6 NASB)

11. You are a chosen people, a royal priesthood, a holy nation, a people belonging to God, that you may declare the praises of him who called you out of darkness into his wonderful light. Once you were not a people, but now you are the people of God; once you had not received mercy, but now you have received mercy. (1 Peter 2:9–10 NIV)

Chapter 32: Is there also a future kingdom—*two* kingdoms?

1. How great is the love the Father has lavished on us, that we should be called children of God! And that is what we are! The reason the world does not know us is that it did not know him. (1 John 3:1 NIV)

2. You are from below, but I am from above. You belong to this world, but I don't. (John 8:23 CEV)

3. If you belonged to the world, it would love you as its own. As it is, you do not belong to the world, but I have chosen you out of the world. That is why the world hates you. (John 15:19 NIV)

4. He was given authority, glory and sovereign power; all peoples, nations and men of every language worshiped him. His dominion is an everlasting dominion that will not pass away, and his kingdom is one that will never be destroyed. (Daniel 7:14 NIV)

5. When the seven thunders uttered their voices, I was about to write; but I heard a voice from heaven saying to me, "Seal up the things which the seven thunders uttered, and do not write them." (Revelation 10:4 NKJV)

6. I saw an angel coming down from heaven, holding the key of the abyss and a great chain in his hand. And he laid hold of the dragon, the serpent of old, who is the devil and Satan, and bound him for a thousand years; and he threw him into the abyss, and shut it and sealed it over him, so that he would not deceive the nations any longer, until the thousand years were completed; after these things he must be released for a short time. (Revelation 20:1–3 NASB)

7. Blessed and holy are those who share in the first resurrection. For them the second death holds no power, but they will be priests of God and of Christ and will reign with him a thousand years. (Revelation 20:6 NLT)

8. This is the covenant that I will make with the house of Israel after those days, says the LORD: I will put my law within them, and I will write it on their hearts; and I will be their God, and they shall be my people. No longer shall they teach one another, or say to each other, "Know the LORD," for they shall all know me, from the least of them to the greatest, says the LORD; for I will forgive their iniquity, and remember their sin no more. (Jeremiah 31:33–34 NRSV)

9. Jesus must stay in heaven until God makes all things new, just as his holy prophets promised long ago. (Acts 3:21 CEV)

10. He made known to us the mystery of his will according to his good pleasure, which he purposed in Christ, to be put into effect when the times will have reached their fulfillment—to bring all things in heaven and on earth together under one head, even Christ. (Ephesians 1:9–10 NIV)

11. The people begged for a king, and God gave them Saul son of Kish, a man of the tribe of Benjamin, who reigned for forty years. But God removed Saul and replaced him with David, a man about whom God said, "I have found David son of Jesse, a man after my own heart. He will do everything I want him to do." And it is one of King David's descendants, Jesus, who is God's promised Savior of Israel! (Acts 13:21–23 NLT)

12. I will appoint Peace as your overseer and Righteousness as your taskmaster. Violence shall no more be heard in your land, devastation or destruction within your borders; you shall call your walls Salvation, and your gates Praise. (Isaiah 60:17–18 NRSV)

Chapter 33: Jesus, are You the only way to heaven?

1. Based on John 14:6 NIV: Jesus answered, "I am the way and the truth and the life. No one comes to the Father except through me."

2. Jesus said to them again, "Most assuredly, I say to you, I am the door of the sheep." (John 10:7 NKJV)

3. There is salvation in no one else; for there is no other name under heaven that has been given among men by which we must be saved. (Acts 4:12 NASB)

4. A voice from heaven said, "This is my own dear Son, and I am pleased with him." (Matthew 3:17 CEV)

5. In the beginning the Word already existed. The Word was with God, and the Word was God. (John 1:1 NLT)

6. He is the kind of high priest we need because he is holy and blameless, unstained by sin. He has been set apart from sinners and has been given the highest place of honor in heaven. (Hebrews 7:26 NLT)

7. For our sake he made him to be sin who knew no sin, so that in him we might become the righteousness of God. (2 Corinthians 5:21 NRSV)

8. You know that He appeared in order to take away sins; and in Him there is no sin. (1 John 3:5 NASB)

9. If you belong to Christ Jesus, you won't be punished. The Holy Spirit will give you life that comes from Christ Jesus and will set you free from sin and death. The Law of Moses cannot do this, because our selfish desires make the Law weak. But God set you free when he sent his own Son to be like us sinners and to be a sacrifice for our sin. God used Christ's body to condemn sin. (Romans 8:1–3 CEV)

10. Behold, I tell you a mystery; we will not all sleep, but we will all be changed, in a moment, in the twinkling of an eye, at the last trumpet; for the trumpet will sound, and the dead will be raised imperishable, and we will be changed. (1 Corinthians 15:51–52 NASB)

11.   Christ died for sins once for all, the righteous for the unrighteous, to bring you to God. (1 Peter 3:18 NIV)

Chapter 34: What will happen to people who don't believe?

1.   This is good and acceptable in the sight of God our Savior, who desires all men to be saved and to come to the knowledge of the truth. (1 Timothy 2:3–4 NKJV)

2.   Whoever believes in the Son has eternal life; whoever disobeys the Son will not see life, but must endure God's wrath. (John 3:36 NRSV)

3.   The fool has said in his heart, "There is no God," they are corrupt, and have committed abominable injustice; there is no one who does good. (Psalm 53:1 NASB)

4.   We are confident, yes, well pleased rather to be absent from the body and to be present with the Lord. (2 Corinthians 5:8 NKJV)

5.   For their sakes I sanctify Myself, that they themselves also may be sanctified in truth. I do not ask on behalf of these alone, but for those also who believe in Me through their word; that they may all be one; even as You, Father, are in Me and I in You, that they also may be in Us, so that the world may believe that You sent Me. (John 17:19–21 NASB)

6.   Based on Revelation 20:11–15 NIV: I saw a great white throne and him who was seated on it. Earth and sky fled from his presence, and there was no place for them. And I saw the dead, great and small, standing before the throne, and books were opened. Another book was opened, which is the book of life. The dead were judged according to what they had done as recorded in the books. The sea gave up the dead that were in it, and death and Hades gave up the dead that were in them, and each person was judged according to what he had done. Then death and Hades were thrown into the lake of fire. The lake of fire is the second death. If anyone's name was not found written in the book of life, he was thrown into the lake of fire.

7.   He who did not spare His own Son, but delivered Him up for us all, how shall He not with Him also freely give us all things? (Romans 8:32 NKJV)

8.   Even when we were God's enemies, he made peace with us, because his Son died for us. Yet something even greater than friendship is ours. Now that we are at peace with God, we will be saved by his Son's life. And in addition to everything else, we are happy because God sent our Lord Jesus Christ to make peace with us. (Romans 5:10–11 CEV)

9.   In the same way, I tell you, there is joy in the presence of the angels of God over one sinner who repents. (Luke 15:10 NASB)

Chapter 35: What is heaven like?

1.   I know a man in Christ who fourteen years ago—whether in the body I do not know, or out of the body I do not know, God knows—such a man was caught

up to the third heaven. And I know how such a man—whether in the body or apart from the body I do not know, God knows—was caught up into Paradise and heard inexpressible words, which a man is not permitted to speak. (2 Corinthians 12:2–5 NASB)

2. Jesus did many other things as well. If every one of them were written down, I suppose that even the whole world would not have room for the books that would be written. (John 21:25 NIV)

3. Let not your heart be troubled; you believe in God, believe also in Me. In My Father's house are many mansions; if it were not so, I would have told you. I go to prepare a place for you. And if I go and prepare a place for you, I will come again and receive you to Myself; that where I am, there you may be also. And where I go you know, and the way you know. (John 14:1–4 NKJV)

4. Yes, we are fully confident, and we would rather be away from these earthly bodies, for then we will be at home with the Lord. (2 Corinthians 5:8 NLT)

5. I saw the holy city, new Jerusalem, coming down out of heaven from God, made ready as a bride adorned for her husband. And I heard a loud voice from the throne, saying, "Behold, the tabernacle of God is among men, and He will dwell among them, and they shall be His people, and God Himself will be among them, and He will wipe away every tear from their eyes; and there will no longer be any death; there will no longer be any mourning, or crying, or pain; the first things have passed away. (Revelation 21:2–4 NASB)

6. Our bodies are like tents that we live in here on earth. But when these tents are destroyed, we know that God will give each of us a place to live. These homes will not be buildings that someone has made, but they are in heaven and will last forever. While we are here on earth, we sigh because we want to live in that heavenly home. We want to put it on like clothes and not be naked. (2 Corinthians 5:1–3 CEV)

7. These tents we now live in are like a heavy burden, and we groan. But we don't do this just because we want to leave these bodies that will die. It is because we want to change them for bodies that will never die. God is the one who makes all of this possible. He has given us his Spirit to make us certain that he will do it. (2 Corinthians 5:4–5 CEV)

8. Be glad in that day and leap for joy, for behold, your reward is great in heaven. For in the same way their fathers used to treat the prophets. (Luke 6:23 NASB)

9. Men will say, "Surely the righteous still are rewarded; surely there is a God who judges the earth." (Psalm 58:11 NIV)

10. Our citizenship is in heaven, from which we also eagerly wait for the Savior, the Lord Jesus Christ. (Philippians 3:20 NKJV)

11. Without any doubt, the mystery of our religion is great: He was revealed in flesh, vindicated in spirit, seen by angels, proclaimed among Gentiles, believed in throughout the world, taken up in glory. (1 Timothy 3:16 NRSV)

12. What we suffer now is nothing compared to the glory he will reveal to us later. (Romans 8:18 NLT)

13. No longer will a man teach his neighbor, or a man his brother, saying, "Know the LORD," because they will all know me, from the least of them to the greatest," declares the LORD. "For I will forgive their wickedness and will remember their sins no more." (Jeremiah 31:34 NIV)

Chapter 36: What will we do for eternity?

1. Now we see in a mirror, dimly, but then face to face. Now I know in part, but then I shall know just as I also am known. (1 Corinthians 13:12 NKJV)

2. There will no longer be any curse; and the throne of God and of the Lamb will be in it, and His bond-servants will serve Him; they will see His face, and His name will be on their foreheads. (Revelation 22:3–4 NASB)

3. I heard a loud voice from heaven saying, "Behold, the tabernacle of God is with men, and He will dwell with them, and they shall be His people. God Himself will be with them and be their God. (Revelation 21:3 NKJV)

4. These little troubles are getting us ready for an eternal glory that will make all our troubles seem like nothing. Things that are seen don't last forever, but things that are not seen are eternal. That's why we keep our minds on the things that cannot be seen. (2 Corinthians 4:17–18 CEV)

5. When everything is ready, I will come and get you, so that you will always be with me where I am. (John 14:3 NLT)

6. He raised us from the dead along with Christ and seated us with him in the heavenly realms because we are united with Christ Jesus. (Ephesians 2:6 NLT)

7. When I was a child, I talked like a child, I thought like a child, I reasoned like a child. When I became a man, I put childish ways behind me. Now we see but a poor reflection as in a mirror; then we shall see face to face. Now I know in part; then I shall know fully, even as I am fully known. (1 Corinthians 13:11–12 NIV)

8. He humbled Himself by becoming obedient to the point of death, even death on a cross. For this reason also, God highly exalted Him, and bestowed on Him the name which is above every name, so that at the name of Jesus every knee will bow, of those who are in heaven and on earth and under the earth, and that every tongue will confess that Jesus Christ is Lord, to the glory of God the Father. (Philippians 2:8–11 NASB)

Chapter 37: What will we look like in heaven?

1. Our citizenship is in heaven. And we eagerly await a Savior from there, the Lord Jesus Christ, who, by the power that enables him to bring everything under his control, will transform our lowly bodies so that they will be like his glorious body. (Philippians 3:20–21 NIV)

2.   There are also celestial bodies and terrestrial bodies; but the glory of the celestial is one, and the glory of the terrestrial is another. There is one glory of the sun, another glory of the moon, and another glory of the stars; for one star differs from another star in glory. (1 Corinthians 15:40–41 NKJV)

3.   As is the earthy, so also are those who are earthy; and as is the heavenly, so also are those who are heavenly. Just as we have borne the image of the earthy, we will also bear the image of the heavenly. (1 Corinthians 15:48–49 NASB)

4.   Around that throne were 24 thrones, and on the thrones sat 24 elders dressed in white clothes, with gold crowns on their heads. (Revelation 4:4 HCSB)

5.   Jesus said to her, "Woman, why are you weeping? Whom are you looking for?" Supposing him to be the gardener, she said to him, "Sir, if you have carried him away, tell me where you have laid him, and I will take him away." Jesus said to her, "Mary!" She turned and said to him in Hebrew, "Rabbouni!" (which means Teacher). (John 20:15–17 NRSV)

6.   Two of them were going to a village called Emmaus, about seven miles from Jerusalem. They were talking with each other about everything that had happened. As they talked and discussed these things with each other, Jesus himself came up and walked along with them; but they were kept from recognizing him. (Luke 24:13–16 NIV)

7.   Jesus Himself stood in the midst of them, and said to them, "Peace to you." But they were terrified and frightened, and supposed they had seen a spirit. And He said to them, "Why are you troubled? And why do doubts arise in your hearts? Behold My hands and My feet, that it is I Myself. Handle Me and see, for a spirit does not have flesh and bones as you see I have." (Luke 24:36–39 NKJV)

8.   They gave Him a piece of a broiled fish; and He took it and ate it before them. (Luke 24:42–43 NASB)

9.   Six days later Jesus took with Him Peter and James and John his brother, and led them up on a high mountain by themselves. And He was transfigured before them; and His face shone like the sun, and His garments became as white as light. And behold, Moses and Elijah appeared to them, talking with Him. (Matthew 17:1–3 NASB)

10.   Based on Matthew 22:24–28 NLT: Teacher, Moses said, "If a man dies without children, his brother should marry the widow and have a child who will carry on the brother's name." Well, suppose there were seven brothers. The oldest one married and then died without children, so his brother married the widow. But the second brother also died, and the third brother married her. This continued with all seven of them. Last of all, the woman also died. So tell us, whose wife will she be in the resurrection? For all seven were married to her.

11.   Jesus replied, "Your mistake is that you don't know the Scriptures, and you don't know the power of God. For when the dead rise, they will neither marry nor be given in marriage. In this respect they will be like the angels in heaven." (Matthew 22:29–30 NLT)

Chapter 38: Is there really such a place as hell?

1. I saw the dead, great and small, standing before the throne, and books were opened. Another book was opened, which is the book of life. The dead were judged according to what they had done as recorded in the books. (Revelation 20:12 NIV)

2. He will say to those on his left, "Depart from me, you who are cursed, into the eternal fire prepared for the devil and his angels." (Matthew 25:41 NIV)

3. Because of your hardness and unrepentant heart you are storing up wrath for yourself in the day of wrath, when God's righteous judgment is revealed. (Romans 2:5 HCSB)

4. He will punish those who do not know God and do not obey the gospel of our Lord Jesus. They will be punished with everlasting destruction and shut out from the presence of the Lord and from the majesty of his power. (2 Thessalonians 1:8–9 NIV)

5. Based and adapted from a quote attributed to C. S. Lewis.

6. You people of Chorazin are in for trouble! You people of Bethsaida are in for trouble too! If the miracles that took place in your towns had happened in Tyre and Sidon, the people there would have turned to God long ago. They would have dressed in sackcloth and put ashes on their heads. I tell you that on the day of judgment the people of Tyre and Sidon will get off easier than you will. People of Capernaum, do you think you will be honored in heaven? You will go down to hell! If the miracles that took place in your town had happened in Sodom, that town would still be standing. So I tell you that on the day of judgment the people of Sodom will get off easier than you. (Matthew 11:21–24 CEV)

7. Enter by the narrow gate; for wide is the gate and broad is the way that leads to destruction, and there are many who go in by it. Because narrow is the gate and difficult is the way which leads to life, and there are few who find it. (Matthew 7:13–14 NKJV)

8. While you have the light, believe in the light, that you may become sons of light. (John 12:35 NKJV)

Chapter 39: Is Satan for real?

1. Be self-controlled and alert. Your enemy the devil prowls around like a roaring lion looking for someone to devour. (1 Peter 5:8 NIV)

2. The Lord said, "Simon, Simon! Indeed, Satan has asked for you, that he may sift you as wheat. But I have prayed for you, that your faith should not fail; and when you have returned to Me, strengthen your brethren." (Luke 22:31–32 NKJV)

3. Jesus, full of the Holy Spirit, returned from the Jordan River. He was led by the Spirit in the wilderness, where he was tempted by the devil for forty days. Jesus ate nothing all that time and became very hungry. (Luke 4:1–2 NLT)

4. The devil said to him, "If you are the Son of God, change this stone into a loaf of bread." But Jesus told him, "No! The Scriptures say, 'People do not live by

bread alone.' Then the devil took him up and revealed to him all the kingdoms of the world in a moment of time. "I will give you the glory of these kingdoms and authority over them," the devil said, "because they are mine to give to anyone I please. I will give it all to you if you will worship me." Jesus replied, "The Scriptures say, 'You must worship the LORD your God and serve only him.'" Then the devil took him to Jerusalem, to the highest point of the Temple, and said, "If you are the Son of God, jump off!" (Luke 4:3–9 NLT)

5.   How you have fallen from heaven, O morning star, son of the dawn! You have been cast down to the earth, you who once laid low the nations! You said in your heart, "I will ascend to heaven; I will raise my throne above the stars of God; I will sit enthroned on the mount of assembly, on the utmost heights of the sacred mountain." (Isaiah 14:12–13 NIV)

6.   I will ascend above the tops of the clouds; I will make myself like the Most High. (Isaiah 14:14 NIV)

7.   I saw a large red dragon with seven heads and ten horns, with seven crowns on his heads. His tail swept away one-third of the stars in the sky, and he threw them to the earth. He stood in front of the woman as she was about to give birth, ready to devour her baby as soon as it was born. (Revelation 12:3–4 NLT)

8.   He said to them, "I watched Satan fall from heaven like a flash of lightning." (Luke 10:18 NRSV)

9.   You belong to your father, the devil, and you want to carry out your father's desire. He was a murderer from the beginning, not holding to the truth, for there is no truth in him. When he lies, he speaks his native language, for he is a liar and the father of lies. (John 8:44 NIV)

10.   He showed me Joshua the high priest standing before the angel of the LORD, and Satan standing at his right hand to accuse him. (Zechariah 3:1 NASB)

11.   The great dragon was cast out, that serpent of old, called the Devil and Satan, who deceives the whole world; he was cast to the earth, and his angels were cast out with him. Then I heard a loud voice saying in heaven, "Now salvation, and strength, and the kingdom of our God, and the power of His Christ have come, for the accuser of our brethren, who accused them before our God day and night, has been cast down." (Revelation 12:9–10 NKJV)

12.   Submit yourselves, then, to God. Resist the devil, and he will flee from you. (James 4:7 NIV)

13.   Put on the full armor of God so that you can take your stand against the devil's schemes. (Ephesians 6:11 NIV)

14.   I will rescue you from both your own people and the Gentiles. Yes, I am sending you to the Gentiles to open their eyes, so they may turn from darkness to light and from the power of Satan to God. Then they will receive forgiveness for their sins and be given a place among God's people, who are set apart by faith in me. (Acts 26:17–18 NLT)

15.   What then shall we say to these things? If God is for us, who is against us? He who did not spare His own Son, but delivered Him over for us all, how will He not also with Him freely give us all things? Who will bring a charge against God's elect? God

is the one who justifies; who is the one who condemns? Christ Jesus is He who died, yes, rather who was raised, who is at the right hand of God, who also intercedes for us. Who will separate us from the love of Christ? Will tribulation, or distress, or persecution, or famine, or nakedness, or peril, or sword? (Romans 8:31–35 NASB)

Chapter 40: Who really rules this earth, God—You or Satan?

1.   God saw all that he had made, and it was very good. And there was evening, and there was morning—the sixth day. (Genesis 1:31 NIV)

2.   The earth is the LORD's, and all its fullness, the world and those who dwell therein. (Psalm 24:1 NKJV)

3.   We are not fighting against humans. We are fighting against forces and authorities and against rulers of darkness and powers in the spiritual world. (Ephesians 6:12 CEV)

4.   Now is the time for judgment on this world; now the prince of this world will be driven out. (John 12:31 NIV)

5.   I will not speak with you much longer, for the prince of this world is coming. He has no hold on me, but the world must learn that I love the Father and that I do exactly what my Father has commanded me. (John 14:30–31 NIV)

6.   When he comes, he will convict the world of guilt in regard to sin and righteousness and judgment: in regard to sin, because men do not believe in me; in regard to righteousness, because I am going to the Father, where you can see me no longer; and in regard to judgment, because the prince of this world now stands condemned. (John 16:8–11 NIV)

7.   Once you were dead because of your disobedience and your many sins. You used to live in sin, just like the rest of the world, obeying the devil—the commander of the powers in the unseen world. He is the spirit at work in the hearts of those who refuse to obey God. All of us used to live that way, following the passionate desires and inclinations of our sinful nature. By our very nature we were subject to God's anger, just like everyone else. (Ephesians 2:1–3 NLT)

8.   Satan, who is the god of this world, has blinded the minds of those who don't believe. They are unable to see the glorious light of the Good News. They don't understand this message about the glory of Christ, who is the exact likeness of God. (2 Corinthians 4:4 NLT)

9.   We wanted to come to you—certainly I, Paul, did, again and again—but Satan stopped us. (1 Thessalonians 2:18 NIV)

10.   To keep me from becoming conceited because of these surpassingly great revelations, there was given me a thorn in my flesh, a messenger of Satan, to torment me. (2 Corinthians 12:7 NIV)

11.   We do this so that we may not be outwitted by Satan; for we are not ignorant of his designs. (2 Corinthians 2:11 NRSV)

12.   These people are false apostles. They are deceitful workers who disguise themselves as apostles of Christ. But I am not surprised! Even Satan disguises himself as an angel of light. So it is no wonder that his servants also disguise

themselves as servants of righteousness. In the end they will get the punishment their wicked deeds deserve. (2 Corinthians 11:13–15 NLT)

13. The God of peace will crush Satan under your feet shortly. (Romans 16:20 NKJV)

Chapter 41: Are we unique?

1. The LORD God took a handful of soil and made a man. God breathed life into the man, and the man started breathing. (Genesis 2:7 CEV).

2. The LORD God had formed out of the ground all the beasts of the field and all the birds of the air. He brought them to the man to see what he would name them; and whatever the man called each living creature, that was its name. (Genesis 2:19 NIV)

3. God said, "Let the waters swarm with fish and other life. Let the skies be filled with birds of every kind." . . . Then God said, "Let the earth produce every sort of animal, each producing offspring of the same kind—livestock, small animals that scurry along the ground, and wild animals." And that is what happened. (Genesis 1:20, 24 NLT)

4. God created man in His own image, in the image of God He created him; male and female He created them. (Genesis 1:27 NASB)

5. The LORD God formed man of the dust of the ground, and breathed into his nostrils the breath of life; and man became a living being. (Genesis 2:7 NKJV)

6. God is spirit, and his worshipers must worship in spirit and in truth. (John 4:24 NIV)

7. Based on Psalm 8:3-4 NIV: When I consider your heavens, the work of your fingers, the moon and the stars, which you have set in place, what is man that you are mindful of him?

8. You have made him a little lower than God, and You crown him with glory and majesty! (Psalm 8:5 NASB)

9. God blessed them, and God said to them, "Be fruitful and multiply; fill the earth and subdue it; have dominion over the fish of the sea, over the birds of the air, and over every living thing that moves on the earth." (Genesis 1:28 NKJV)

Chapter 42: Is being unique good or bad?

1. George Santayana, *Reason in Common Sense* (New York: Charles Scribner's Sons, 1905), 284.

2. The account can be found in 2 Samuel 11–12.

3. The account can be found in Genesis 3.

4. The good man brings good things out of the good stored up in him, and the evil man brings evil things out of the evil stored up in him. (Matthew 12:35 NIV)

5. Matthew 28:19–20 NKJV.

Chapter 43: Why are there two sexes?

1. The man gave names to all the livestock, the birds of the air and all the beasts of the field. But for Adam no suitable helper was found. (Genesis 2:20 NIV)

2. The LORD God caused a deep sleep to fall on Adam, and he slept; and He took one of his ribs, and closed up the flesh in its place. Then the rib which the LORD God had taken from man He made into a woman, and He brought her to the man. (Genesis 2:21–22 NKJV)

3. Based on Genesis 2:23 NASB: The man said, "This is now bone of my bones, and flesh of my flesh; she shall be called Woman, because she was taken out of Man"; Adam called his wife's name Eve, because she was the mother of all living. (Genesis 3:20 NKJV))

4. This explains why a man leaves his father and mother and is joined to his wife, and the two are united into one. (Genesis 2:24 NLT)

5. God showed his love for us when he sent his only Son into the world to give us life. Real love isn't our love for God, but his love for us. God sent his Son to be the sacrifice by which our sins are forgiven. (1 John 4:9–10 CEV)

6. All this is from God, who reconciled us to himself through Christ and gave us the ministry of reconciliation: that God was reconciling the world to himself in Christ, not counting men's sins against them. (2 Corinthians 5:18–19 NIV)

7. A husband should love his wife as much as Christ loved the church and gave his life for it. (Ephesians 5:25 CEV)

8. For husbands, this means love your wives, just as Christ showed the church. He gave up his life for her. (Ephesians 5:25 NLT)

9. Each of you, however, should love his wife as himself, and a wife should respect her husband. (Ephesians 5:33 NRSV)

10. When the woman saw that the fruit of the tree was good for food and pleasing to the eye, and also desirable for gaining wisdom, she took some and ate it. She also gave some to her husband, who was with her, and he ate it. (Genesis 3:6 NIV)

11. Cain talked with Abel his brother; and it came to pass, when they were in the field, that Cain rose up against Abel his brother and killed him. (Genesis 4:8 NKJV)

12. To the unmarried and the widows I say: It is good for them to stay unmarried, as I am. (1 Corinthians 7:8 NIV)

13. When Jesus came into Peter's home, He saw his mother-in-law lying sick in bed with a fever. (Matthew 8:14 NASB)

Chapter 44: What is our biggest problem?

1. Do not be like Cain, who belonged to the evil one and murdered his brother. And why did he murder him? Because his own actions were evil and his brother's were righteous. (1 John 3:12 NIV)

2. We are tempted by our own desires that drag us off and trap us. Our desires make us sin, and when sin is finished with us, it leaves us dead. (James 1:14–15 CEV)

3. The serpent was more cunning than any beast of the field which the LORD God had made. (Genesis 3:1 NKJV)

4. All that is in the world, the lust of the flesh and the lust of the eyes and the boastful pride of life, is not from the Father, but is from the world. (1 John 2:16 NASB)

5. Based on Genesis 3:1 NIV: He said to the woman, "Did God really say, 'You must not eat from any tree in the garden'?"

6. Based on Genesis 3:2–3 NIV: The woman said to the serpent, "We may eat fruit from the trees in the garden, but God did say, 'You must not eat fruit from the tree that is in the middle of the garden, and you must not touch it, or you will die.'"

7. Based on Genesis 3:4–5 NIV: "You will not surely die," the serpent said to the woman. "For God knows that when you eat of it your eyes will be opened, and you will be like God, knowing good and evil."

8. When the woman saw that the fruit of the tree was good for food and pleasing to the eye, and also desirable for gaining wisdom, she took some and ate it. She also gave some to her husband, who was with her, and he ate it. (Genesis 3:6 NIV)

9. He has told you, O man, what is good; and what does the LORD require of you, but to do justice, to love kindness, and to walk humbly with your God? (Micah 6:8 NASB)

10. Do to others as you would have them do to you. (Luke 6:31 NIV)

11. Based on Matthew 22:37–40 NLT: Jesus replied, "'You must love the Lord your God with all your heart, all your soul, and all your mind.' This is the first and greatest commandment. A second is equally important: 'Love your neighbor as yourself.' The entire law and all the demands of the prophets are based on these two commandments."

Chapter 45: Why does sin still plague us?

1. If we claim to be without sin, we deceive ourselves and the truth is not in us. If we confess our sins, he is faithful and just and will forgive us our sins and purify us from all unrighteousness. If we claim we have not sinned, we make him out to be a liar and his word has no place in our lives. (1 John 1:8–10 NIV)

2. I have discovered this principle of life—that when I want to do what is right, I inevitably do what is wrong. I love God's law with all my heart. But there is another power within me that is at war with my mind. This power makes me a slave to the sin that is still within me. Oh, what a miserable person I am! Who will free me from this life that is dominated by sin and death? (Romans 7:21–24 NLT)

3. Thank God! The answer is in Jesus Christ our Lord. So you see how it is: In my mind I really want to obey God's law, but because of my sinful nature I am a slave to sin. (Romans 7:25 NLT)

4. All have sinned and fall short of the glory of God. (Romans 3:23 NKJV)

5. Christ carried the burden of our sins. He was nailed to the cross, so that we would stop sinning and start living right. By his cuts and bruises you are healed. You had wandered away like sheep. Now you have returned to the one who is your shepherd and protector. (1 Peter 2:24–25 CEV)

6. I want you to know that through Jesus the forgiveness of sins is proclaimed to you. (Acts 13:38 NIV)

7. What shall we say then? Shall we continue in sin that grace may abound? Certainly not! How shall we who died to sin live any longer in it? (Romans 6:1–2 NKJV)

8. Your word I have treasured in my heart, that I may not sin against You. (Psalm 119:11 NASB)

9. My little children, I am writing these things to you so that you may not sin. But if anyone does sin, we have an advocate with the Father, Jesus Christ the righteous; and he is the atoning sacrifice for our sins, and not for ours only but also for the sins of the whole world. (1 John 2:1–2 NRSV)

10. All who are led by the Spirit of God are children of God. (Romans 8:14 NLT)

11. Jesus presented another parable to them, saying, "The kingdom of heaven may be compared to a man who sowed good seed in his field. But while his men were sleeping, his enemy came and sowed tares among the wheat, and went away. But when the wheat sprouted and bore grain, then the tares became evident also. The slaves of the landowner came and said to him, 'Sir, did you not sow good seed in your field? How then does it have tares?' And he said to them, 'An enemy has done this!' The slaves said to him, 'Do you want us, then, to go and gather them up?' But he said, 'No; for while you are gathering up the tares, you may uproot the wheat with them. Allow both to grow together until the harvest; and in the time of the harvest I will say to the reapers, "First gather up the tares and bind them in bundles to burn them up; but gather the wheat into my barn."'" (Matthew 13:24–30 NASB)

12. You are the salt of the earth. But if the salt loses its saltiness, how can it be made salty again? It is no longer good for anything, except to be thrown out and trampled by men. (Matthew 5:13 NIV)

13. You are the light of the world. A city on a hill cannot be hidden. Neither do people light a lamp and put it under a bowl. Instead they put it on its stand, and it gives light to everyone in the house. In the same way, let your light shine before men, that they may see your good deeds and praise your Father in heaven. (Matthew 5:14–16 NIV)

Chapter 46: How can we experience peace?

1. A heart at peace gives life to the body, but envy rots the bones. (Proverbs 14:30 NIV)

2. Be anxious for nothing, but in everything by prayer and supplication with thanksgiving let your requests be made known to God. And the peace of God,

which surpasses all comprehension, will guard your hearts and your minds in Christ Jesus. (Philippians 4:6–7 NASB)

3. The LORD gives his people strength. The LORD blesses them with peace. (Psalm 29:11 NLT)

4. To us a child is born, to us a son is given, and the government will be on his shoulders. And he will be called Wonderful Counselor, Mighty God, Everlasting Father, Prince of Peace. (Isaiah 9:6 NIV)

5. The woman, fearing and trembling, knowing what had happened to her, came and fell down before Him and told Him the whole truth. And He said to her, "Daughter, your faith has made you well. Go in peace, and be healed of your affliction." (Mark 5:33–34 NKJV)

6. Based on Luke 10:5 CEV: As soon as you enter a home, say, "God bless this home with peace."

7. Peace I leave with you, My peace I give to you; not as the world gives do I give to you. Let not your heart be troubled, neither let it be afraid. (John 14:27–28 NKJV)

8. Let the peace that comes from Christ rule in your hearts. For as members of one body you are called to live in peace. And always be thankful. (Colossians 3:15 NLT)

9. These things I have spoken to you, so that in Me you may have peace. In the world you have tribulation, but take courage; I have overcome the world. (John 16:33 NASB)

10. I am with you always, even to the end of the age. (Matthew 28:20 NASB)

Chapter 47: Why should we pray?

1. Now to him who is able to do immeasurably more than all we ask or imagine, according to his power that is at work within us, to him be glory in the church and in Christ Jesus throughout all generations, for ever and ever! Amen. (Ephesians 3:20–21 NIV)

2. At midnight Paul and Silas were praying and singing hymns to God, and the prisoners were listening to them. Suddenly there was a great earthquake, so that the foundations of the prison were shaken; and immediately all the doors were opened and everyone's chains were loosed. (Acts 16:25–26 NKJV)

3. It came about when Moses was coming down from Mount Sinai (and the two tablets of the testimony were in Moses' hand as he was coming down from the mountain), that Moses did not know that the skin of his face shone because of his speaking with Him. (Exodus 34:29 NASB)

4. Immediately after this, Jesus insisted that his disciples get back into the boat and cross to the other side of the lake, while he sent the people home. After sending them home, he went up into the hills by himself to pray. Night fell while he was there alone. (Matthew 14:22–23 NLT)

5. When you pray, do not be like the hypocrites, for they love to pray standing in the synagogues and on the street corners to be seen by men. I tell you the truth, they have received their reward in full. But when you pray, go into your

NOTES

room, close the door and pray to your Father, who is unseen. Then your Father, who sees what is done in secret, will reward you. (Matthew 6:5–6 NIV)

6. Always be joyful and never stop praying. Whatever happens, keep thanking God because of Jesus Christ. This is what God wants you to do. (1 Thessalonians 5:16–18 CEV)

7. Jesus spoke these words, lifted up His eyes to heaven, and said: "Father, the hour has come. Glorify Your Son, that Your Son also may glorify You, as You have given Him authority over all flesh, that He should give eternal life to as many as You have given Him. And this is eternal life, that they may know You, the only true God, and Jesus Christ whom You have sent. I have glorified You on the earth. I have finished the work which You have given Me to do. And now, O Father, glorify Me together with Yourself, with the glory which I had with You before the world was." (John 17:1–5 NKJV)

8. If any of you lacks wisdom, he should ask God, who gives generously to all without finding fault, and it will be given to him. (James 1:5 NIV)

Chapter 48: God, should we pray to You or Jesus?

1. This is the confidence we have in approaching God: that if we ask anything according to his will, he hears us. And if we know that he hears us—whatever we ask—we know that we have what we asked of him. (1 John 5:14–15 NIV)

2. The LORD spoke to Moses face to face, as a man speaks to his friend. (Exodus 33:11 NKJV)

3. I heard the voice of the Lord saying, "Whom shall I send? And who will go for us?" And I said, "Here am I. Send me!" (Isaiah 6:8 NIV)

4. You have dealt well with Your servant, O LORD, according to Your word. Teach me good discernment and knowledge, for I believe in Your commandments. Before I was afflicted I went astray, but now I keep Your word. You are good and do good; teach me Your statutes. (Psalm 119:65–68 NASB)

5. Peter, filled with the Holy Spirit, said to them, "Rulers and elders of our people, are we being questioned today because we've done a good deed for a crippled man? Do you want to know how he was healed? Let me clearly state to all of you and to all the people of Israel that he was healed by the powerful name of Jesus Christ the Nazarene, the man you crucified but whom God raised from the dead." (Acts 4:8–10 NLT)

6. I and My Father are one. (John 10:30 NKJV)

7. In this manner, therefore, pray: Our Father in heaven, hallowed be Your name. (Matthew 6:9 NKJV)

8. God decided in advance to adopt us into his own family by bringing us to himself through Jesus Christ. This is what he wanted to do, and it gave him great pleasure. (Ephesians 1:5 NLT)

9. Based on John 16:24 NRSV: Until now you have not asked for anything in my name. Ask and you will receive, so that your joy may be complete.

10.   There is one God, and one mediator also between God and men, the man Christ Jesus, who gave Himself as a ransom for all, the testimony given at the proper time. (1 Timothy 2:5–6 NASB)

11.   The LORD is far from the wicked but he hears the prayer of the righteous. (Proverbs 15:29 NIV)

Chapter 49: God, how do You want to be worshipped?

1.   Shout for joy to the LORD, all the earth. Worship the LORD with gladness; come before him with joyful songs. Know that the LORD is God. It is he who made us, and we are his; we are his people, the sheep of his pasture. Enter his gates with thanksgiving and his courts with praise; give thanks to him and praise his name. For the LORD is good and his love endures forever; his faithfulness continues through all generations. (Psalm 100 NIV)

2.   David danced before the LORD with all his might; and David was wearing a linen ephod. So David and all the house of Israel brought up the ark of the LORD with shouting and with the sound of the trumpet. (2 Samuel 6:14–15 NKJV)

3.   Come, let us worship and bow down, let us kneel before the LORD our Maker. (Psalm 95:6 NASB)

4.   Jesus told this story to some who had great confidence in their own righteousness and scorned everyone else: "Two men went to the Temple to pray. One was a Pharisee, and the other was a despised tax collector. The Pharisee stood by himself and prayed this prayer: 'I thank you, God, that I am not a sinner like everyone else. For I don't cheat, I don't sin, and I don't commit adultery. I'm certainly not like that tax collector! I fast twice a week, and I give you a tenth of my income.' But the tax collector stood at a distance and dared not even lift his eyes to heaven as he prayed. Instead, he beat his chest in sorrow, saying, 'O God, be merciful to me, for I am a sinner.' I tell you, this sinner, not the Pharisee, returned home justified before God. For those who exalt themselves will be humbled, and those who humble themselves will be exalted." (Luke 18:9–14 NLT)

5.   Sing to the LORD with thanksgiving; make music to our God on the harp. (Psalm 147:7 NIV)

6.   Let us continually offer the sacrifice of praise to God, that is, the fruit of our lips, giving thanks to His name. But do not forget to do good and to share, for with such sacrifices God is well pleased. (Hebrews 13:15–16 NKJV)

7.   I acknowledged my sin to You, and my iniquity I did not hide; I said, "I will confess my transgressions to the LORD"; and You forgave the guilt of my sin. (Psalm 32:5 NASB)

8.   We should keep on encouraging each other to be thoughtful and to do helpful things. Some people have gotten out of the habit of meeting for worship, but we must not do that. We should keep on encouraging each other, especially since you know that the day of the Lord's coming is getting closer. (Hebrews 10:24–25 CEV)

Chapter 50: How can we love the unlovable?

1.   Based on John 21:15 NIV: When they had finished eating, Jesus said to Simon Peter, "Simon son of John, do you truly love me more than these?"

2.   Based on John 21:15 NIV: "Yes, Lord," he said, "you know that I love you." (John 21:15 NIV)

3.   Behold, a leper came and worshiped Him, saying, "Lord, if You are willing, You can make me clean." Then Jesus put out His hand and touched him, saying, "I am willing; be cleansed." Immediately his leprosy was cleansed. (Matthew 8:2–3 NKJV)

4.   There was a woman in the city who was a sinner; and when she learned that He was reclining at the table in the Pharisee's house, she brought an alabaster vial of perfume, and standing behind Him at His feet, weeping, she began to wet His feet with her tears, and kept wiping them with the hair of her head, and kissing His feet and anointing them with the perfume. (Luke 7:37–38 NASB)

5.   When the Pharisee who had invited Him saw this, he spoke to himself, saying, "This Man, if He were a prophet, would know who and what manner of woman this is who is touching Him, for she is a sinner." (Luke 7:39 NKJV)

6.   Jesus answered, "I will dip this piece of bread in the sauce and give it to the one I was talking about." Then Jesus dipped the bread and gave it to Judas, the son of Simon Iscariot. (John 13:26 CEV)

7.   Even though I was once a blasphemer and a persecutor and a violent man, I was shown mercy because I acted in ignorance and unbelief. The grace of our Lord was poured out on me abundantly, along with the faith and love that are in Christ Jesus. (1 Timothy 1:13–14 NIV)

Chapter 51: God, are we confused about what You want?

1.   You were like sheep going astray, but now you have returned to the Shepherd and Overseer of your souls. (1 Peter 2:25 NIV)

2.   What do you think? If a man has a hundred sheep, and one of them goes astray, does he not leave the ninety-nine and go to the mountains to seek the one that is straying? And if he should find it, assuredly, I say to you, he rejoices more over that sheep than over the ninety-nine that did not go astray. Even so it is not the will of your Father who is in heaven that one of these little ones should perish. (Matthew 18:12–14 NKJV)

3.   Jesus said, "Come to me, all of you who are weary and carry heavy burdens, and I will give you rest. Take my yoke upon you. Let me teach you, because I am humble and gentle at heart, and you will find rest for your souls. For my yoke is easy to bear, and the burden I give you is light." (Matthew 11:28–30 NLT)

4.   It was for freedom that Christ set us free; therefore keep standing firm and do not be subject again to a yoke of slavery. (Galatians 5:1 NASB)

5.   For this reason also, since the day we heard this, we haven't stopped praying for you. We are asking that you may be filled with the knowledge of His will in all wisdom and spiritual understanding, so that you may walk worthy of

the Lord, fully pleasing to Him, bearing fruit in every good work and growing in the knowledge of God. (Colossians 1:9–10 HCSB)

6.   He has told you, O man, what is good; and what does the LORD require of you but to do justice, to love kindness, and to walk humbly with your God? (Micah 6:8 NASB)

7.   People of Israel, what does the LORD your God want from you? The LORD wants you to respect and follow him, to love and serve him with all your heart and soul, and to obey his laws and teachings that I am giving you today. Do this, and all will go well for you. (Deuteronomy 10:12–13 CEV)

8.   He has rescued us from the power of darkness and transferred us into the kingdom of his beloved Son, in whom we have redemption, the forgiveness of sins. (Colossians 1:13–14 NRSV)

9.   The Lord is not slow in keeping his promise, as some understand slowness. He is patient with you, not wanting anyone to perish, but everyone to come to repentance. (2 Peter 3:9 NIV)

10.   What profit is it to a man if he gains the whole world, and loses his own soul? Or what will a man give in exchange for his soul? (Matthew 16:26 NKJV)

11.   You are to be perfect, as your heavenly Father is perfect. (Matthew 5:48 NASB)

12.   I concluded there is nothing better than to be happy and enjoy ourselves as long as we can. And people should eat and drink and enjoy the fruits of their labor, for these are gifts from God. (Ecclesiastes 3:12–13 NLT)

13.   You know when I sit and when I rise; you perceive my thoughts from afar. You discern my going out and my lying down; you are familiar with all my ways. (Psalm 139:2–3 NIV)

Chapter 52: What should our political role be?

1.   The authorities that exist have been established by God. (Romans 13:1 NIV)

2.   Herod, when he saw that he was deceived by the wise men, was exceedingly angry; and he sent forth and put to death all the male children who were in Bethlehem and in all its districts, from two years old and under, according to the time which he had determined from the wise men. (Matthew 2:16 NKJV)

3.   Every person is to be in subjection to the governing authorities. (Romans 13:1 NASB)

4.   Anyone who rebels against authority is rebelling against what God has instituted, and they will be punished. (Romans 13:2 NLT)

5.   "Well, then," Jesus said, "give to Caesar what belongs to Caesar, and give to God what belongs to God." His reply completely amazed them. (Mark 12:17 NLT)

6.   This is also why you pay taxes, for the authorities are God's servants, who give their full time to governing. Give everyone what you owe him: If you owe taxes, pay taxes; if revenue, then revenue; if respect, then respect; if honor, then honor. (Romans 13:6–7 NIV)

7. Pilate said to Him, "You do not speak to me? Do You not know that I have authority to release You, and I have authority to crucify You?" Jesus answered, "You would have no authority over Me, unless it had been given you from above; for this reason he who delivered Me to you has the greater sin." (John 19:10–11 NASB)

8. Remind your people to obey the rulers and authorities and not to be rebellious. They must always be ready to do something helpful and not say cruel things or argue. They should be gentle and kind to everyone. (Titus 3:1–2 CEV)

Chapter 53: Does choice extend to abortion?

1. When he comes, he will convince the world of its sin, and of God's righteousness, and of the coming judgment. (John 16:8 NLT)

2. Trust in the LORD with all your heart and lean not on your own understanding; in all your ways acknowledge him, and he will make your paths straight. (Proverbs 3:5–6 NIV)

3. Jesus answered and said to her, "Martha, Martha, you are worried and troubled about many things. But one thing is needed, and Mary has chosen that good part, which will not be taken away from her." (Luke 10:41–42 NKJV)

4. By faith Moses, when he had grown up, refused to be called the son of Pharaoh's daughter, choosing rather to endure ill-treatment with the people of God than to enjoy the passing pleasures of sin, considering the reproach of Christ greater riches than the treasures of Egypt; for he was looking to the reward. (Hebrews 11:24–26 NASB)

5. Based on Joshua 24:15 NLT: If you refuse to serve the LORD, then choose today whom you will serve. Would you prefer the gods your ancestors served beyond the Euphrates? Or will it be the gods of the Amorites in whose land you now live? But as for me and my family, we will serve the LORD.

6. Do not envy the violent and do not choose any of their ways; for the perverse are an abomination to the LORD, but the upright are in his confidence. (Proverbs 3:31–32 NRSV)

7. You may think you are on the right road and still end up dead. (Proverbs 14:12 CEV)

8. You formed my inward parts; You covered me in my mother's womb. I will praise You, for I am fearfully and wonderfully made; marvelous are Your works, and that my soul knows very well. (Psalm 139:13–14 NKJV)

9. Your eyes have seen my unformed substance; and in Your book were all written the days that were ordained for me, when as yet there was not one of them. (Psalm 139:16 NASB)

10. Do to others as you would have them do to you. (Luke 6:31 NIV)

Chapter 54: God, do you love or hate homosexuals?

1. If you really keep the royal law found in Scripture, "Love your neighbor as yourself," you are doing right. (James 2:8 NIV)

2.   The scribes and the Pharisees brought a woman caught in adultery, and having set her in the center of the court, they said to Him, "Teacher, this woman has been caught in adultery, in the very act. Now in the Law Moses commanded us to stone such women; what then do You say?" (John 8:3–5 NASB)

3.   When they continued asking Him, He raised Himself up and said to them, "He who is without sin among you, let him throw a stone at her first." (John 8:7 NKJV)

4.   There is more happiness in heaven because of one sinner who turns to God than over ninety-nine good people who don't need to. (Luke 15:7 CEV)

5.   I tell you that anyone who looks at a woman lustfully has already committed adultery with her in his heart. (Matthew 5:28 NIV)

6.   He created them male and female, and He blessed them and named them Man in the day when they were created. (Genesis 5:2 NASB)

7.   Do you not know that the wicked will not inherit the kingdom of God? Do not be deceived: Neither the sexually immoral nor idolaters nor adulterers nor male prostitutes nor homosexual offenders nor thieves nor the greedy nor drunkards nor slanderers nor swindlers will inherit the kingdom of God. (1 Corinthians 6:9–10 NIV)

8.   Some of you were once like that. But you were cleansed; you were made holy; you were made right with God by calling on the name of the Lord Jesus Christ and by the Spirit of our God. (1 Corinthians 6:11 NLT)

9.   No temptation has seized you except what is common to man. And God is faithful; he will not let you be tempted beyond what you can bear. But when you are tempted, he will also provide a way out so that you can stand up under it. (1 Corinthians 10:13 NIV)

10.   Do not judge so that you will not be judged. For in the way you judge, you will be judged; and by your standard of measure, it will be measured to you. Why do you look at the speck that is in your brother's eye, but do not notice the log that is in your own eye? Or how can you say to your brother, "Let me take the speck out of your eye," and behold, the log is in your own eye? You hypocrite, first take the log out of your own eye, and then you will see clearly to take the speck out of your brother's eye. (Matthew 7:1–5 NASB)

Chapter 55: Is taking care of our planet spiritual or political?

1.   The earth is the LORD's, and everything in it, the world, and all who live in it; for he founded it upon the seas and established it upon the waters. (Psalm 24:1–2 NIV)

2.   God blessed them; and God said to them, "Be fruitful and multiply, and fill the earth, and subdue it; and rule over the fish of the sea and over the birds of the sky and over every living thing that moves on the earth." (Genesis 1:28 NASB)

3.   God said, "Behold, I have given you every plant yielding seed that is on the surface of all the earth, and every tree which has fruit yielding seed; it shall be food for you; and to every beast of the earth and to every bird of the sky and

to every thing that moves on the earth which has life, I have given every green plant for food"; and it was so. (Genesis 1:29–30 NASB)

4. God saw all that He had made, and behold, it was very good. And there was evening and there was morning, the sixth day. (Genesis 1:31 NASB)

5. Yours, O LORD, is the greatness, the power, the glory, the victory, and the majesty. Everything in the heavens and on earth is yours, O LORD, and this is your kingdom. We adore you as the one who is over all things. Wealth and honor come from you alone, for you rule over everything. Power and might are in your hand, and at your discretion people are made great and given strength. (1 Chronicles 29:11–12 NLT)

6. God's eternal power and character cannot be seen. But from the beginning of creation, God has shown what these are like by all he has made. That's why those people don't have any excuse. (Romans 1:20 CEV)

7. He makes grass grow for the cattle, and plants for man to cultivate— bringing forth food from the earth: wine that gladdens the heart of man, oil to make his face shine, and bread that sustains his heart. (Psalm 104:14–15 NIV)